Lucky☆Star

4

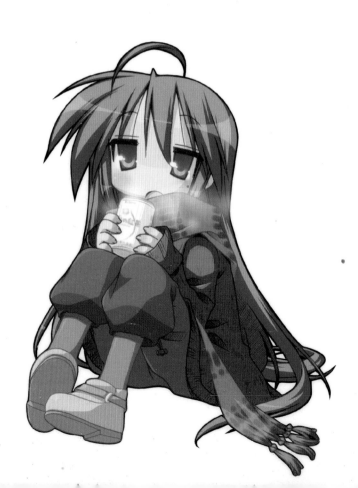

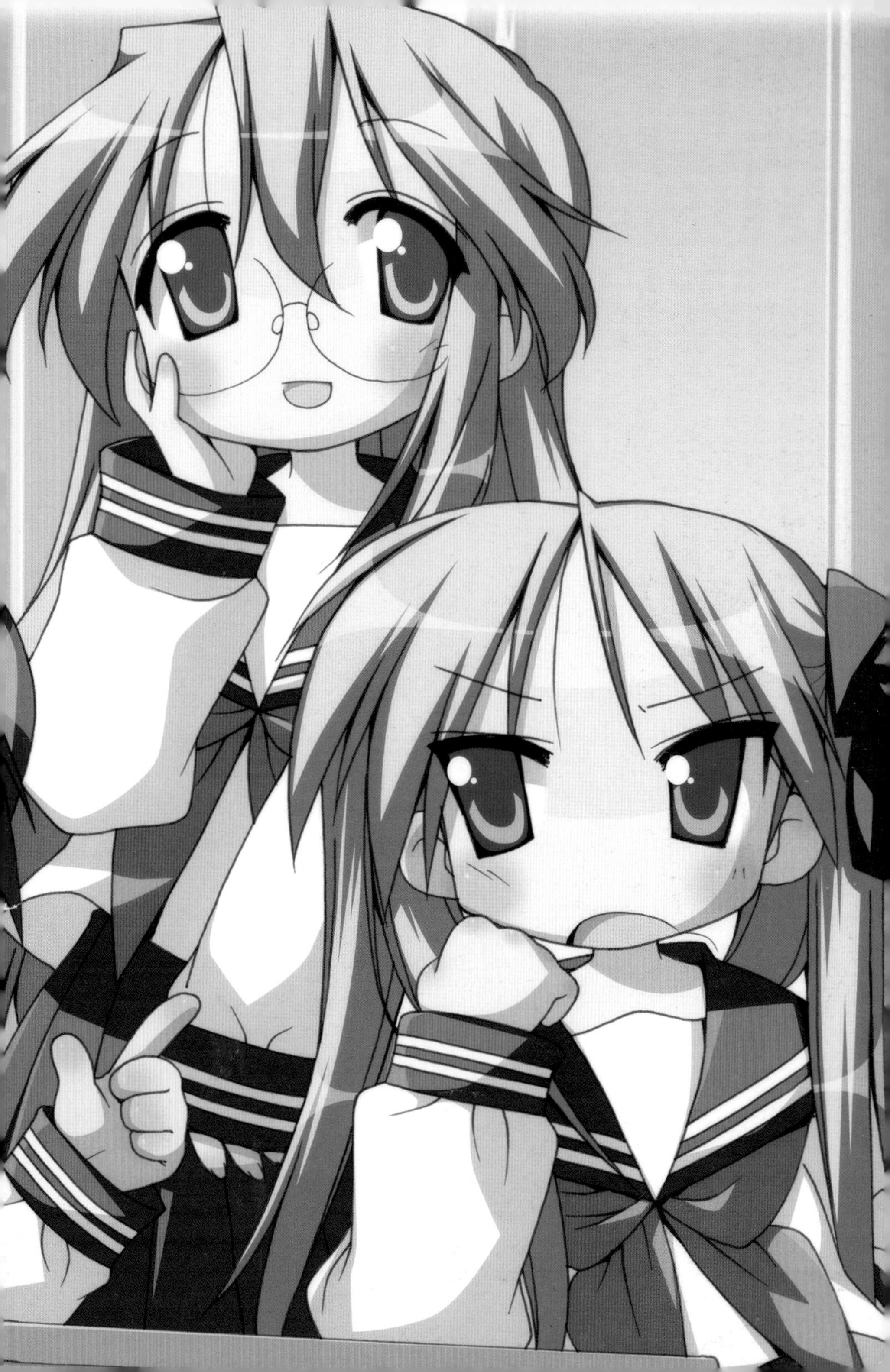

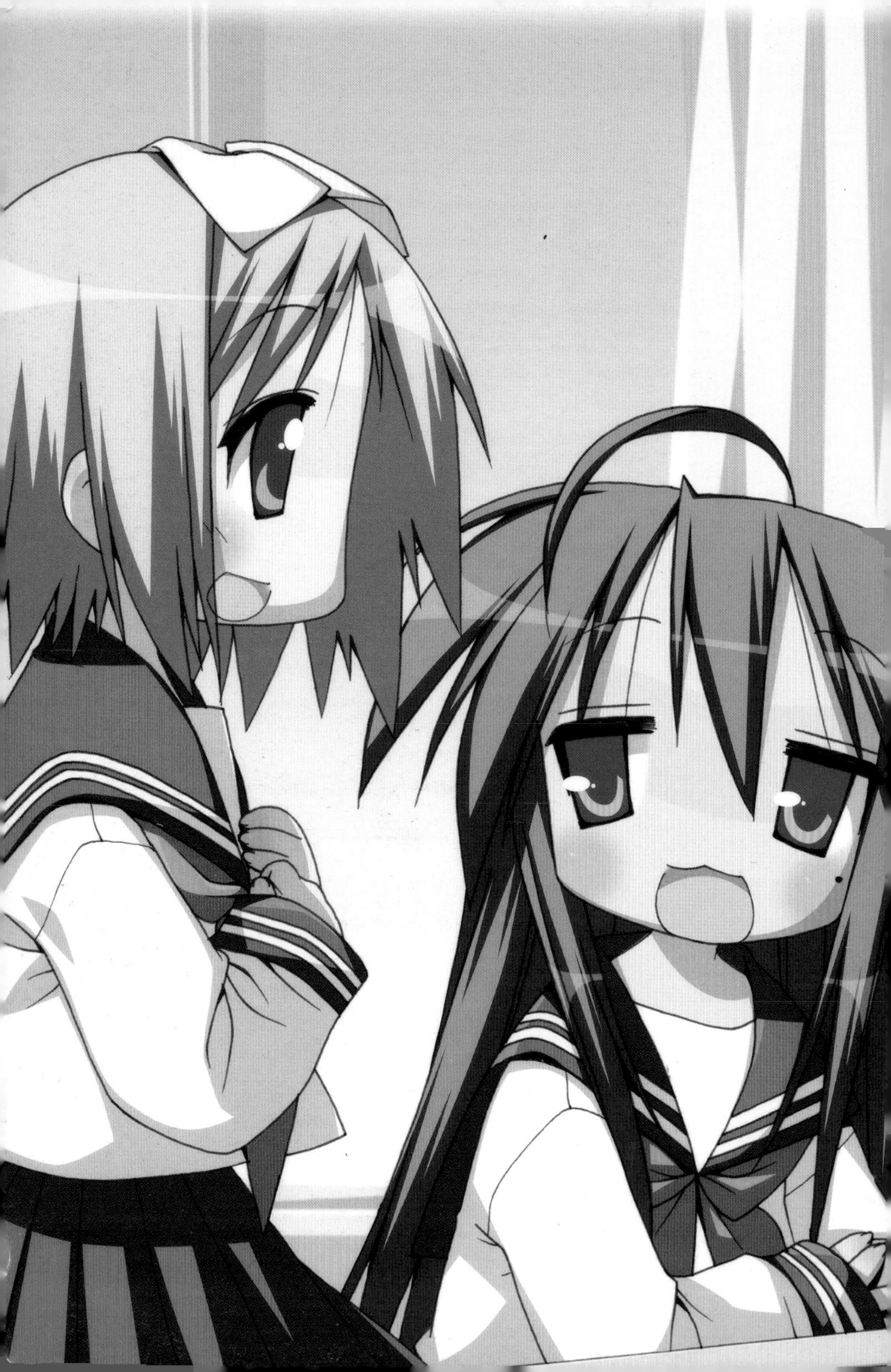

contents

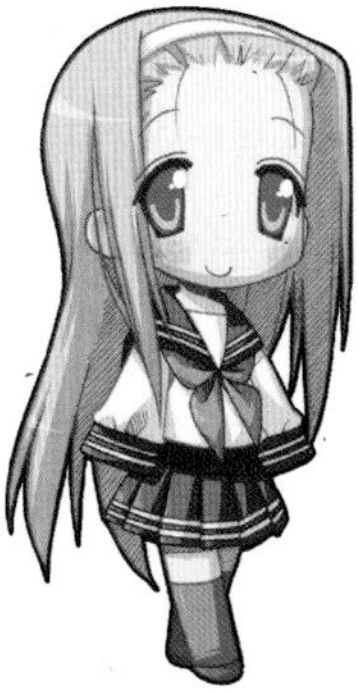

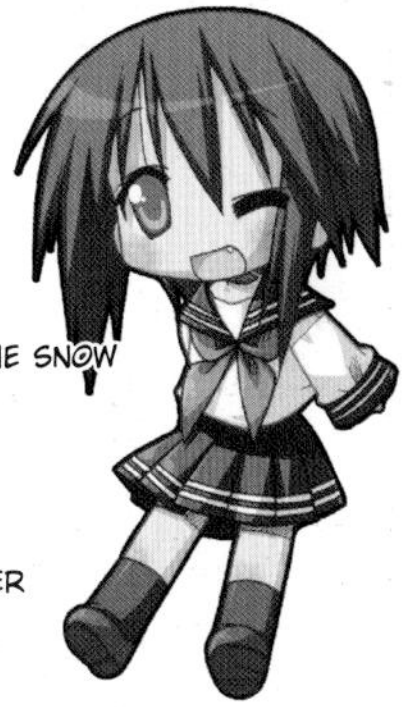

Lucky☆Star

episode 88 removed from the world

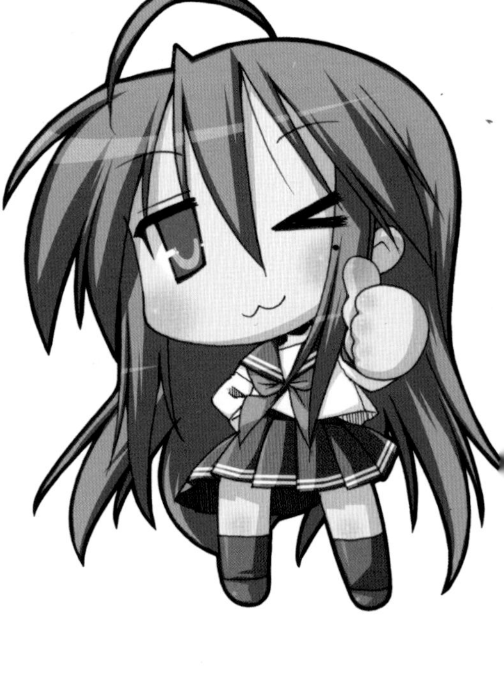

●Comptiq, July 2006 issue

process is important

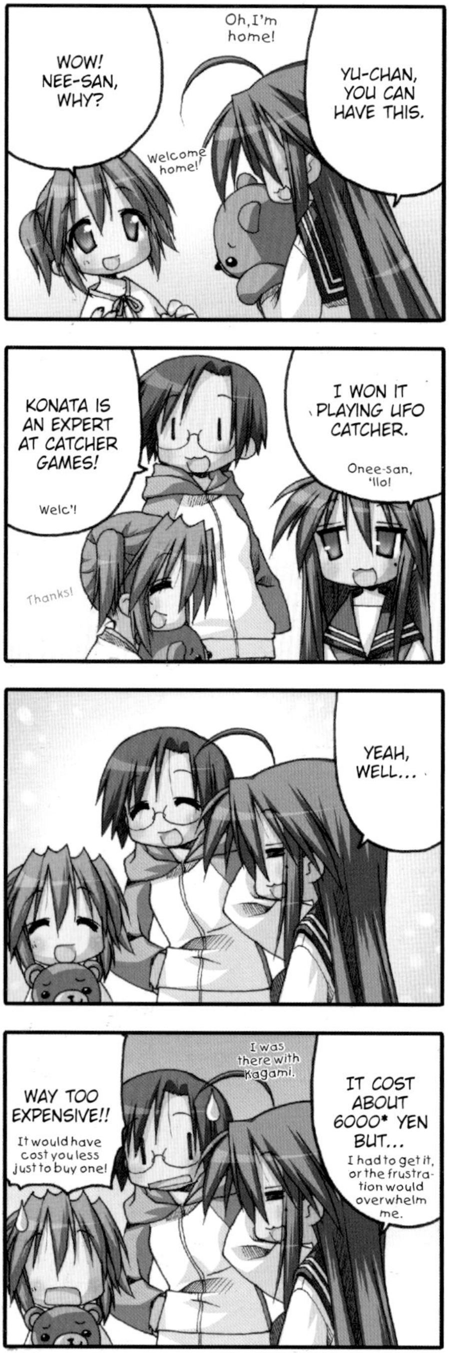
Oh, I'm home!
YU-CHAN, YOU CAN HAVE THIS.
WOW! NEE-SAN, WHY?
Welcome home!
I WON IT PLAYING UFO CATCHER.
Onee-san, 'llo!
KONATA IS AN EXPERT AT CATCHER GAMES!
Welc'!
Thanks!
YEAH, WELL...
I was there with Kagami.
IT COST ABOUT 6000* YEN BUT...
I had to get it, or the frustration would overwhelm me.
WAY TOO EXPENSIVE!!
It would have cost you less just to buy one!

*ABOUT $60

Autumn Sky

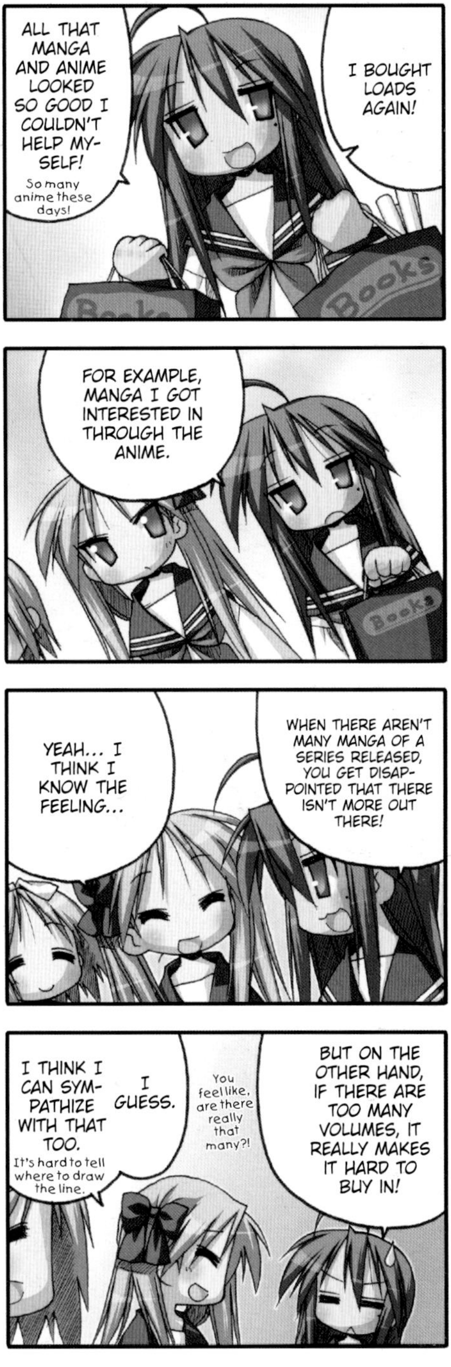
I BOUGHT LOADS AGAIN!
ALL THAT MANGA AND ANIME LOOKED SO GOOD I COULDN'T HELP MY-SELF!
So many anime these days!
FOR EXAMPLE, MANGA I GOT INTERESTED IN THROUGH THE ANIME.
WHEN THERE AREN'T MANY MANGA OF A SERIES RELEASED, YOU GET DISAP-POINTED THAT THERE ISN'T MORE OUT THERE!
YEAH... I THINK I KNOW THE FEELING...
BUT ON THE OTHER HAND, IF THERE ARE TOO MANY VOLUMES, IT REALLY MAKES IT HARD TO BUY IN!
You feel like, are there really that many?!
I GUESS.
I THINK I CAN SYM-PATHIZE WITH THAT TOO.
It's hard to tell where to draw the line.

never ever cross the line

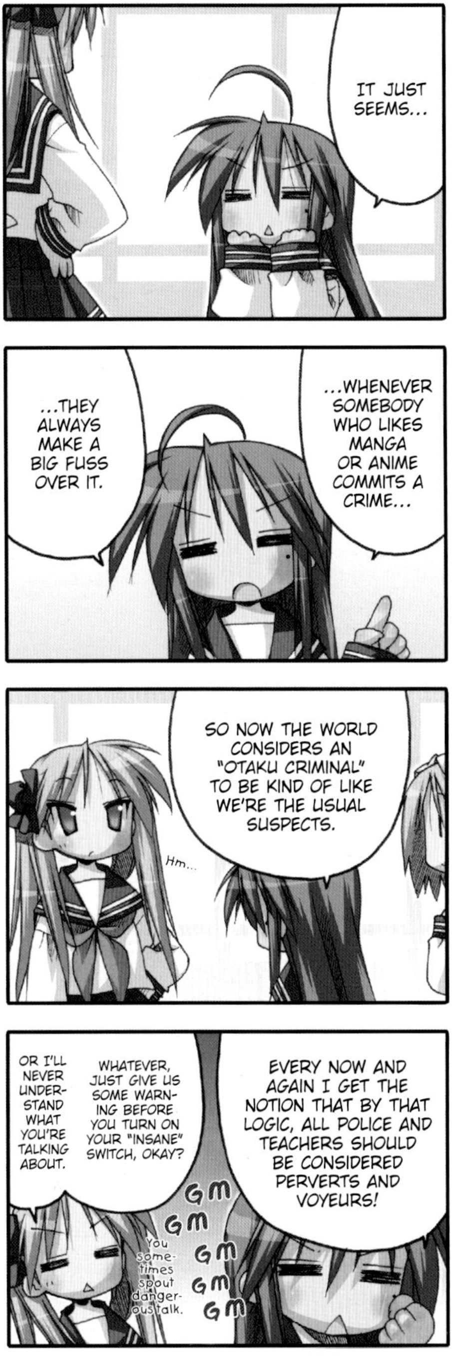
IT JUST SEEMS...
...WHENEVER SOMEBODY WHO LIKES MANGA OR ANIME COMMITS A CRIME...
...THEY ALWAYS MAKE A BIG FUSS OVER IT.
SO NOW THE WORLD CONSIDERS AN "OTAKU CRIMINAL" TO BE KIND OF LIKE WE'RE THE USUAL SUSPECTS.
Hm...
EVERY NOW AND AGAIN I GET THE NOTION THAT BY THAT LOGIC, ALL POLICE AND TEACHERS SHOULD BE CONSIDERED PERVERTS AND VOYEURS!
GM GM GM GM GM
You some-times spout danger-ous talk.
WHATEVER, JUST GIVE US SOME WARN-ING BEFORE YOU TURN ON YOUR "INSANE" SWITCH, OKAY?
OR I'LL NEVER UNDER-STAND WHAT YOU'RE TALKING ABOUT.

don't cool down

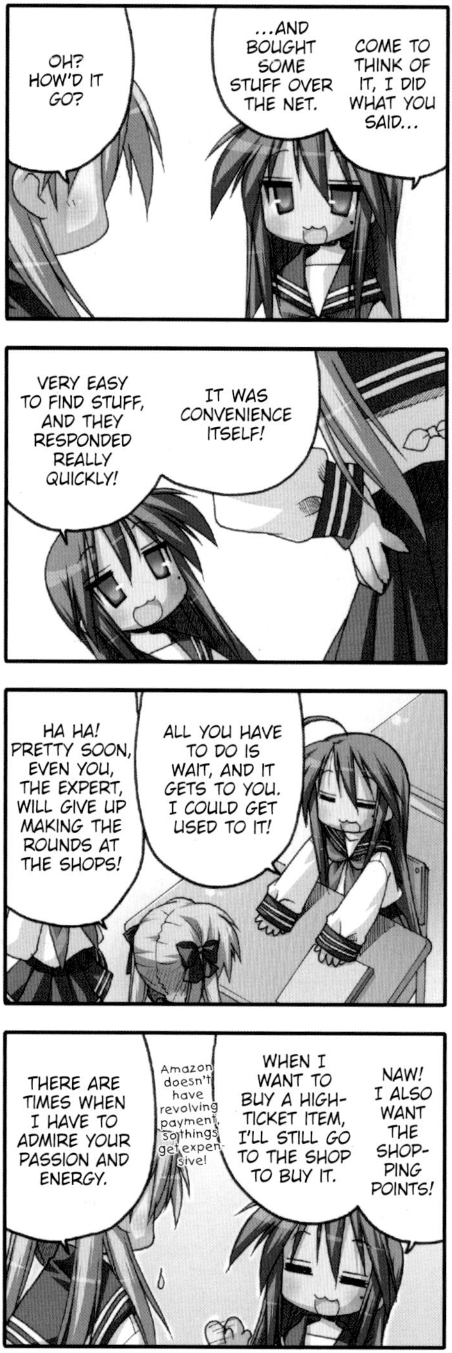
COME TO THINK OF IT, I DID WHAT YOU SAID...
...AND BOUGHT SOME STUFF OVER THE NET.
OH? HOW'D IT GO?
IT WAS CONVENIENCE ITSELF!
VERY EASY TO FIND STUFF, AND THEY RESPONDED REALLY QUICKLY!
ALL YOU HAVE TO DO IS WAIT, AND IT GETS TO YOU. I COULD GET USED TO IT!
HA HA! PRETTY SOON, EVEN YOU, THE EXPERT, WILL GIVE UP MAKING THE ROUNDS AT THE SHOPS!
NAW! I ALSO WANT THE SHOP-PING POINTS!
WHEN I WANT TO BUY A HIGH-TICKET ITEM, I'LL STILL GO TO THE SHOP TO BUY IT.
Amazon doesn't have revolving payment, so things get expen-sive!
THERE ARE TIMES WHEN I HAVE TO ADMIRE YOUR PASSION AND ENERGY.

true-feelings mode

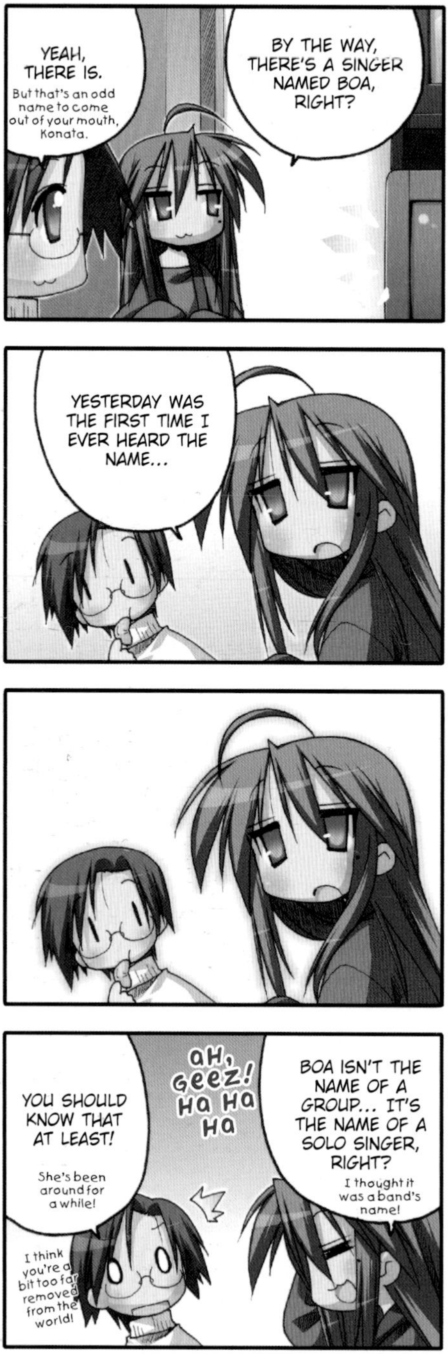
BY THE WAY, THERE'S A SINGER NAMED BOA, RIGHT?
YEAH, THERE IS.
But that's an odd name to come out of your mouth, Konata.
YESTERDAY WAS THE FIRST TIME I EVER HEARD THE NAME...
BOA ISN'T THE NAME OF A GROUP... IT'S THE NAME OF A SOLO SINGER, RIGHT?
I thought it was a band's name!
aH, GEEZ! Ha Ha Ha
YOU SHOULD KNOW THAT AT LEAST!
She's been around for a while!
I think you're a bit too far removed from the world!

2004 WINTER COMP FESTIVAL

true-feelings mode

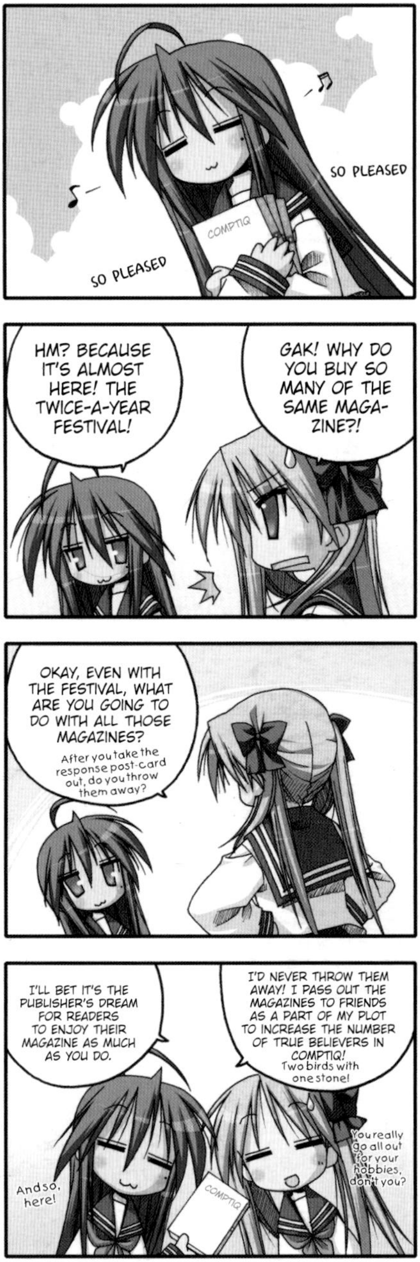
SO PLEASED
SO PLEASED
COMPTIQ
GAK! WHY DO YOU BUY SO MANY OF THE SAME MAGA-ZINE?!
HM? BECAUSE IT'S ALMOST HERE! THE TWICE-A-YEAR FESTIVAL!
OKAY, EVEN WITH THE FESTIVAL, WHAT ARE YOU GOING TO DO WITH ALL THOSE MAGAZINES? After you take the response post-card out, do you throw them away?
I'D NEVER THROW THEM AWAY! I PASS OUT THE MAGAZINES TO FRIENDS AS A PART OF MY PLOT TO INCREASE THE NUMBER OF TRUE BELIEVERS IN COMPTIQ! Two birds with one stone!
I'LL BET IT'S THE PUBLISHER'S DREAM FOR READERS TO ENJOY THEIR MAGAZINE AS MUCH AS YOU DO.
You really go all out for your hobbies, don't you?
COMPTIQ
And so, here!

room in one's heart

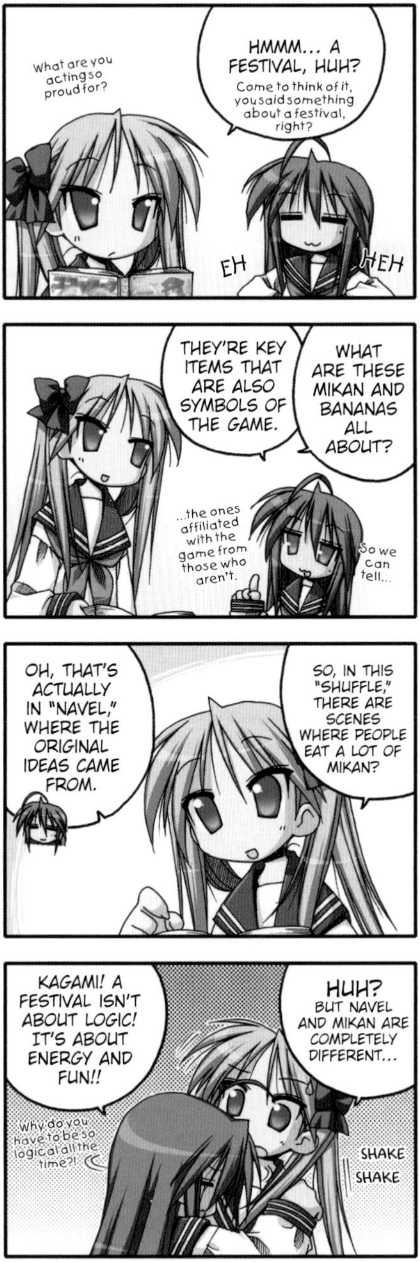
HMMM... A FESTIVAL, HUH? Come to think of it, you said something about a festival, right?
What are you acting so proud for?
EH HEH
WHAT ARE THESE MIKAN AND BANANAS ALL ABOUT?
THEY'RE KEY ITEMS THAT ARE ALSO SYMBOLS OF THE GAME.
So we can tell...
...the ones affiliated with the game from those who aren't.
SO, IN THIS "SHUFFLE," THERE ARE SCENES WHERE PEOPLE EAT A LOT OF MIKAN?
OH, THAT'S ACTUALLY IN "NAVEL," WHERE THE ORIGINAL IDEAS CAME FROM.
HUH? BUT NAVEL AND MIKAN ARE COMPLETELY DIFFERENT...
KAGAMI! A FESTIVAL ISN'T ABOUT LOGIC! IT'S ABOUT ENERGY AND FUN!!
SHAKE
SHAKE
Why do you have to be so logical all the time?!

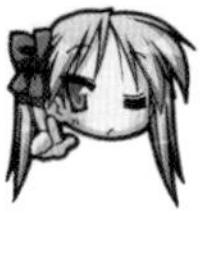

● These were drawn especially for the 2004 Winter Comp Festival ●

Lucky☆Star

episode 89
daily fun

●Comptiq, July 2006 issue

the strongest character

HOME ROOM...
CHATTER
EVERYONE! PLEASE! PLEASE BE QUIET!
We're not getting anywhere!
CHATTER
SOMETIME THEY SEEM LIKE GRADE-SCHOOL KIDS!
CHATTER
MIYUKI-SAN! WE HAVE NO INTENTION OF BECOMING THE TYPE OF ADULTS THAT PASSIVELY TAKE OTHER PEOPLE'S ORDERS!
We aren't fools like those types who turn right when somebody says, "Turn right," or shut up when we're ordered to!
YEAH, IZUMI! WELL SPOKEN!!
WILL YOU GUYS SHAPE UP AND...
I FEEL THAT IS AN EXCELLENT MENTAL ATTITUDE.
THEREFORE, I WILL NOW ENTERTAIN OPINIONS REGARDING THE SUBJECT FROM ALL OF YOU!
GM GM GM GM GM GM
EH? IS SHE ANGRY?!
SHE'S SMILING, BUT I GET THE FEELING SHE'S ANGRY!
And it scares me!
HUS——SSH

measure of confidence

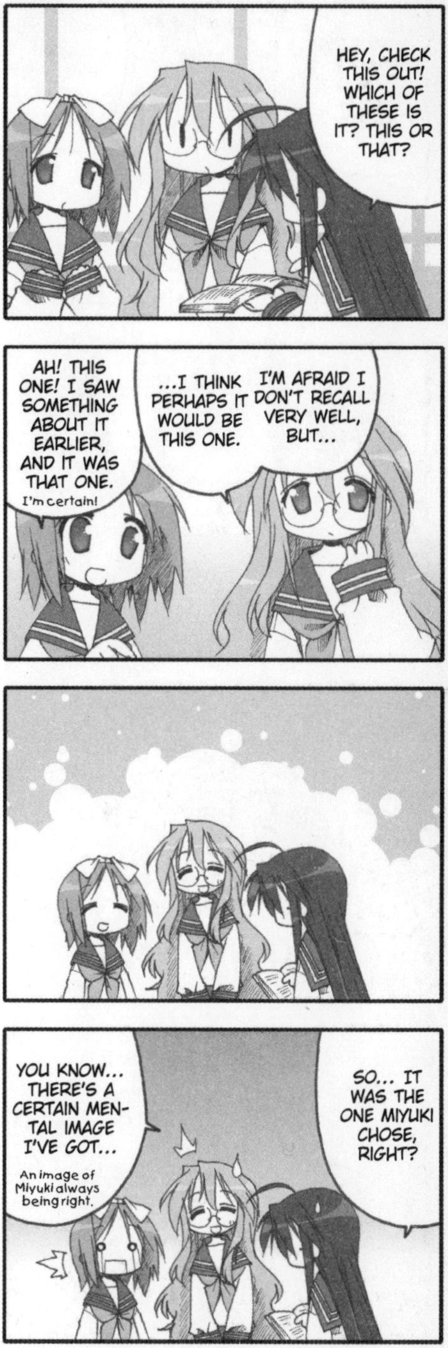

HEY, CHECK THIS OUT! WHICH OF THESE IS IT? THIS OR THAT?
I'M AFRAID I DON'T RECALL VERY WELL, BUT...
...I THINK PERHAPS IT WOULD BE THIS ONE.
AH! THIS ONE! I SAW SOMETHING ABOUT IT EARLIER, AND IT WAS THAT ONE.
I'm certain!
SO... IT WAS THE ONE MIYUKI CHOSE, RIGHT?
YOU KNOW... THERE'S A CERTAIN MENTAL IMAGE I'VE GOT...
An image of Miyuki always being right.

and soon she'll forget she bought it

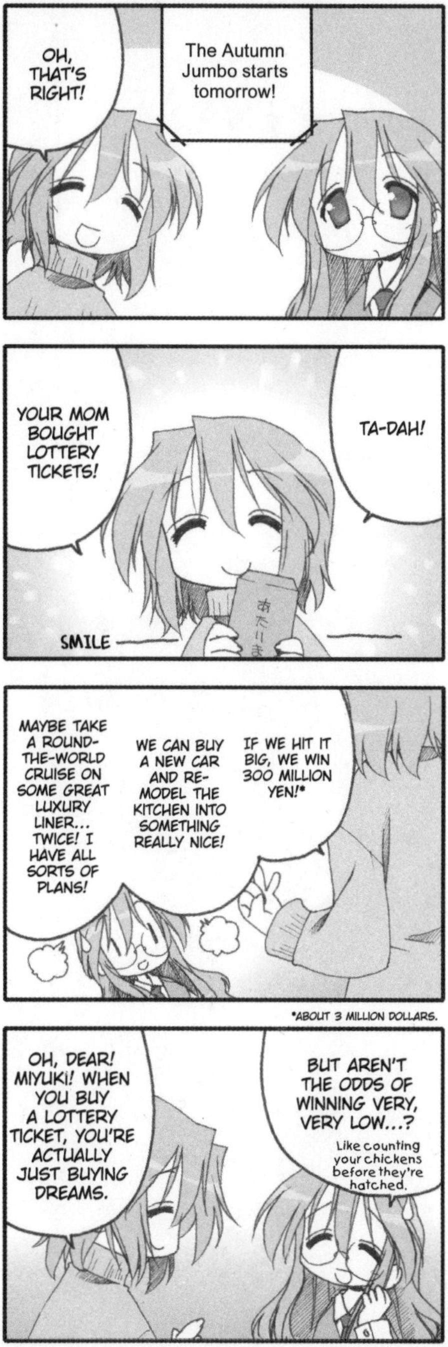

The Autumn Jumbo starts tomorrow!
OH, THAT'S RIGHT!
TA-DAH!
YOUR MOM BOUGHT LOTTERY TICKETS!
SMILE
IF WE HIT IT BIG, WE WIN 300 MILLION YEN!*
WE CAN BUY A NEW CAR AND RE-MODEL THE KITCHEN INTO SOMETHING REALLY NICE!
MAYBE TAKE A ROUND-THE-WORLD CRUISE ON SOME GREAT LUXURY LINER... TWICE! I HAVE ALL SORTS OF PLANS!
*ABOUT 3 MILLION DOLLARS.
BUT AREN'T THE ODDS OF WINNING VERY, VERY LOW...?
Like counting your chickens before they're hatched.
OH, DEAR! MIYUKI! WHEN YOU BUY A LOTTERY TICKET, YOU'RE ACTUALLY JUST BUYING DREAMS.

it figures, doesn't it?

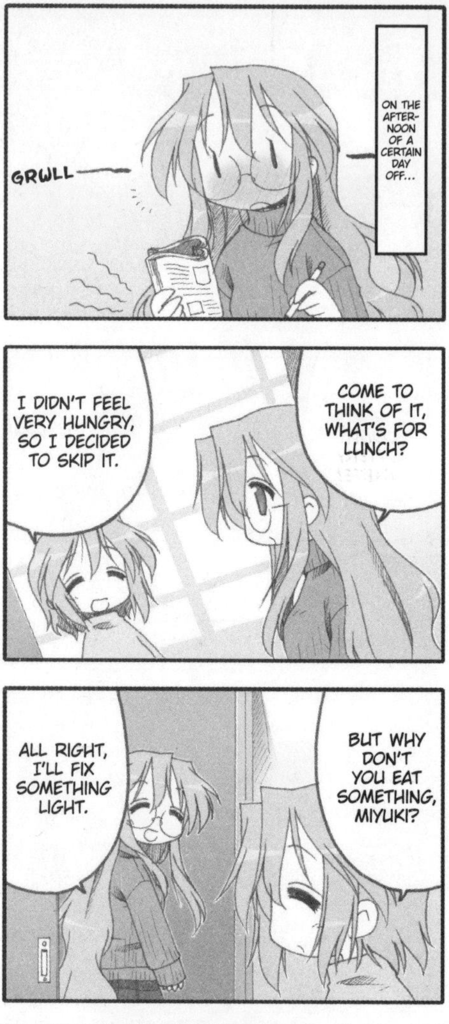
ON THE AFTERNOON OF A CERTAIN DAY OFF...
GRWLL——
COME TO THINK OF IT, WHAT'S FOR LUNCH?
I DIDN'T FEEL VERY HUNGRY, SO I DECIDED TO SKIP IT.
BUT WHY DON'T YOU EAT SOMETHING, MIYUKI?
ALL RIGHT, I'LL FIX SOMETHING LIGHT.
THEN... FIX SOME FOR ME TOO, OKAY?
OKAAAAY.

this figures too

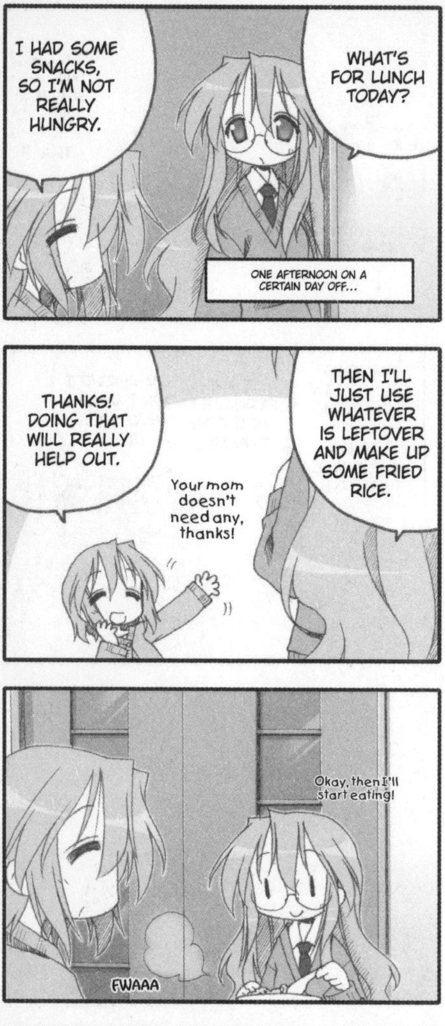
WHAT'S FOR LUNCH TODAY?
I HAD SOME SNACKS, SO I'M NOT REALLY HUNGRY.
ONE AFTERNOON ON A CERTAIN DAY OFF...
THEN I'LL JUST USE WHATEVER IS LEFTOVER AND MAKE UP SOME FRIED RICE.
THANKS! DOING THAT WILL REALLY HELP OUT.
Your mom doesn't need any, thanks!
Okay, then I'll start eating!
FWAAA
YOU KNOW, I THINK I WILL HAVE A LITTLE AFTER ALL!
Its smells great!
OKAAAY.
I thought you'd say that.
Sta——aare

episode 90
an inconvenient truth

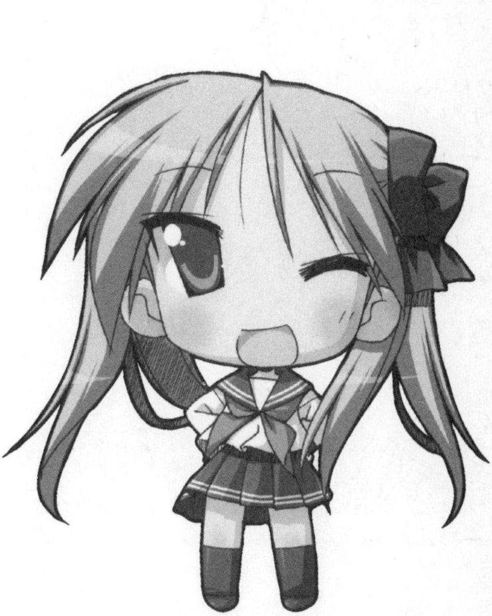

● Comptiq, July 2006 issue

ms. selfish

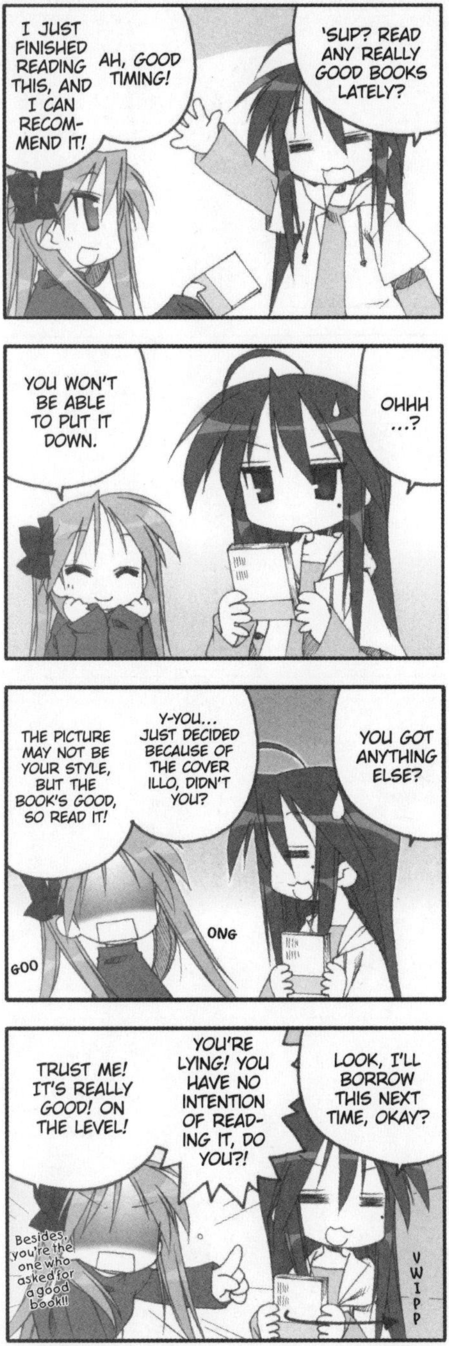
'SUP? READ ANY REALLY GOOD BOOKS LATELY?
AH, GOOD TIMING!
I JUST FINISHED READING THIS, AND I CAN RECOMMEND IT!
OHHH ...?
YOU WON'T BE ABLE TO PUT IT DOWN.
YOU GOT ANYTHING ELSE?
Y-YOU... JUST DECIDED BECAUSE OF THE COVER ILLO, DIDN'T YOU?
THE PICTURE MAY NOT BE YOUR STYLE, BUT THE BOOK'S GOOD, SO READ IT!
ONG
GOO
LOOK, I'LL BORROW THIS NEXT TIME, OKAY?
YOU'RE LYING! YOU HAVE NO INTENTION OF READING IT, DO YOU?!
TRUST ME! IT'S REALLY GOOD! ON THE LEVEL!
VWIPP
Besides, you're the one who asked for a good book!!

self delusion

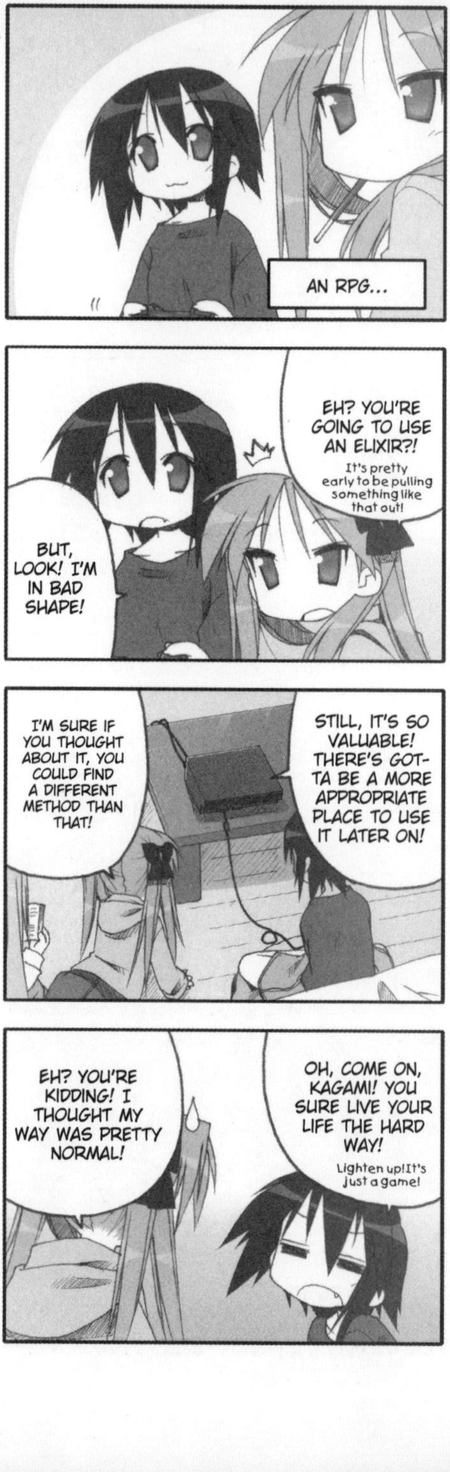
AN RPG...
EH? YOU'RE GOING TO USE AN ELIXIR?!
It's pretty early to be pulling something like that out!
BUT, LOOK! I'M IN BAD SHAPE!
STILL, IT'S SO VALUABLE! THERE'S GOT-TA BE A MORE APPROPRIATE PLACE TO USE IT LATER ON!
I'M SURE IF YOU THOUGHT ABOUT IT, YOU COULD FIND A DIFFERENT METHOD THAN THAT!
OH, COME ON, KAGAMI! YOU SURE LIVE YOUR LIFE THE HARD WAY!
Lighten up! It's just a game!
EH? YOU'RE KIDDING! I THOUGHT MY WAY WAS PRETTY NORMAL!

important business

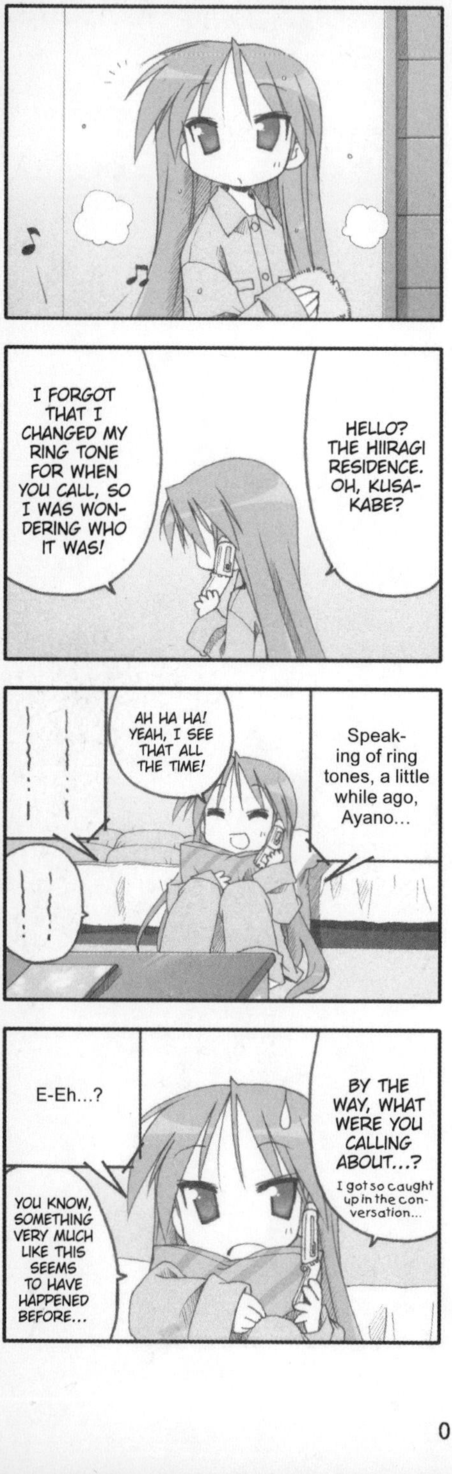
HELLO? THE HIIRAGI RESIDENCE. OH, KUSA-KABE?
I FORGOT THAT I CHANGED MY RING TONE FOR WHEN YOU CALL, SO I WAS WON-DERING WHO IT WAS!
Speak-ing of ring tones, a little while ago, Ayano...
AH HA HA! YEAH, I SEE THAT ALL THE TIME!
BY THE WAY, WHAT WERE YOU CALLING ABOUT...?
I got so caught up in the con-versation...
E-Eh...?
YOU KNOW, SOMETHING VERY MUCH LIKE THIS SEEMS TO HAVE HAPPENED BEFORE...

don't wake me up

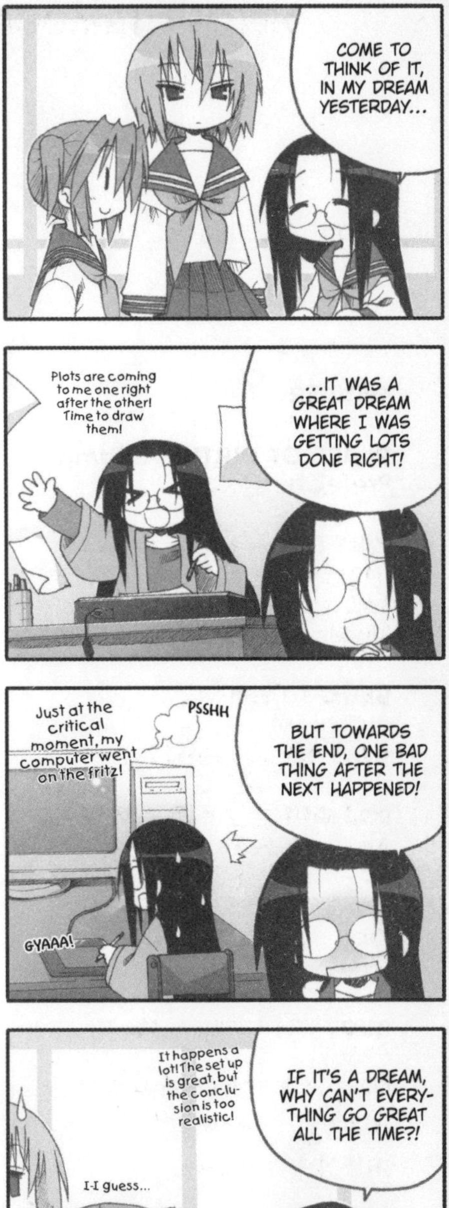
COME TO THINK OF IT, IN MY DREAM YESTERDAY...
...IT WAS A GREAT DREAM WHERE I WAS GETTING LOTS DONE RIGHT!
Plots are coming to me one right after the other! Time to draw them!
BUT TOWARDS THE END, ONE BAD THING AFTER THE NEXT HAPPENED!
PSSHH
Just at the critical moment, my computer went on the fritz!
GYAAA!
IF IT'S A DREAM, WHY CAN'T EVERYTHING GO GREAT ALL THE TIME?!
It happens a lot! The set up is great, but the conclusion is too realistic!
I-I guess...

ms. careless

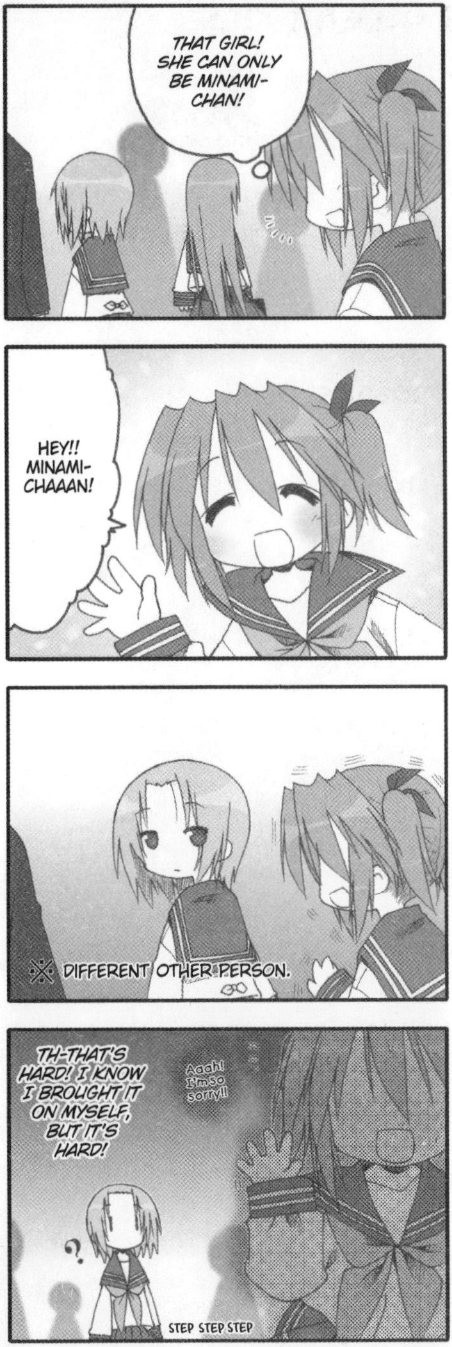
THAT GIRL! SHE CAN ONLY BE MINAMI-CHAN!
HEY!! MINAMI-CHAAAN!
※ DIFFERENT OTHER PERSON.
TH-THAT'S HARD! I KNOW I BROUGHT IT ON MYSELF, BUT IT'S HARD!
Aaah! I'm so sorry!!
STEP STEP STEP

HIYORI TAMURA'S HUMAN FILE

NAME: Konata Izumi

GENDER: ♀

PLACE OF BIRTH: Saitama Prefecture

BIRTHDAY: May 28th
*Her birthday is close to mine, so I feel even more that we're kindred spirits.

BLOOD TYPE: A

STAR SIGN: Gemini

PRESENT RANK: Ryou-ou Academy, 3rd Year, Class B

HANDEDNESS: Ambidextrous
*Sempai sure has some strong specs!

BUST-SIZE RANK: Minimal

FAMILY & POSITION: Father,
☆ Eldest daughter

HOBBIES: Games, Anime, Reading (manga)

LIKES: Chocolate Coronets, Moe
*Come to think of it, she's always eating them.

DISLIKES: Mozuku seaweed, Sports on TV

FAVORITE COLORS: Red, Black

SPECIAL SKILLS: Athletics (although she doesn't like it)
*The fact that she isn't on any team is a point in her favor.

WEAK POINTS: All Things Science

CLUBS: None

CLASS REP: No

HIYORI'S MEMO

An Otaku sempai worthy of respect.
It appears that she has experience in sports and martial arts, but she seems to have come out of the experience with little further interest in it. She is a sempai who tries to avoid any work unrelated to her interests, and relies on Hiiragi-sensei for homework help.

Lucky☆Star

episode 91
machine life

●Comptiq, August 2006 issue

field of vision

WHAT ARE YOU READING?
A MAGAZINE THAT KONA-CHAN LEFT BEHIND.
THIS MANGA DOESN'T DO ANYTHING FOR ME.
EH? I THINK IT'S REALLY INTERESTING! I WAS THINKING ABOUT BUYING THE GRAPHIC NOVELS!
DAYS LATER AT THE BOOK STORE...
HMM... NOW WHERE IS THAT MANGA...?
I KNEW IT! IT'S ONE OF THOSE, RIGHT?
I doubt normal book-stores would have it.
YOU MEAN IT'S SO POPULAR, IT'S SOLD OUT?
IS THAT WHAT YOU TOOK MY STATEMENT TO MEAN?!
I meant they just don't carry it.

beloved daughter

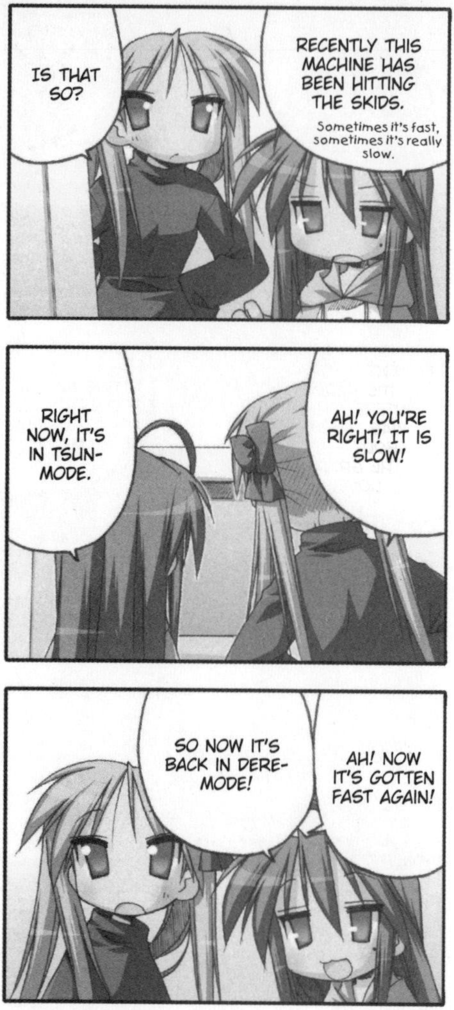
RECENTLY THIS MACHINE HAS BEEN HITTING THE SKIDS.
Sometimes it's fast, sometimes it's really slow.
IS THAT SO?
AH! YOU'RE RIGHT! IT IS SLOW!
RIGHT NOW, IT'S IN TSUN-MODE.
AH! NOW IT'S GOTTEN FAST AGAIN!
SO NOW IT'S BACK IN DERE-MODE!
ALL RIGHT... WHAT HAS ALL THAT BEEN ABOUT?
NOTHING... IT'S JUST THAT MY MACHINE IS SORT OF LIKE A TSUNDERE GIRL, THAT'S ALL!

example

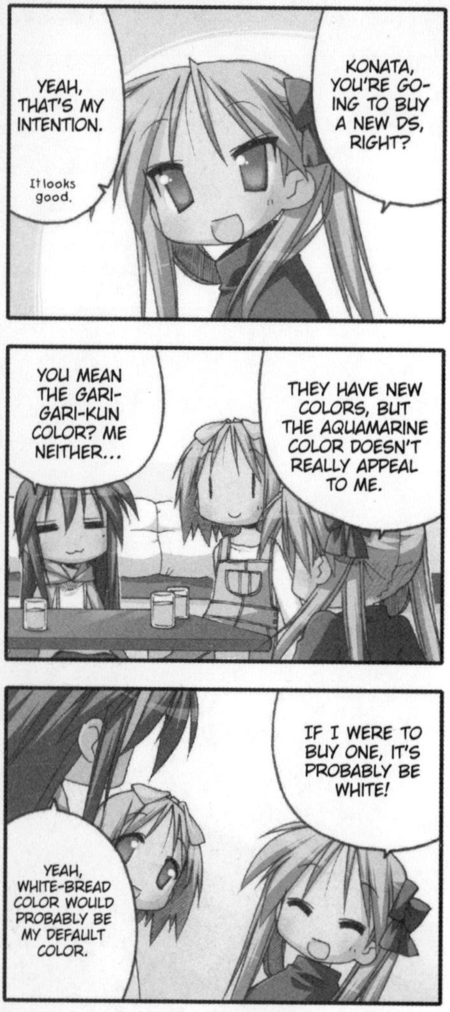
KONATA, YOU'RE GOING TO BUY A NEW DS, RIGHT?
YEAH, THAT'S MY INTENTION.
It looks good.
THEY HAVE NEW COLORS, BUT THE AQUAMARINE COLOR DOESN'T REALLY APPEAL TO ME.
YOU MEAN THE GARI-GARI-KUN COLOR? ME NEITHER...
IF I WERE TO BUY ONE, IT'S PROBABLY BE WHITE!
YEAH, WHITE-BREAD COLOR WOULD PROBABLY BE MY DEFAULT COLOR.
BUT PERSONALLY, I THINK I'LL GO FOR THE SCHOOL SWIMSUIT COLOR...
WAIT! HOLD IT A SECOND.
WHENEVER I TALK TO YOU I GET SORT OF...
...tired...

leaving it to chance

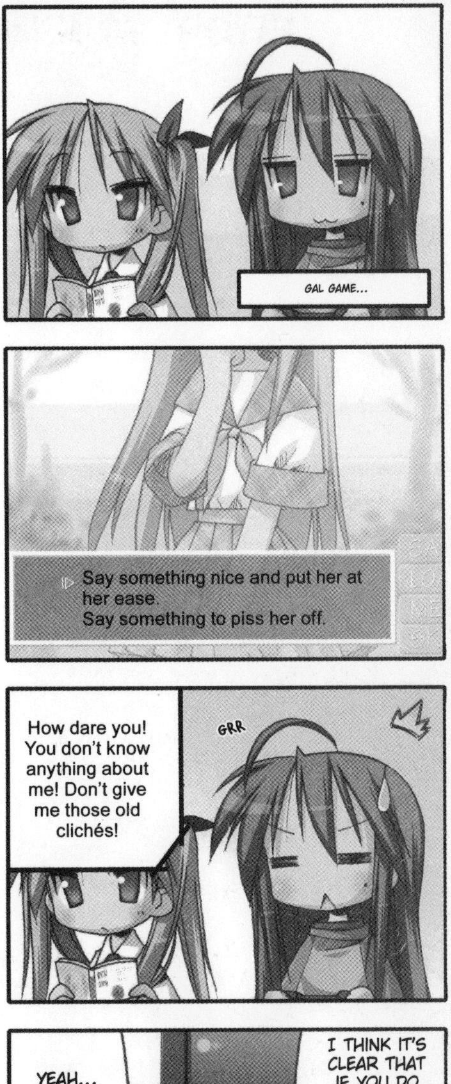
GAL GAME...
Say something nice and put her at her ease.
Say something to piss her off.
GRR
How dare you! You don't know anything about me! Don't give me those old clichés!
I THINK IT'S CLEAR THAT IF YOU DO WHAT'S OBVI-OUS IN THIS GAME, YOU FALL RIGHT INTO THEIR TRAP.
YEAH... I THINK YOU'RE RIGHT.
But I don't see what else I can choose?

or more concretely, something like child pornography

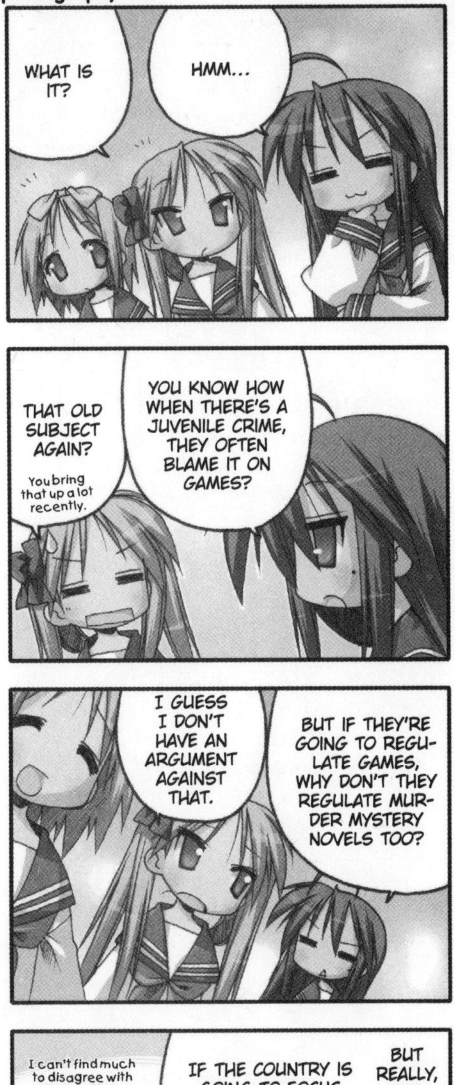
HMM...
WHAT IS IT?
YOU KNOW HOW WHEN THERE'S A JUVENILE CRIME, THEY OFTEN BLAME IT ON GAMES?
THAT OLD SUBJECT AGAIN?
You bring that up a lot recently.
BUT IF THEY'RE GOING TO REGU-LATE GAMES, WHY DON'T THEY REGULATE MUR-DER MYSTERY NOVELS TOO?
I GUESS I DON'T HAVE AN ARGUMENT AGAINST THAT.
BUT REALLY, THE THING I WANT TO SAY THE MOST IS...
IF THE COUNTRY IS GOING TO FOCUS THEIR ATTENTIONS ON THAT SMALL A POINT, DON'T THEY HAVE ANYTHING BETTER TO DO?
I can't find much to disagree with there either.

HIYORI TAMURA'S HUMAN FILE

NAME: Tsukasa Hiiragi

GENDER: ♀

PLACE OF BIRTH: Saitama Prefecture

BIRTHDAY: July 7th

BLOOD TYPE: B

STAR SIGN: Cancer

PRESENT RANK: Ryou-ou Academy, 3rd Year, Class B

HANDEDNESS: Left Handed

BUST-SIZE RANK: Small

FAMILY & POSITION: Father, Mother, Eldest Daughter, Second Daughter, Third Daughter, ☆ Fourth Daughter
*I hear that all the daughters have performed as Miko.

HOBBIES: Cooking (Housework)
*It's her strongest skill too

LIKES: Sweets (especially melons and other fruits), Novel and out-of-the-ordinary thing

DISLIKES: Bell Peppers, Occult, Horror
*I can understand the bell peppers though...

FAVORITE COLORS: White

SPECIAL SKILLS: Housework

WEAK POINTS: Athletics

CLUBS: None

CLASS REP: No

HIYORI'S MEMO

Kagami Hiiragi-sempai's twin sister.
Good around the house and a people person. Has special moe specs in that direction.
Her goal is to become a licensed chef, and she may even be on a higher level than Takara-sempai in that respect.

episode 92
after the dream

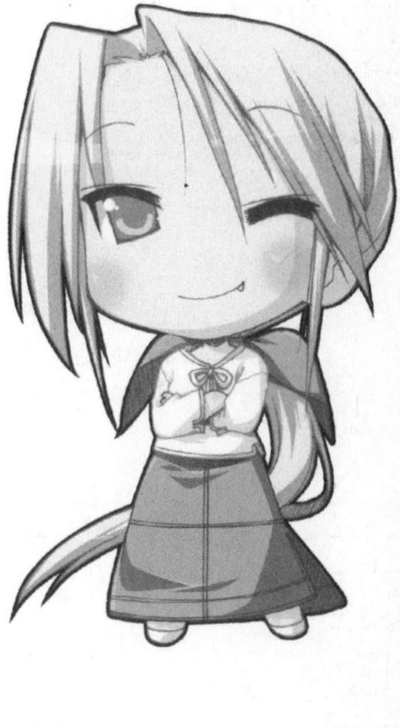

● Comptiq, October 2006 issue

favorite numbers

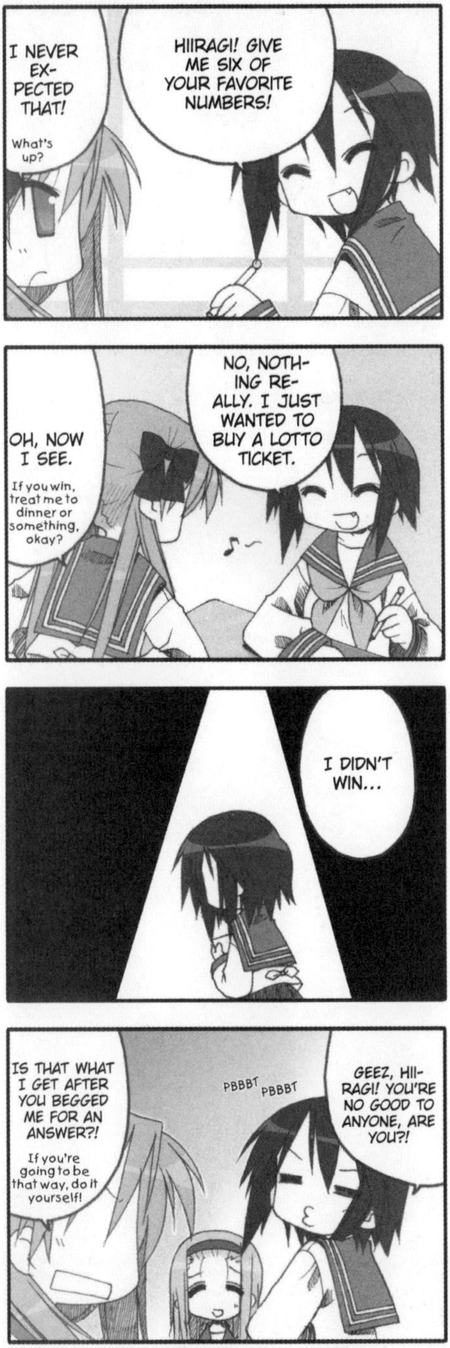
HIIRAGI! GIVE ME SIX OF YOUR FAVORITE NUMBERS!
I NEVER EX-PECTED THAT!
What's up?
NO, NOTH-ING RE-ALLY. I JUST WANTED TO BUY A LOTTO TICKET.
OH, NOW I SEE.
If you win, treat me to dinner or something, okay?
I DIDN'T WIN...
GEEZ, HII-RAGI! YOU'RE NO GOOD TO ANYONE, ARE YOU?!
PBBBT PBBBT
IS THAT WHAT I GET AFTER YOU BEGGED ME FOR AN ANSWER?!
If you're going to be that way, do it yourself!

the star to wish on

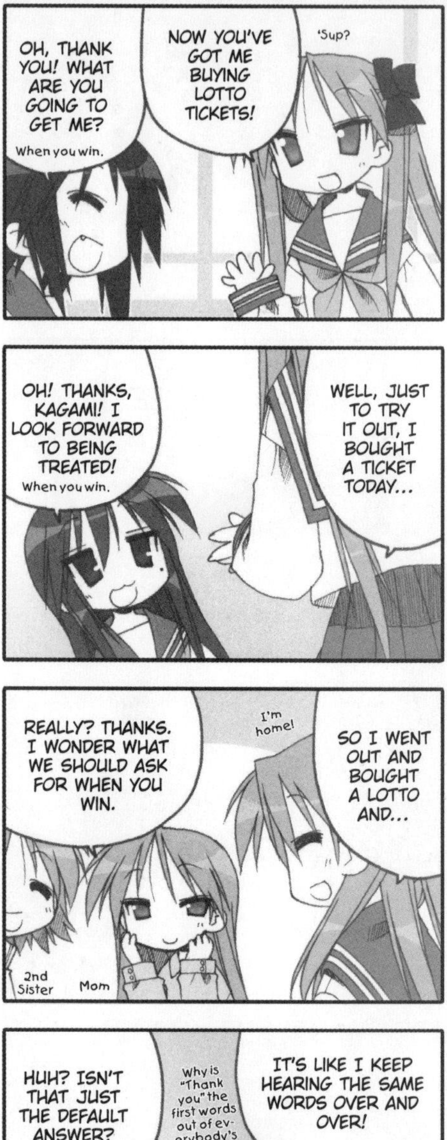
'Sup?
NOW YOU'VE GOT ME BUYING LOTTO TICKETS!
OH, THANK YOU! WHAT ARE YOU GOING TO GET ME?
When you win.
WELL, JUST TO TRY IT OUT, I BOUGHT A TICKET TODAY...
OH! THANKS, KAGAMI! I LOOK FORWARD TO BEING TREATED!
When you win.
SO I WENT OUT AND BOUGHT A LOTTO AND...
I'm home!
REALLY? THANKS. I WONDER WHAT WE SHOULD ASK FOR WHEN YOU WIN.
2nd Sister
Mom
IT'S LIKE I KEEP HEARING THE SAME WORDS OVER AND OVER!
Why is "Thank you" the first words out of everybody's mouths?
HUH? ISN'T THAT JUST THE DEFAULT ANSWER?

junk from the drawers

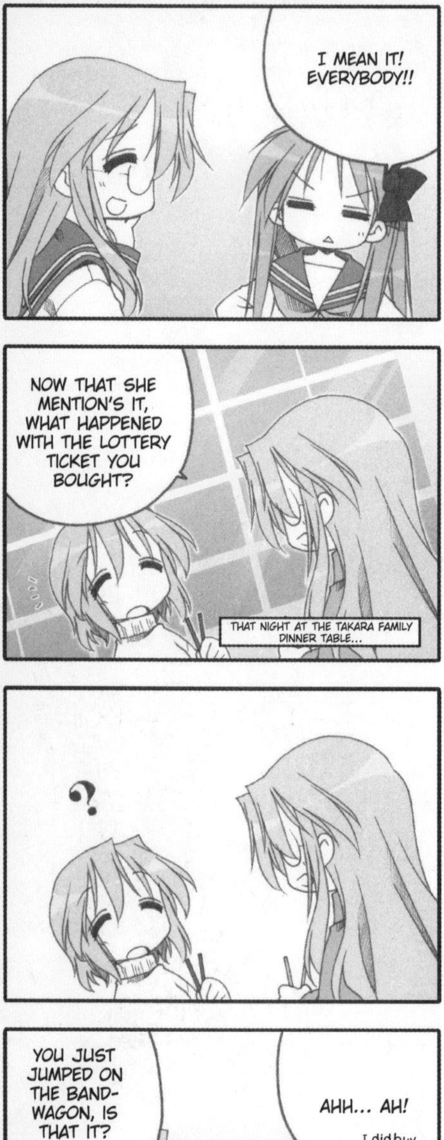
I MEAN IT! EVERYBODY!!
THAT NIGHT AT THE TAKARA FAMILY DINNER TABLE...
NOW THAT SHE MENTION'S IT, WHAT HAPPENED WITH THE LOTTERY TICKET YOU BOUGHT?
?
AHH... AH!
I did buy one once, didn't I?
YOU JUST JUMPED ON THE BAND-WAGON, IS THAT IT?
You bought it, and that was the end of the matter for you, right?
POFF

premiums

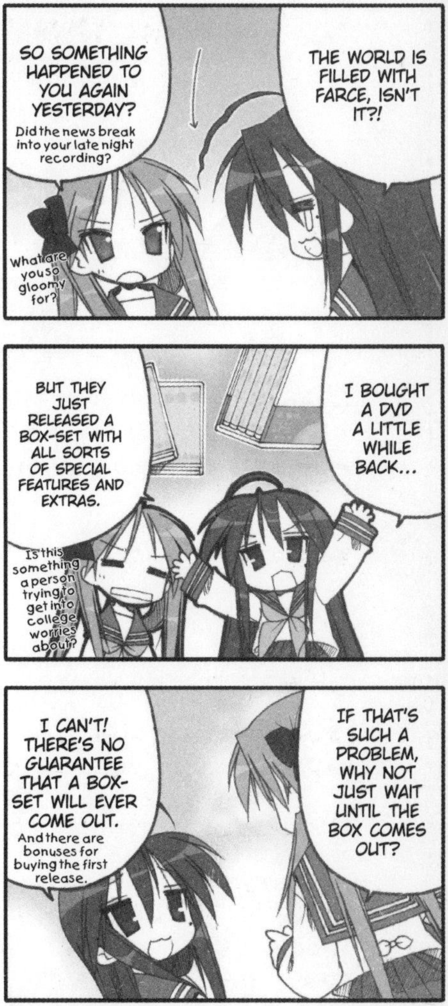
THE WORLD IS FILLED WITH FARCE, ISN'T IT?!
SO SOMETHING HAPPENED TO YOU AGAIN YESTERDAY?
Did the news break into your late night recording?
What are you so gloomy for?
I BOUGHT A DVD A LITTLE WHILE BACK...
BUT THEY JUST RELEASED A BOX-SET WITH ALL SORTS OF SPECIAL FEATURES AND EXTRAS.
Is this something a person trying to get into college worries about?
IF THAT'S SUCH A PROBLEM, WHY NOT JUST WAIT UNTIL THE BOX COMES OUT?
I CAN'T! THERE'S NO GUARANTEE THAT A BOX-SET WILL EVER COME OUT.
And there are bonuses for buying the first release.
HMM... SO THEY'RE OUT TO GET THE REPEAT-BUYER'S MONEY, HUH?
THE ADULT WORLD IS BOTH DIRTY AND CRUEL!

smash and shatter

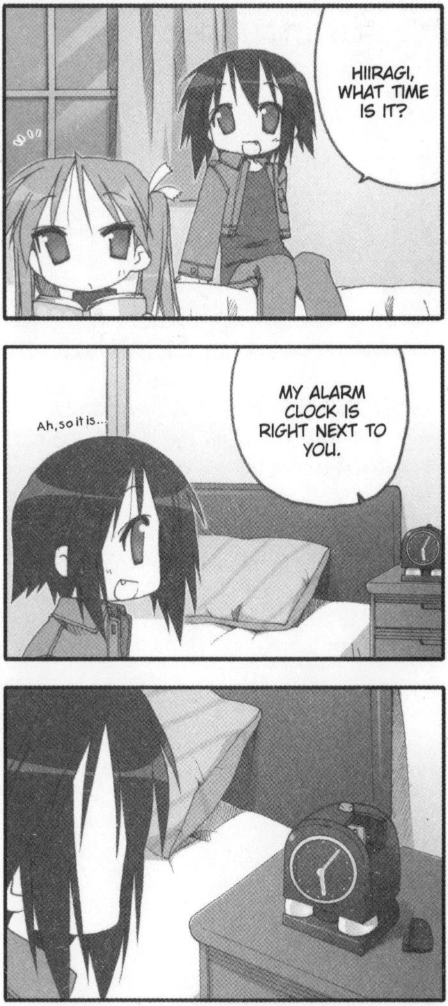
HIIRAGI, WHAT TIME IS IT?
MY ALARM CLOCK IS RIGHT NEXT TO YOU.
Ah, so it is...
THE VIOLENT LEGEND OF EARLY-MORNING HIIRAGI LIVES!!
ZUGEEEN
JUST FOR YOUR INFORMATION, IT ONLY BROKE BECAUSE IT FELL!
GULP

HIYORI TAMURA'S HUMAN FILE

NAME: Kagami Hiiragi

GENDER: ♀

PLACE OF BIRTH: Saitama Prefecture

BIRTHDAY: July 7th

BLOOD TYPE: B

STAR SIGN: Cancer

PRESENT RANK: Ryou-ou Academy, 3rd Year, Class C

HANDEDNESS: Left Handed

BUST-SIZE RANK: Medium
*I thought she was flat, but it turns out she's rounder than expected.

FAMILY & POSITION: Father, Mother, Eldest Daughter, Second Daughter, ☆ Third Daughter, Fourth Daughter

HOBBIES: Reading, Games
*I'd like to hear her lecture on light novels!

LIKES: Snacks (especially of the chocolate variety)

DISLIKES: Shellfish, Bathroom Scales

FAVORITE COLORS: Violet

SPECIAL SKILLS: English

WEAK POINTS: Housework
*High points for fitting her profile.

CLUBS: None

CLASS REP: No
(But she was head of the 1st-Year Reps in her freshman year.)

HIYORI'S MEMO

Tsukasa Hiiragi-sempai's older twin sister.
Plays the wife to everyone.
Great at her part.
She denies this, but no matter how I look at it, she's tsundere!
According to Izumi-sempai, she can be very cute at times.

Lucky☆Star

episode 93
landmines

●Comptiq, August 2006 issue

a secret

TAMURA-SAN, YOU'RE IN *THAT* CIRCLE, AREN'T YOU?
I am, thank you.
OH, YEAH! I'D LIKE TO SEE TAMURA-SAN'S MANGA!
HMM? SURE, IF YOU LIKE...
GWIP
It's very embarrassing!
I DON'T KNOW ABOUT THAT...
COME ON, HIYORIN! DOUJIN ARE THERE FOR OTHER PEOPLE TO SEE!
WHAA! WHERE'S YOUR WAR-RIOR'S MERCY...?!
AT LEAST ONLY SHOW THE STUFF MEANT FOR THE AVERAGE AUDIENCE!
And "Hiyorin" is embarrassing!
?

true colors

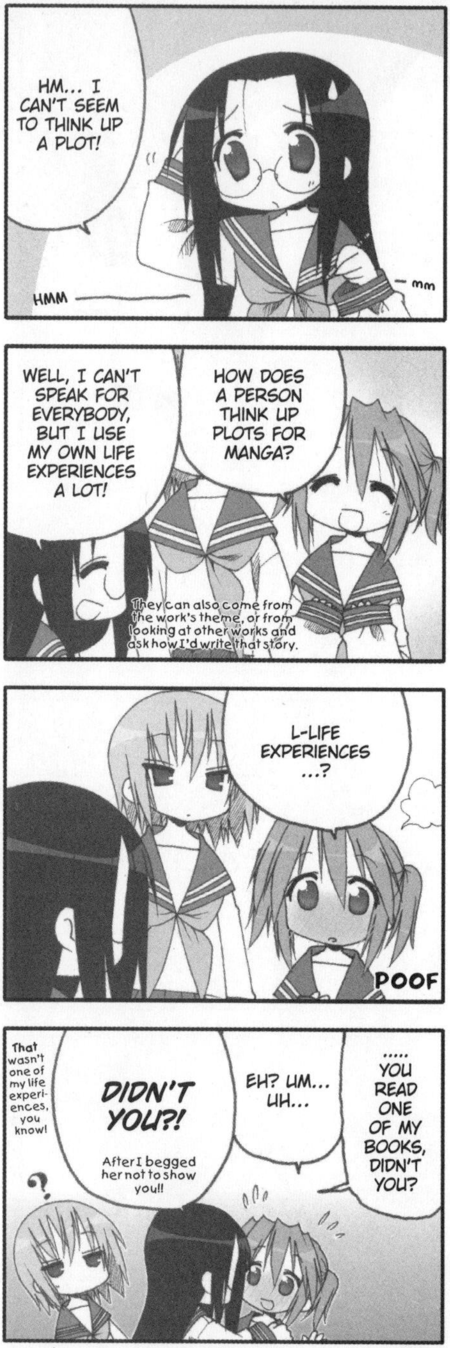
HM... I CAN'T SEEM TO THINK UP A PLOT!
HMM —— mm
HOW DOES A PERSON THINK UP PLOTS FOR MANGA?
WELL, I CAN'T SPEAK FOR EVERYBODY, BUT I USE MY OWN LIFE EXPERIENCES A LOT!
They can also come from the work's theme, or from looking at other works and ask how I'd write that story.
L-LIFE EXPERIENCES ...?
POOF
..... YOU READ ONE OF MY BOOKS, DIDN'T YOU?
EH? UM... UH...
DIDN'T YOU?!
After I begged her not to show you!!
That wasn't one of my life experiences, you know!

an example

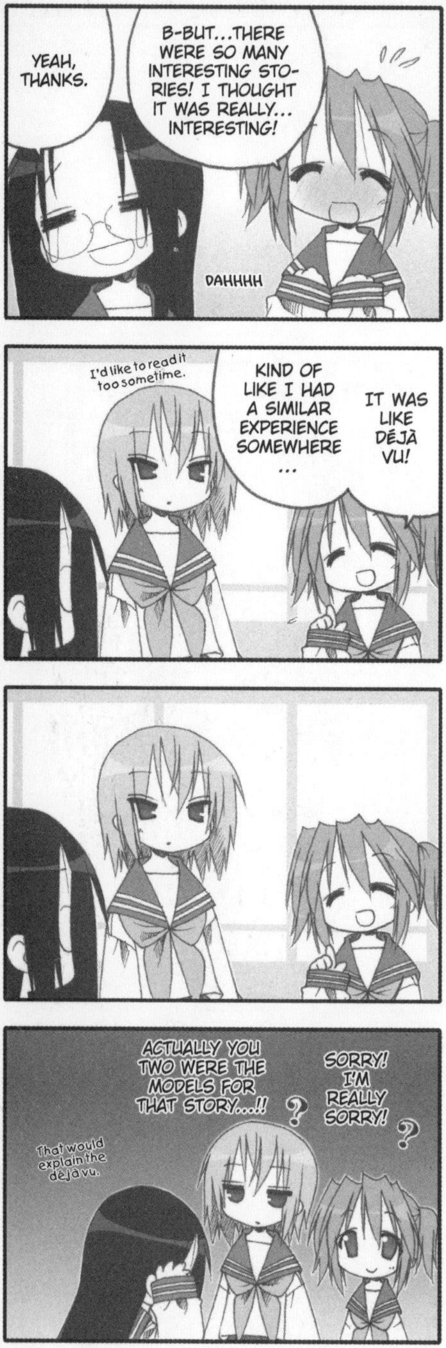
B-BUT...THERE WERE SO MANY INTERESTING STORIES! I THOUGHT IT WAS REALLY... INTERESTING!
YEAH, THANKS.
DAHHHH
IT WAS LIKE DÉJÀ VU!
KIND OF LIKE I HAD A SIMILAR EXPERIENCE SOMEWHERE ...
I'd like to read it too sometime.
SORRY! I'M REALLY SORRY!
ACTUALLY YOU TWO WERE THE MODELS FOR THAT STORY...!!
That would explain the déjà vu.

gone with the wind

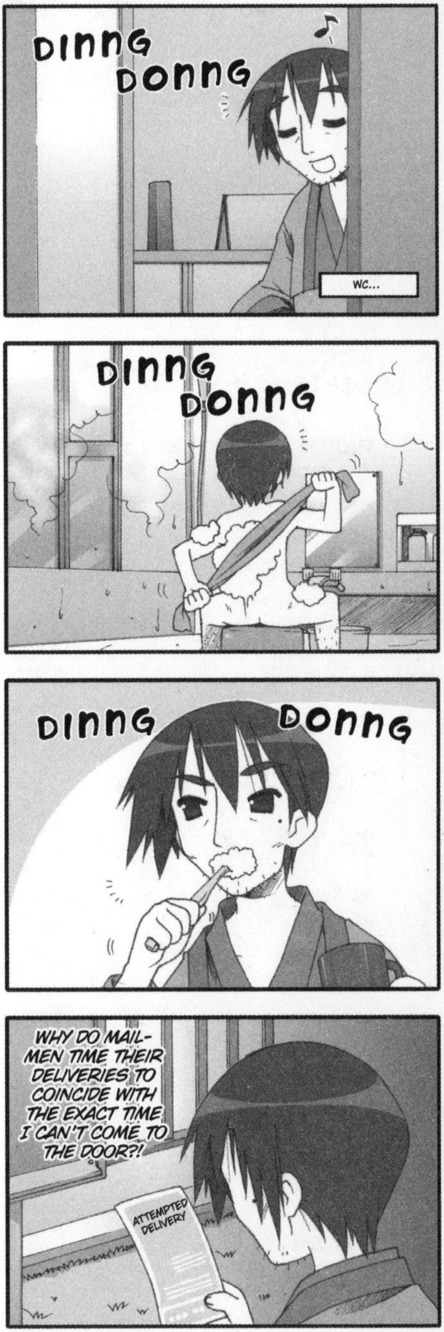
DINNG DONNG
WC...
DINNG DONNG
DINNG DONNG
WHY DO MAIL-MEN TIME THEIR DELIVERIES TO COINCIDE WITH THE EXACT TIME I CAN'T COME TO THE DOOR?!
ATTEMPTED DELIVERY

one's standing

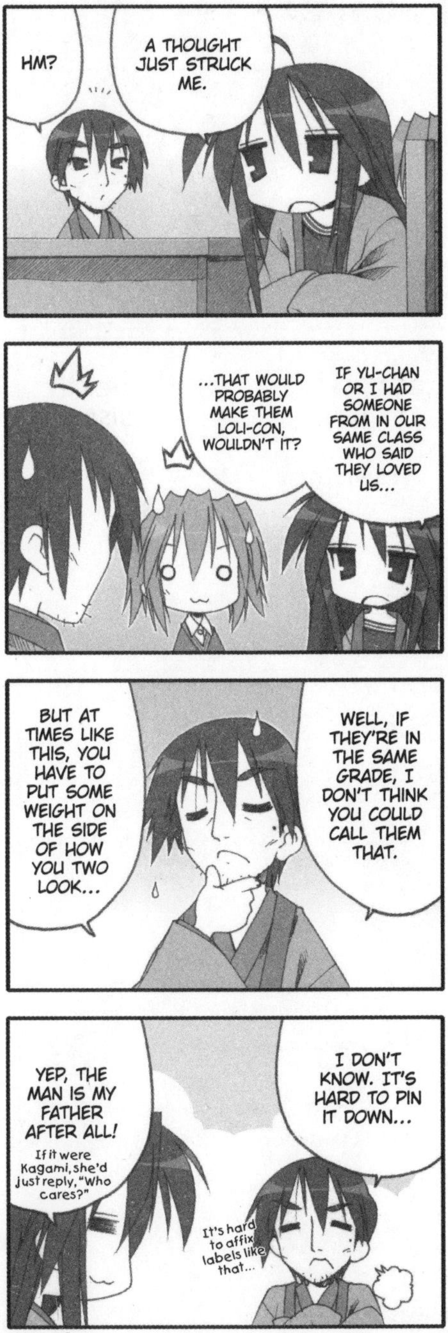
A THOUGHT JUST STRUCK ME.
HM?
IF YU-CHAN OR I HAD SOMEONE FROM IN OUR SAME CLASS WHO SAID THEY LOVED US...
...THAT WOULD PROBABLY MAKE THEM LOLI-CON, WOULDN'T IT?
WELL, IF THEY'RE IN THE SAME GRADE, I DON'T THINK YOU COULD CALL THEM THAT.
BUT AT TIMES LIKE THIS, YOU HAVE TO PUT SOME WEIGHT ON THE SIDE OF HOW YOU TWO LOOK...
I DON'T KNOW. IT'S HARD TO PIN IT DOWN...
YEP, THE MAN IS MY FATHER AFTER ALL!
If it were Kagami, she'd just reply, "Who cares?"
It's hard to affix labels like that...

HIYORI TAMURA'S HUMAN FILE

NAME: Miyuki Takura

GENDER: ♀

PLACE OF BIRTH: Tokyo

BIRTHDAY: October 25th

BLOOD TYPE: O

STAR SIGN: Scorpio

PRESENT RANK: Ryou-ou Academy, 3rd Year, Class B

HANDEDNESS: Left Handed

BUST-SIZE RANK: Giant

FAMILY & POSITION: Father, Mother, ☆ Eldest daughter

HOBBIES: Reading, Games that are purely mental exercises

LIKES: Chawan-mushi, Japanese-style snacks, Study (anything to increase her knowledge)
*I wish I could do that!

DISLIKES: Raw Fish Dishes, Doctors (especially dentists)
*I can understand that!

FAVORITE COLORS: Orange

SPECIAL SKILLS: None to speak of

WEAK POINTS: None to speak of

CLUBS: None

CLASS REP: Head of the 3rd-Year Reps
*And the student-body president. A familiar pattern.

HIYORI'S MEMO

She has a beautiful body, great manners, can both study and do sports, and on top of that, she wears glasses and has an impossible bust size!
A princess with high marks for affability.
To be blunt, her existence is not fair!
A neighbor to Iwasaki-san, and they share a sisterly-like relationship.

Lucky☆Star

episode 94
as a customer

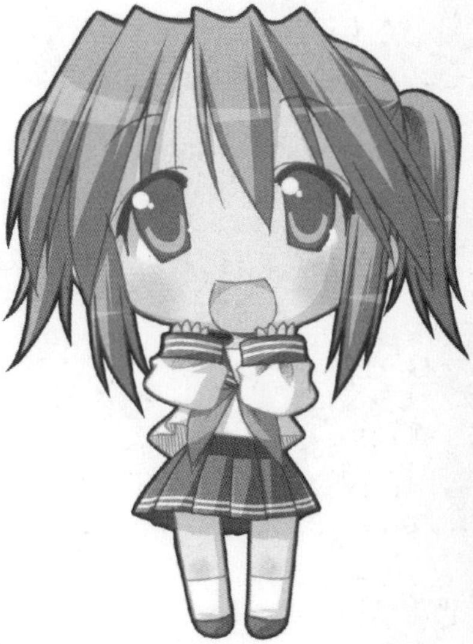

● Comptiq, September 2006 issue

a benefit

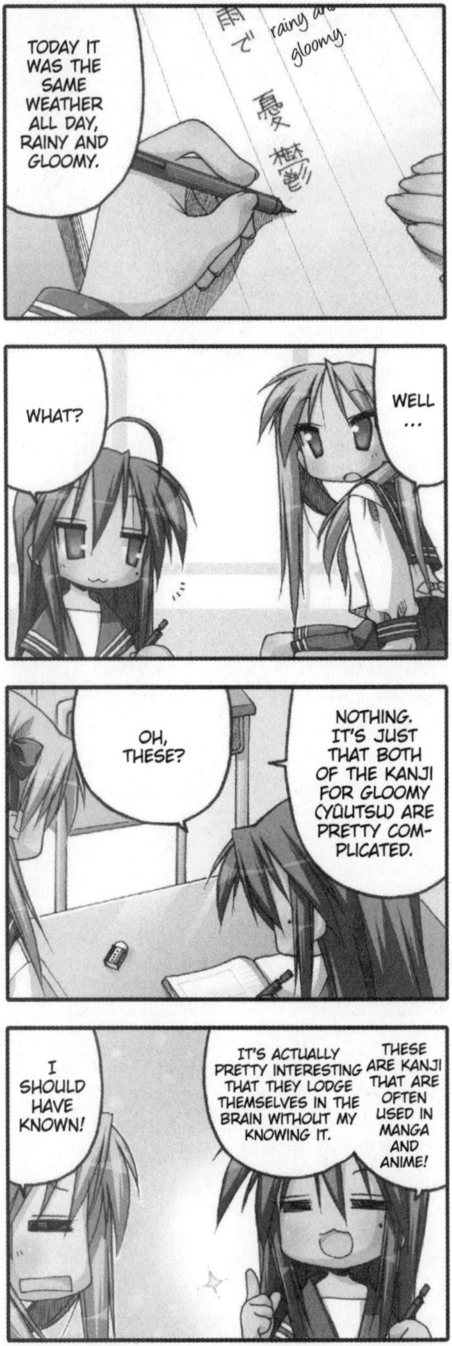

雨で rainy and gloomy.
憂鬱
TODAY IT WAS THE SAME WEATHER ALL DAY, RAINY AND GLOOMY.
WELL ...
WHAT?
NOTHING. IT'S JUST THAT BOTH OF THE KANJI FOR GLOOMY (YÛUTSU) ARE PRETTY COMPLICATED.
OH, THESE?
THESE ARE KANJI THAT ARE OFTEN USED IN MANGA AND ANIME!
IT'S ACTUALLY PRETTY INTERESTING THAT THEY LODGE THEMSELVES IN THE BRAIN WITHOUT MY KNOWING IT.
I SHOULD HAVE KNOWN!

just sort of

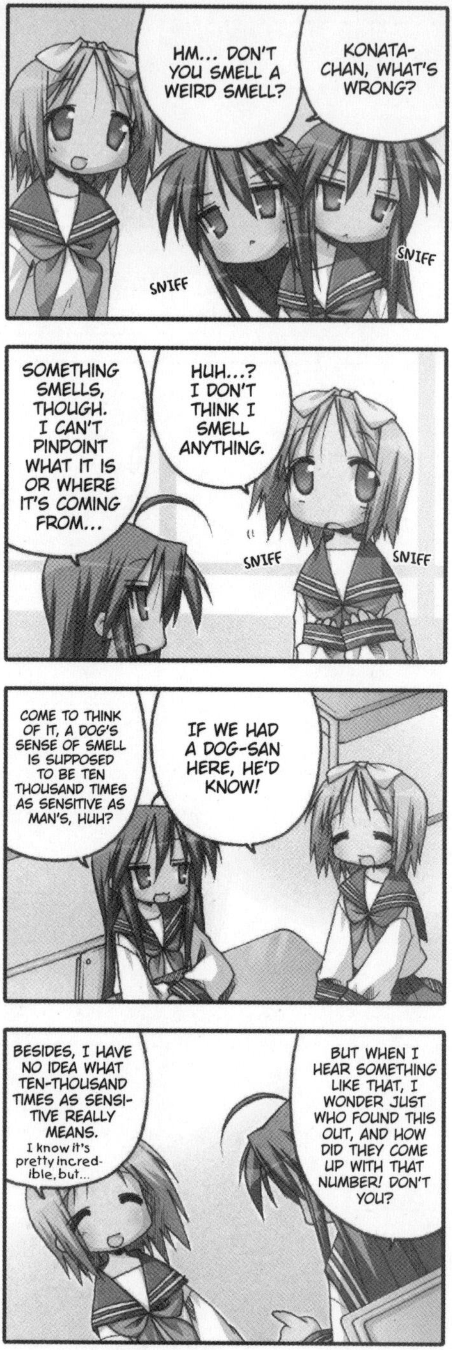
KONATA-CHAN, WHAT'S WRONG?
HM... DON'T YOU SMELL A WEIRD SMELL?
SNIFF
SNIFF
HUH...? I DON'T THINK I SMELL ANYTHING.
SOMETHING SMELLS, THOUGH. I CAN'T PINPOINT WHAT IT IS OR WHERE IT'S COMING FROM...
SNIFF
SNIFF
IF WE HAD A DOG-SAN HERE, HE'D KNOW!
COME TO THINK OF IT, A DOG'S SENSE OF SMELL IS SUPPOSED TO BE TEN THOUSAND TIMES AS SENSITIVE AS MAN'S, HUH?
BUT WHEN I HEAR SOMETHING LIKE THAT, I WONDER JUST WHO FOUND THIS OUT, AND HOW DID THEY COME UP WITH THAT NUMBER! DON'T YOU?
BESIDES, I HAVE NO IDEA WHAT TEN-THOUSAND TIMES AS SENSITIVE REALLY MEANS.
I know it's pretty incredible, but...

the target item

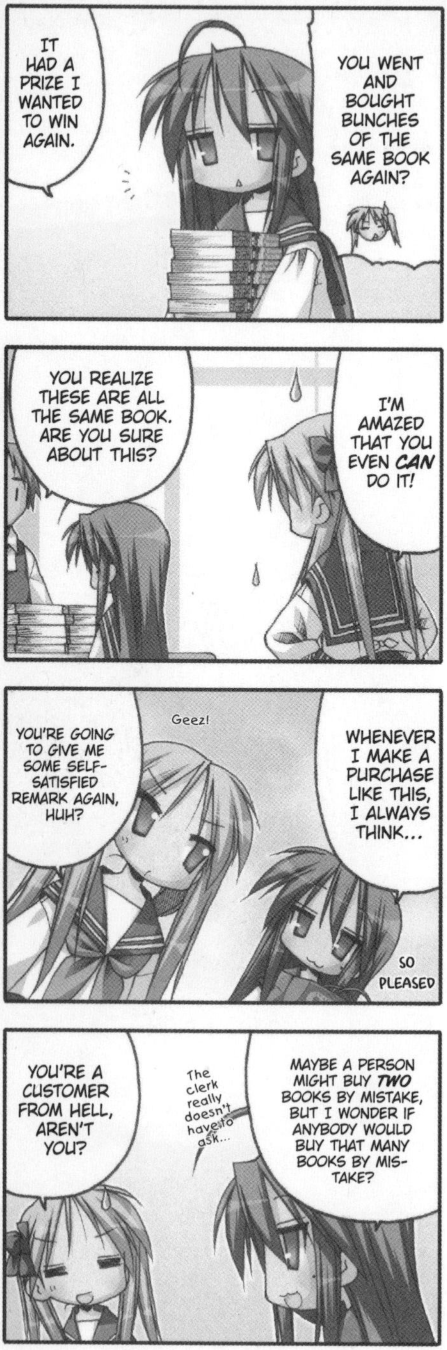
YOU WENT AND BOUGHT BUNCHES OF THE SAME BOOK AGAIN?
IT HAD A PRIZE I WANTED TO WIN AGAIN.
I'M AMAZED THAT YOU EVEN CAN DO IT!
YOU REALIZE THESE ARE ALL THE SAME BOOK. ARE YOU SURE ABOUT THIS?
WHENEVER I MAKE A PURCHASE LIKE THIS, I ALWAYS THINK...
Geez!
YOU'RE GOING TO GIVE ME SOME SELF-SATISFIED REMARK AGAIN, HUH?
SO PLEASED
MAYBE A PERSON MIGHT BUY TWO BOOKS BY MISTAKE, BUT I WONDER IF ANYBODY WOULD BUY THAT MANY BOOKS BY MISTAKE?
The clerk really doesn't have to ask...
YOU'RE A CUSTOMER FROM HELL, AREN'T YOU?

the throughway

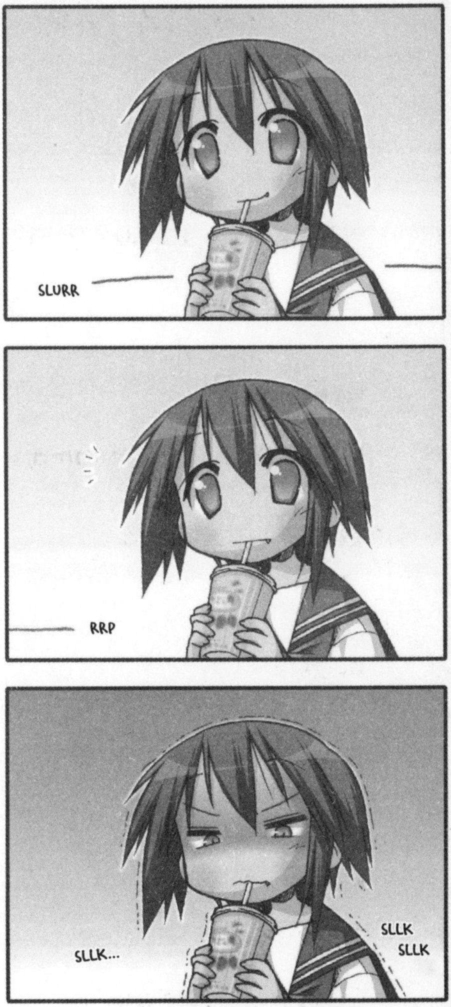
SLURR
RRP
SLLK SLLK
SLLK...
DAMN! YOU'VE BEAT-EN ME AGAIN, PULPY FRUIT DRINKS!
HAHHH ...
I lose!
AH, IT'S CAUGHT IN THE STRAW, HUH?

questor

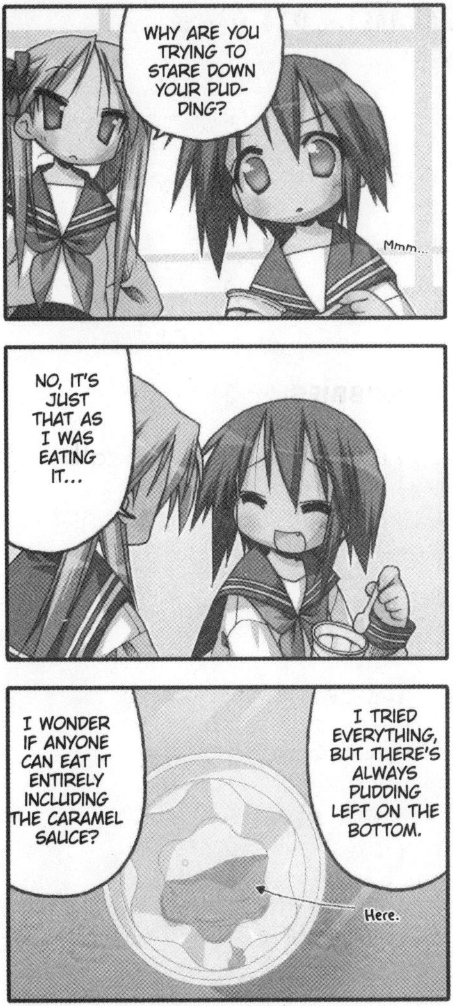
WHY ARE YOU TRYING TO STARE DOWN YOUR PUD-DING?
Mmm...
NO, IT'S JUST THAT AS I WAS EATING IT...
I TRIED EVERYTHING, BUT THERE'S ALWAYS PUDDING LEFT ON THE BOTTOM.
I WONDER IF ANYONE CAN EAT IT ENTIRELY INCLUDING THE CARAMEL SAUCE?
Here.
THAT'S WHAT I WAS THINKING, ANYWAY.
I can never seem to find a way.
I ENVY YOU AND YOUR COMPLETE LACK OF WORRIES.

HIYORI TAMURA'S HUMAN FILE

NAME: Misao Kusakabe

GENDER: ♀

PLACE OF BIRTH: Saitama Prefecture

BIRTHDAY: July 20th
*A day that predicts a high-energy life.

BLOOD TYPE: B

STAR SIGN: Cancer

PRESENT RANK: Ryou-ou Academy, 3rd Year, Class C

HANDEDNESS: Left Handed

BUST-SIZE RANK: Medium

FAMILY & POSITION:
Grandfather, Grandmother, Father, Mother,
☆ Eldest daughter

HOBBIES: All Sports

LIKES: Hamburgers, Meatballs, The Sun
*She's kind of like grade-school boys that way.

DISLIKES: Konnyaku, Vegetables, Rain

FAVORITE COLORS: Yellow

SPECIAL SKILLS: Athletics

WEAK POINTS: World History, Math

CLUBS: Track & Field Club
*Her skills put her in the lower reaches of the upper echelon.

CLASS REP: Athletics Rep

HIYORI'S MEMO

Kagami Hiiragi-sempai's classmate and a childhood friend of Minegishi-sempai.
If I had to choose, I'd say she was more like the guy in the relationship.
Optimistic and always having fun.
Her fangs are a cute individual characteristic.

episode 95
think well of me, you all

● Comptiq, September 2006 issue

WE ALL WENT AS A FAMILY TO KARAOKE YESTERDAY!
REALLY?
RECENTLY IT'S GETTING NORMAL TO SEE GAME THEME-SONGS AMONG THE SELECTIONS.
I sure was surprised!
AH, THAT...
WELL, THERE WERE SOME TITLES IN THE PAST THAT GOT REALLY FAMOUS, SO THAT NOW, EVEN MINOR HITS ARE INCLUDED.
REALLY ...?
YOU KNOW, THERE ARE MINOR HITS RECENTLY TOO, KAGAMI.
REALLY ...?
What are you trying to say to me?

i need you

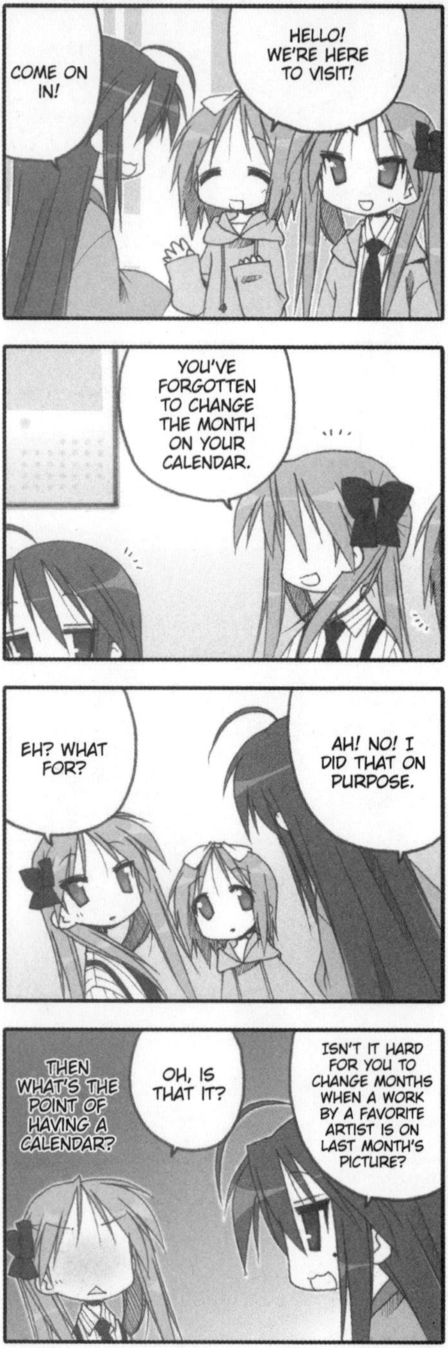
HELLO! WE'RE HERE TO VISIT!
COME ON IN!
YOU'VE FORGOTTEN TO CHANGE THE MONTH ON YOUR CALENDAR.
AH! NO! I DID THAT ON PURPOSE.
EH? WHAT FOR?
ISN'T IT HARD FOR YOU TO CHANGE MONTHS WHEN A WORK BY A FAVORITE ARTIST IS ON LAST MONTH'S PICTURE?
OH, IS THAT IT?
THEN WHAT'S THE POINT OF HAVING A CALENDAR?

lucky strike

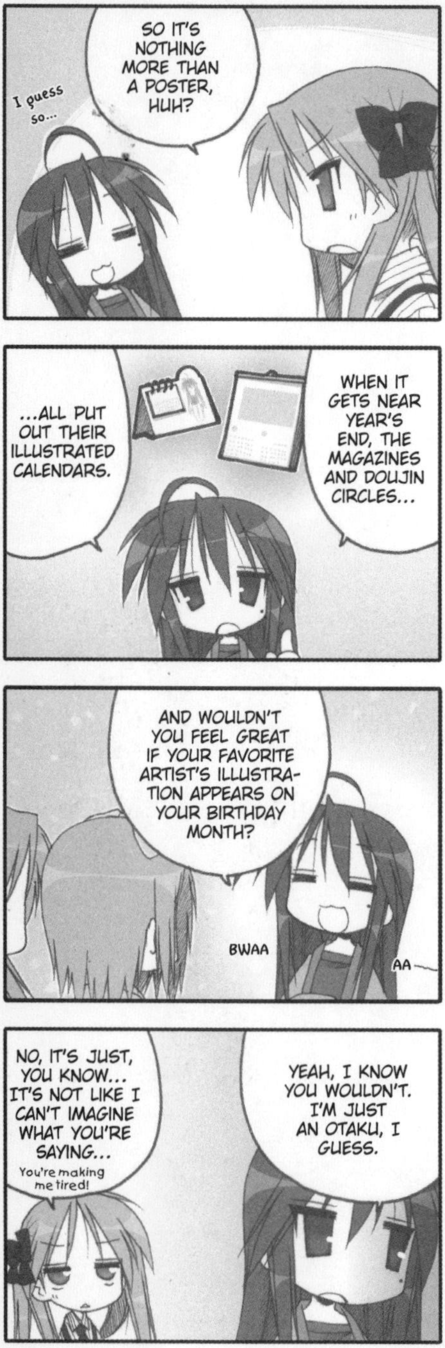
SO IT'S NOTHING MORE THAN A POSTER, HUH?
I guess so...
WHEN IT GETS NEAR YEAR'S END, THE MAGAZINES AND DOUJIN CIRCLES...
...ALL PUT OUT THEIR ILLUSTRATED CALENDARS.
AND WOULDN'T YOU FEEL GREAT IF YOUR FAVORITE ARTIST'S ILLUSTRATION APPEARS ON YOUR BIRTHDAY MONTH?
BWAA
AA—
YEAH, I KNOW YOU WOULDN'T. I'M JUST AN OTAKU, I GUESS.
NO, IT'S JUST, YOU KNOW... IT'S NOT LIKE I CAN'T IMAGINE WHAT YOU'RE SAYING...
You're making me tired!

ms. precision

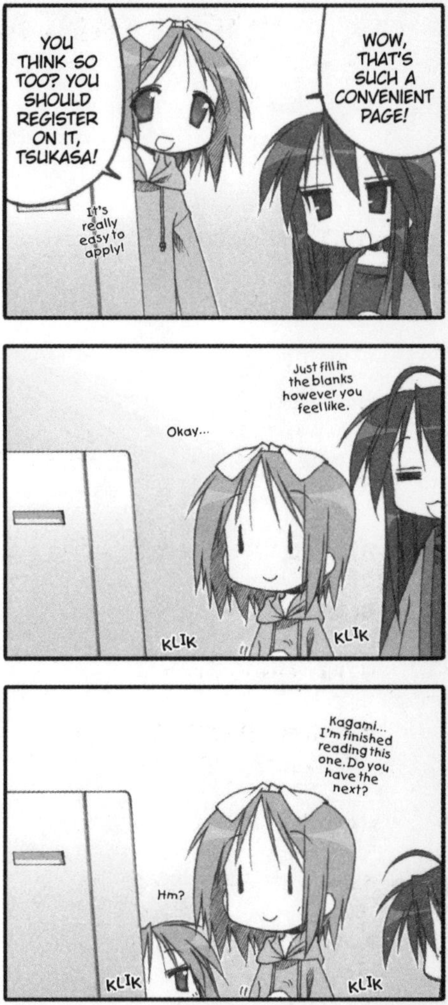
WOW, THAT'S SUCH A CONVENIENT PAGE!
YOU THINK SO TOO? YOU SHOULD REGISTER ON IT, TSUKASA!
It's really easy to apply!
Just fill in the blanks however you feel like.
Okay...
KLIK
KLIK
Kagami... I'm finished reading this one. Do you have the next?
Hm?
KLIK
KLIK
YOU'RE STILL ON THAT PAGE?!
THE TERMS OF USE ARE SO LONG...
EH?! YOU READ ALL THAT?!

full consent

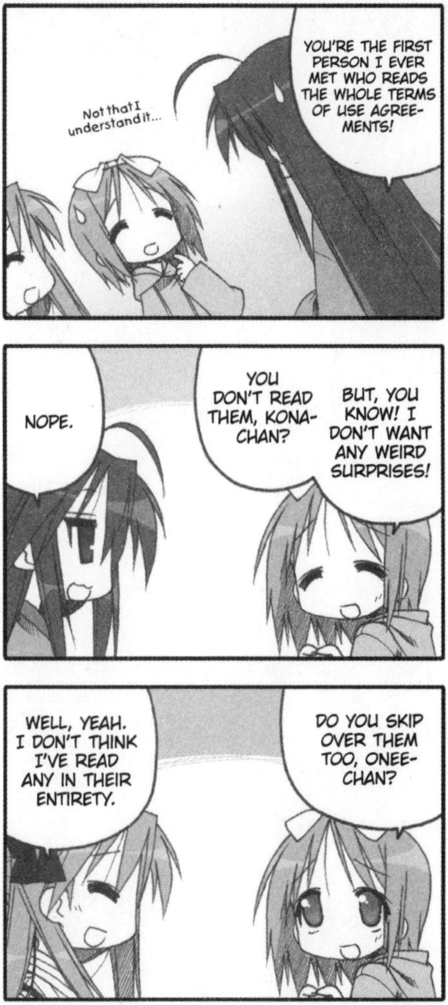
YOU'RE THE FIRST PERSON I EVER MET WHO READS THE WHOLE TERMS OF USE AGREEMENTS!
Not that I understand it...
BUT, YOU KNOW! I DON'T WANT ANY WEIRD SURPRISES!
YOU DON'T READ THEM, KONA-CHAN?
NOPE.
DO YOU SKIP OVER THEM TOO, ONEE-CHAN?
WELL, YEAH. I DON'T THINK I'VE READ ANY IN THEIR ENTIRETY.
KAGAMI, NICE WORDS, BUT THEY'RE MISLEADING.
OH, SHUT UP!
I'm not lying!
BUT THE GIST IS THAT YOU'VE NEVER READ THEM!

HIYORI TAMURA'S HUMAN FILE

NAME: Ayano Minegishi

GENDER: ♀

PLACE OF BIRTH: Saitama Prefecture

BIRTHDAY: November 4th

BLOOD TYPE: AB

STAR SIGN: Scorpio

PRESENT RANK: Ryou-ou Academy, 3rd Year, Class C

HANDEDNESS: Left Handed

BUST-SIZE RANK: Medium

FAMILY & POSITION: Father, Mother, ☆ Eldest Daughter, Second Daughter

HOBBIES: Window Shopping, Walks, Making Sweets
*Sure is feminine!

LIKES: Tofu, Gyoza

DISLIKES: Spicy Foods, Cigarette Smoke

FAVORITE COLORS: Yellow

SPECIAL SKILLS: Japanese Class

WEAK POINTS: Math

CLUBS: Tea Club
*Ah, she'd look good in kimono!

CLASS REP: Discipline Committee
*There's an image of discipline committee members of being really strict.

HIYORI'S MEMO

Kagami Hiiragi-sempai's classmate and Kusakabe-sempai's childhood friend. She's the female of the relationship.
She gives off the image of a modest young lady, but she can be blunt in her way of speech.
Her forehead shines!

episode 96
a world overflowing with smiles

● Comptique, September 2006 issue

a cry from the heart

DAD, IF YOU COULD BE RE-BORN, WHAT WOULD YOU LIKE TO BE?
HM... MAYBE A CUTE GIRL?
H-HUUH?
I SEE THAT OPINION ON THE NET AT TIMES, BUT WHY?
It's kind of creepy.
THERE ARE ALL SORTS OF DIS-COUNTS, LIKE FOR FOOD OR LEISURE ACTIVITIES, OR THOSE LADY'S DAY SALES.
DON'T YOU THINK THAT BEING A GIRL IS JUST NOT FAIR?
There's no "Men's day," you know!
DAD, YOU USU-ALLY SEEM SER-INE, BUT YOU'VE GOT SOME ODD WHINEY QUALITIES TOO, HUH?

that's exactly right

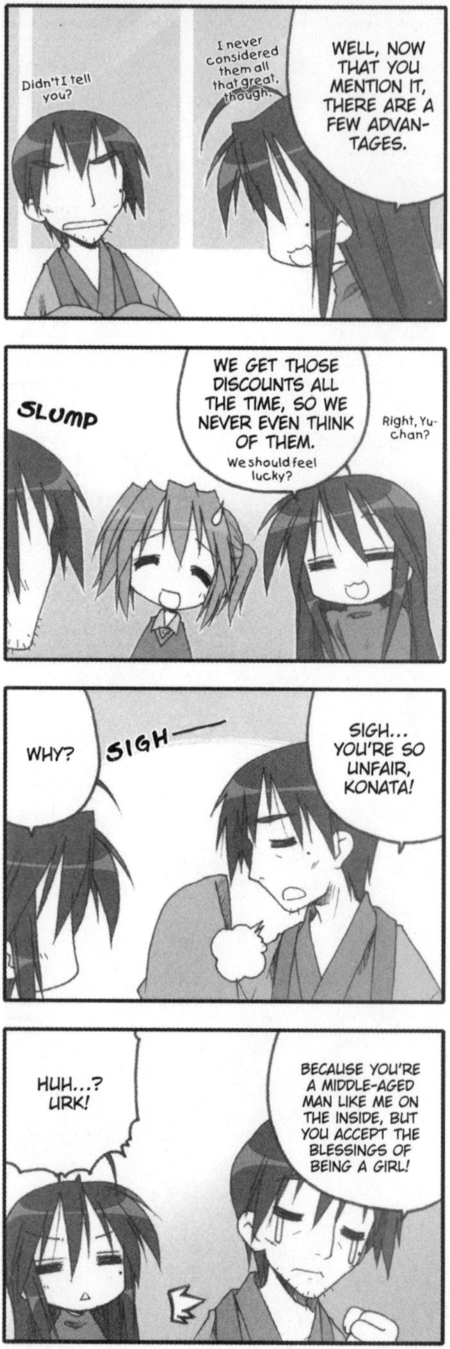
WELL, NOW THAT YOU MENTION IT, THERE ARE A FEW ADVANTAGES.
I never considered them all that great, though.
Didn't I tell you?
Right, Yu-chan?
WE GET THOSE DISCOUNTS ALL THE TIME, SO WE NEVER EVEN THINK OF THEM.
We should feel lucky?
SLUMP
SIGH... YOU'RE SO UNFAIR, KONATA!
SIGH—
WHY?
BECAUSE YOU'RE A MIDDLE-AGED MAN LIKE ME ON THE INSIDE, BUT YOU ACCEPT THE BLESSINGS OF BEING A GIRL!
HUH...? URK!

recharging

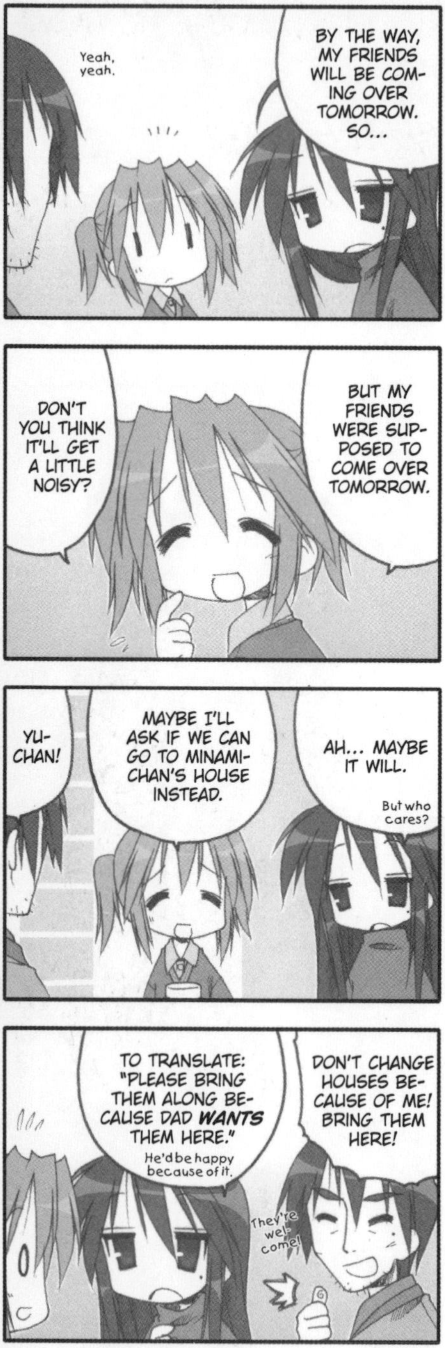
BY THE WAY, MY FRIENDS WILL BE COMING OVER TOMORROW. SO...
Yeah, yeah.
BUT MY FRIENDS WERE SUPPOSED TO COME OVER TOMORROW.
DON'T YOU THINK IT'LL GET A LITTLE NOISY?
AH... MAYBE IT WILL.
But who cares?
MAYBE I'LL ASK IF WE CAN GO TO MINAMI-CHAN'S HOUSE INSTEAD.
YU-CHAN!
DON'T CHANGE HOUSES BECAUSE OF ME! BRING THEM HERE!
They're welcome!
TO TRANSLATE: "PLEASE BRING THEM ALONG BECAUSE DAD **WANTS** THEM HERE."
He'd be happy because of it.

spoilers

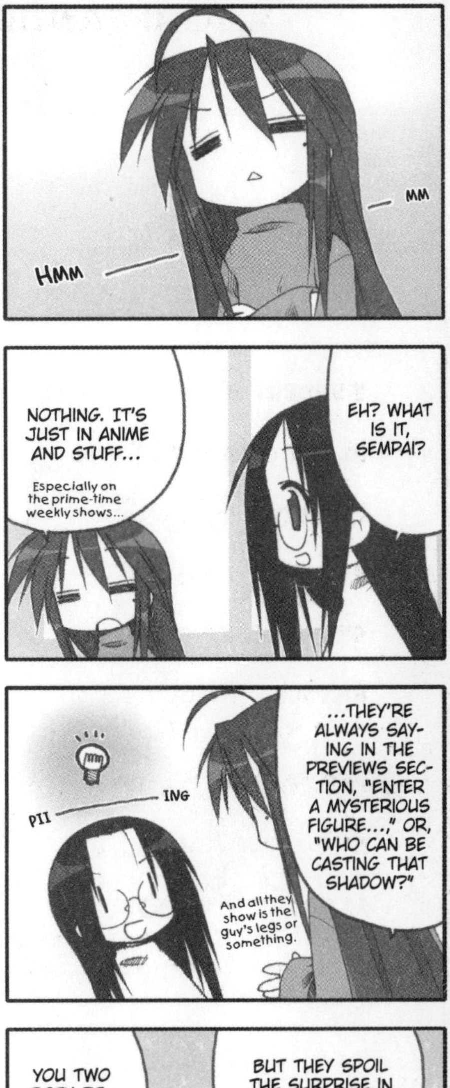
MM
HMM
EH? WHAT IS IT, SEMPAI?
NOTHING. IT'S JUST IN ANIME AND STUFF...
Especially on the prime-time weekly shows...
...THEY'RE ALWAYS SAY-ING IN THE PREVIEWS SEC-TION, "ENTER A MYSTERIOUS FIGURE...," OR, "WHO CAN BE CASTING THAT SHADOW?"
ING
PII
And all they show is the guy's legs or something.
Why do you think that is?
BUT THEY SPOIL THE SURPRISE IN THE TITLE OF THE NEXT EPISODE.
Like, "Enter: XX-san!" or some-thing like that.
It ruins the whole thing.
YOU TWO BOTH RE-ALLY ENJOY LIFE, DON'T YOU?

you, the optimist

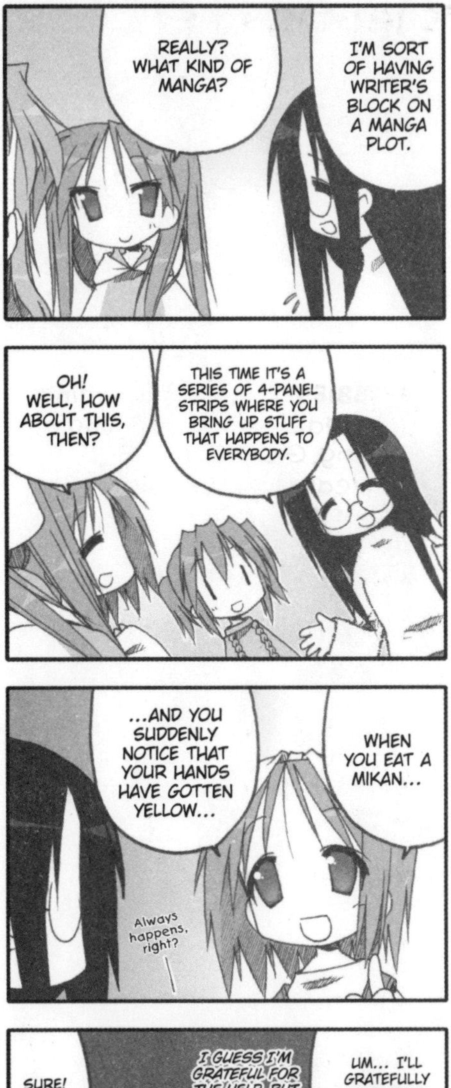
I'M SORT OF HAVING WRITER'S BLOCK ON A MANGA PLOT.
REALLY? WHAT KIND OF MANGA?
THIS TIME IT'S A SERIES OF 4-PANEL STRIPS WHERE YOU BRING UP STUFF THAT HAPPENS TO EVERYBODY.
OH! WELL, HOW ABOUT THIS, THEN?
WHEN YOU EAT A MIKAN...
...AND YOU SUDDENLY NOTICE THAT YOUR HANDS HAVE GOTTEN YELLOW...
Always happens, right?
UM... I'LL GRATEFULLY USE YOUR IDEA...IF I CAN SOMEHOW FIGURE OUT A WAY IT MIGHT WORK.
I GUESS I'M GRATEFUL FOR THE HELP, BUT TO BE BLUNT, IT'S REALLY SUB-PAR!
SURE! AND FOR YOUR NEXT STRIP...
Here's something else that always happens to me...

HIYORI TAMURA'S HUMAN FILE

NAME: Kou Yasaka

GENDER: ♀

PLACE OF BIRTH: Tokyo

BIRTHDAY: February 3rd

BLOOD TYPE: B

STAR SIGN: Aquarius

PRESENT RANK: Ryou-ou Academy, 2rd Year, Class F

HANDEDNESS: Left Handed

BUST-SIZE RANK: Large

FAMILY & POSITION: Father, Mother, Eldest Son, ☆ Eldest Daughter, Second Son

HOBBIES: Doujinshi, Reading (manga), People Watching, Talking, Gambling
*I'd really like her to stop some of her gambling.

LIKES: Curry, Sweets

DISLIKES: Nothing comes to mind

FAVORITE COLORS: Yellow

SPECIAL SKILLS: Japanese Class

WEAK POINTS: English

CLUBS: Animation Research Club
*Please be good to me!

CLASS REP: Student Body Government (Treasurer)
*I know it's rude to say, but I really wonder about that.

HIYORI'S MEMO

My sempai in the Animation Research Club.
She seems to be very chummy with the Ryou-ou Academy teachers, and often goes to their offices.
It isn't like she's scary or anything, but I can't seem to be able to say no to her.
A big-hearted person with great energy.

episode 97
killer smile

● Comptiq, October 2006 issue

unconscious movement

!
HEY, LOOK, KONA-CHAN! YESTERDAY, I FOUND THIS ONE REALLY LONG HAIR!
OHH
PLL
UCK
IT WAS MY GOOD-LUCK CHARM!
I-I'M SORRY! WHENEVER I SEE ONE OF THOSE, I FIND MYSELF PLUCKING IT OUT.
So it was a charm...?

the key to happiness

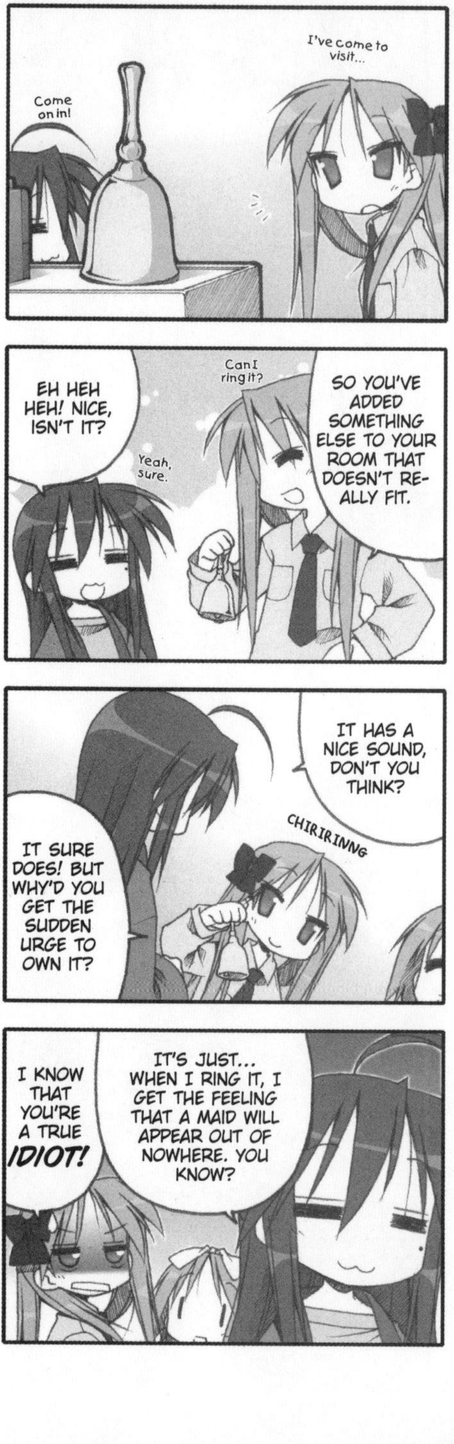
I've come to visit...
Come on in!
SO YOU'VE ADDED SOMETHING ELSE TO YOUR ROOM THAT DOESN'T REALLY FIT.
Can I ring it?
EH HEH HEH! NICE, ISN'T IT?
Yeah, sure.
IT HAS A NICE SOUND, DON'T YOU THINK?
CHIRIRINNG
IT SURE DOES! BUT WHY'D YOU GET THE SUDDEN URGE TO OWN IT?
IT'S JUST... WHEN I RING IT, I GET THE FEELING THAT A MAID WILL APPEAR OUT OF NOWHERE. YOU KNOW?
I KNOW THAT YOU'RE A TRUE *IDIOT!*

defeat

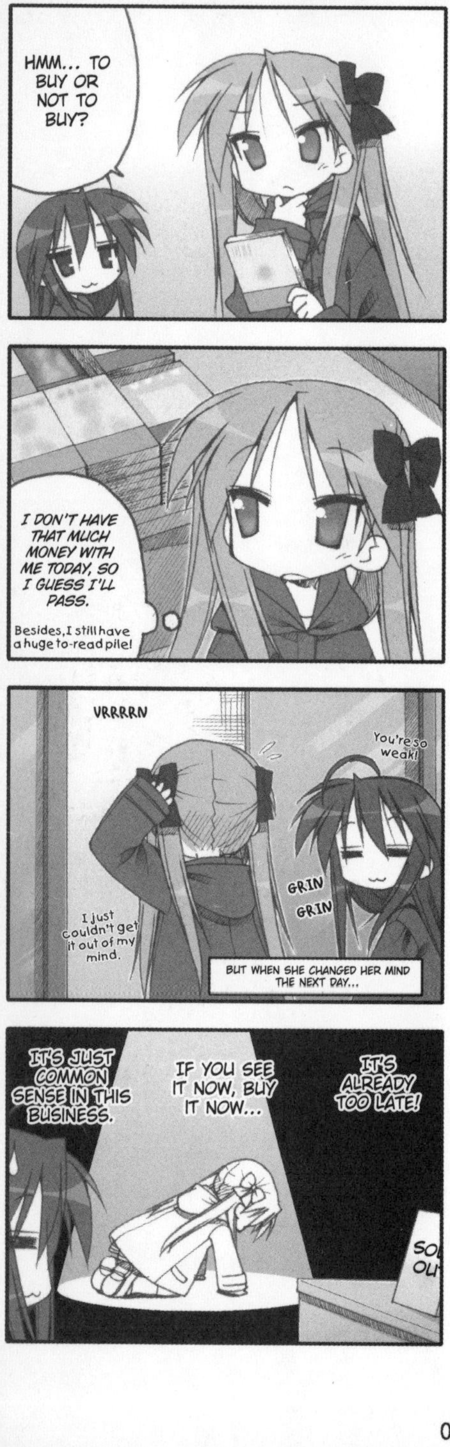
HMM... TO BUY OR NOT TO BUY?
I DON'T HAVE THAT MUCH MONEY WITH ME TODAY, SO I GUESS I'LL PASS.
Besides, I still have a huge to-read pile!
BUT WHEN SHE CHANGED HER MIND THE NEXT DAY...
You're so weak!
VRRRRN
GRIN
GRIN
I just couldn't get it out of my mind.
IT'S ALREADY TOO LATE!
IF YOU SEE IT NOW, BUY IT NOW...
IT'S JUST COMMON SENSE IN THIS BUSINESS.

a storm of smiles

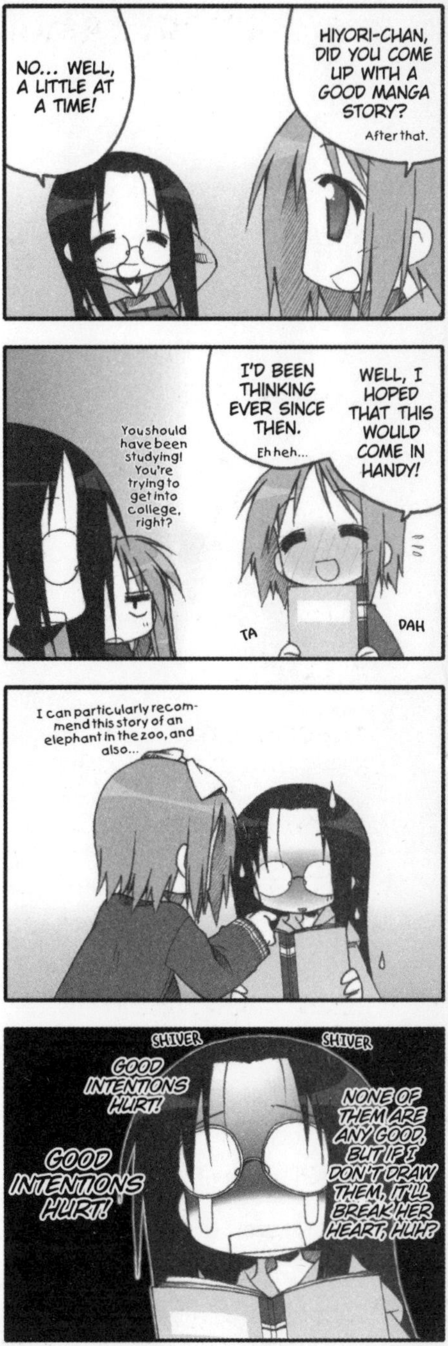
HIYORI-CHAN, DID YOU COME UP WITH A GOOD MANGA STORY?
After that.
NO... WELL, A LITTLE AT A TIME!
WELL, I HOPED THAT THIS WOULD COME IN HANDY!
I'D BEEN THINKING EVER SINCE THEN.
Eh heh...
You should have been studying! You're trying to get into college, right?
TA
DAH
I can particularly recommend this story of an elephant in the zoo, and also...
SHIVER
SHIVER
NONE OF THEM ARE ANY GOOD, BUT IF I DON'T DRAW THEM, IT'LL BREAK HER HEART, HUH?
GOOD INTENTIONS HURT!
GOOD INTENTIONS HURT!

a thorn bush of smiles

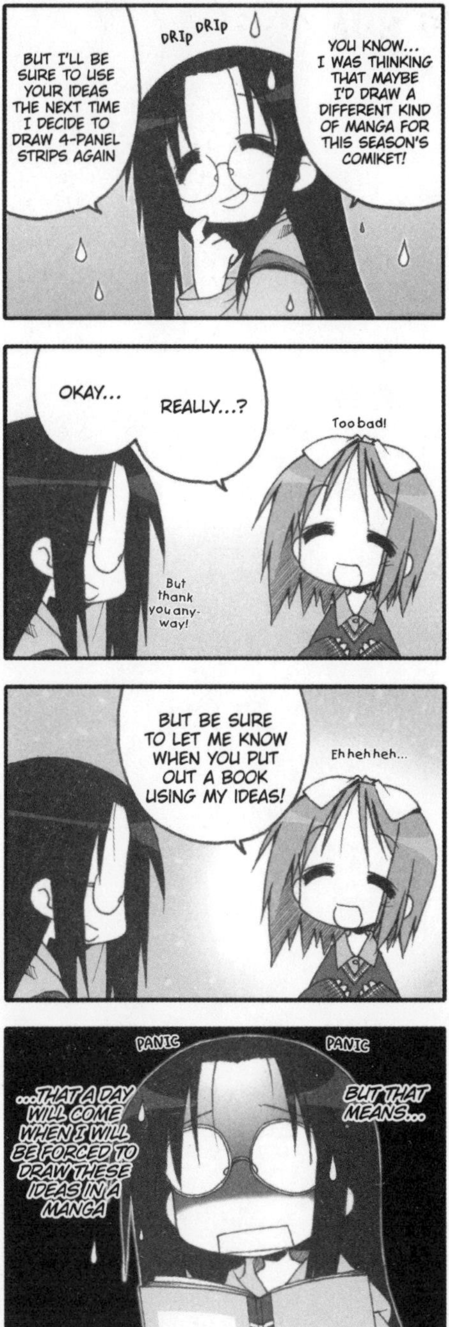
YOU KNOW... I WAS THINKING THAT MAYBE I'D DRAW A DIFFERENT KIND OF MANGA FOR THIS SEASON'S COMIKET!
DRIP DRIP
BUT I'LL BE SURE TO USE YOUR IDEAS THE NEXT TIME I DECIDE TO DRAW 4-PANEL STRIPS AGAIN
Too bad!
OKAY...
REALLY...?
But thank you anyway!
Eh heh heh...
BUT BE SURE TO LET ME KNOW WHEN YOU PUT OUT A BOOK USING MY IDEAS!
PANIC
PANIC
BUT THAT MEANS...
...THAT A DAY WILL COME WHEN I WILL BE FORCED TO DRAW THESE IDEAS IN A MANGA

HIYORI TAMURA'S HUMAN FILE

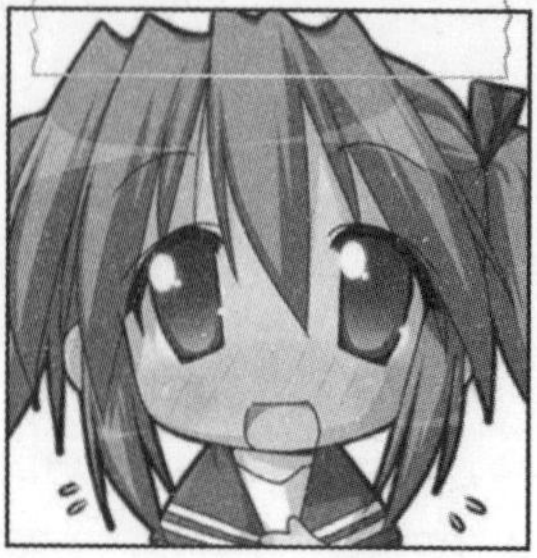

NAME: Yutaka Kobayakawa

GENDER: ♀

PLACE OF BIRTH: Saitama Prefecture

BIRTHDAY: December 20th

BLOOD TYPE: A

STAR SIGN: Sagittarius

PRESENT RANK: Ryou-ou Academy, 1st Year, Class D

HANDEDNESS: Left Handed

BUST-SIZE RANK: Minimal

FAMILY & POSITION: Father, Mother, Eldest Daughter, ☆ Second Daughter

HOBBIES: Internet
*Apparently it's like her toy.

LIKES: Hot Foods (like oden), Animals

DISLIKES: Milk, Her Sickly Physique, Aggressive People
*She's sickly, which gets her points, but for her...

FAVORITE COLORS: Cherry-Blossom Pink

SPECIAL SKILLS: Japanese Class

WEAK POINTS: Athletics

CLUBS: None

CLASS REP: No
*She ran for the position, but didn't get elected. (^_^;)

HIYORI'S MEMO

She and Iwasaki-san together have taken me under their wings.
She's cute in so many ways!
Has a sister who is living out in society. Kobayakawa-san is presently staying at Izumi-sempai's place.
Has a sickly constitution, and spends a lot of time in the Health Office.
Well, anyway, I want us to stay friends.

Lucky☆Star

episode 98 marvelous plot sources

● Comptiq, October 2006 issue

you're ms. expressionless

UME-BOSHI! ...
MUNCH MUNCH
PINNG
ANTICIPATION
Please
Not my taste.
AND THE MYSTERY...
CRESTFALLEN
...REMAINS A MYSTERY
ZUIPPP
MUNNNCH
MUNNNCH

mascot

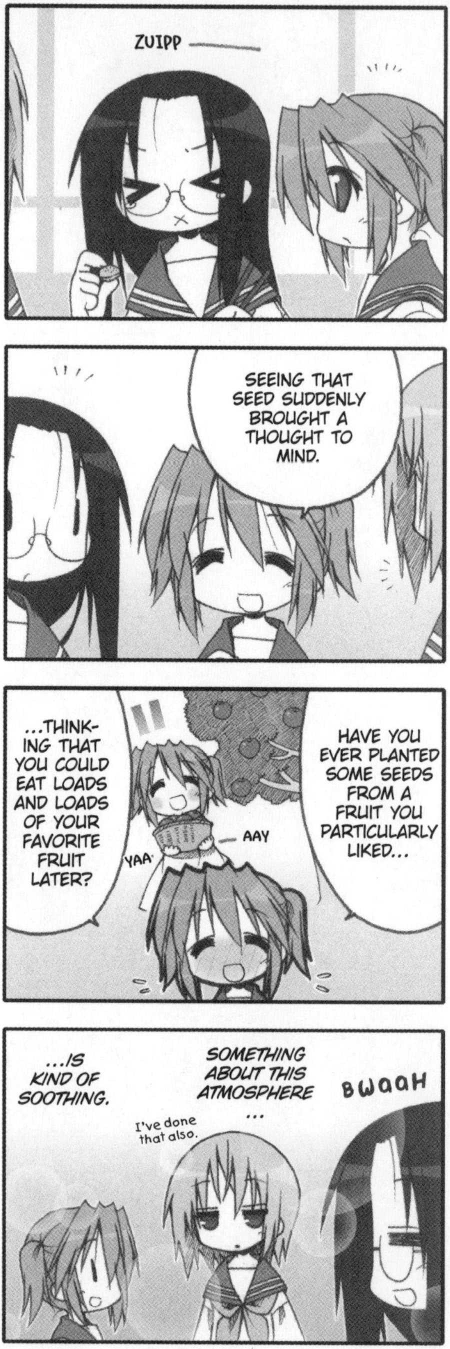
ZUIPP
SEEING THAT SEED SUDDENLY BROUGHT A THOUGHT TO MIND.
HAVE YOU EVER PLANTED SOME SEEDS FROM A FRUIT YOU PARTICULARLY LIKED...
...THINKING THAT YOU COULD EAT LOADS AND LOADS OF YOUR FAVORITE FRUIT LATER?
AAY
YAA
BWAAH
SOMETHING ABOUT THIS ATMOSPHERE ...
...IS KIND OF SOOTHING.
I've done that also.

tiny animal

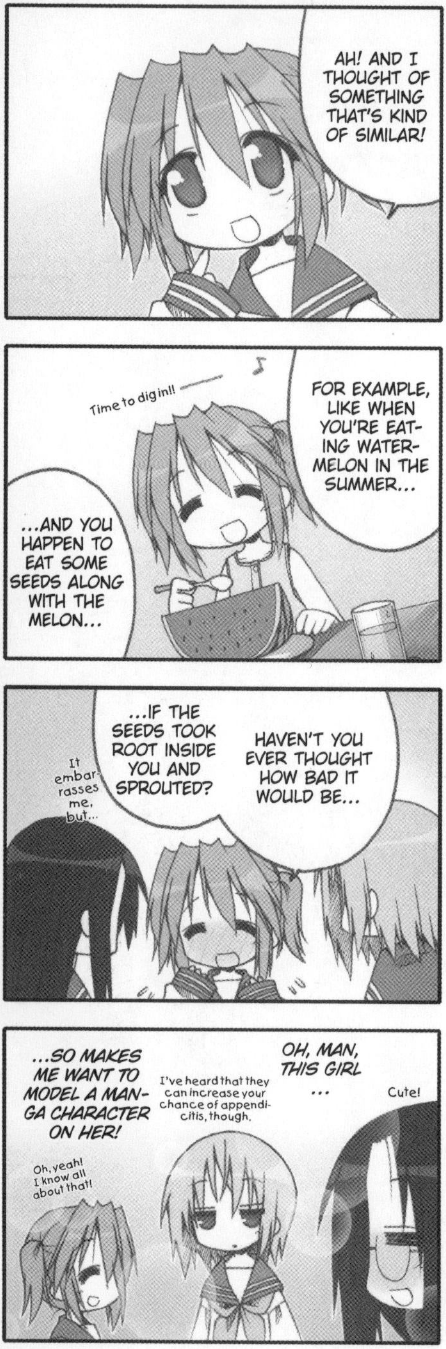
AH! AND I THOUGHT OF SOMETHING THAT'S KIND OF SIMILAR!
FOR EXAMPLE, LIKE WHEN YOU'RE EAT-ING WATER-MELON IN THE SUMMER...
Time to dig in!!
...AND YOU HAPPEN TO EAT SOME SEEDS ALONG WITH THE MELON...
HAVEN'T YOU EVER THOUGHT HOW BAD IT WOULD BE...
...IF THE SEEDS TOOK ROOT INSIDE YOU AND SPROUTED?
It embar-rasses me, but...
Cute!
OH, MAN, THIS GIRL ...
I've heard that they can increase your chance of appendi-citis, though.
...SO MAKES ME WANT TO MODEL A MAN-GA CHARACTER ON HER!
Oh, yeah! I know all about that!

case in point

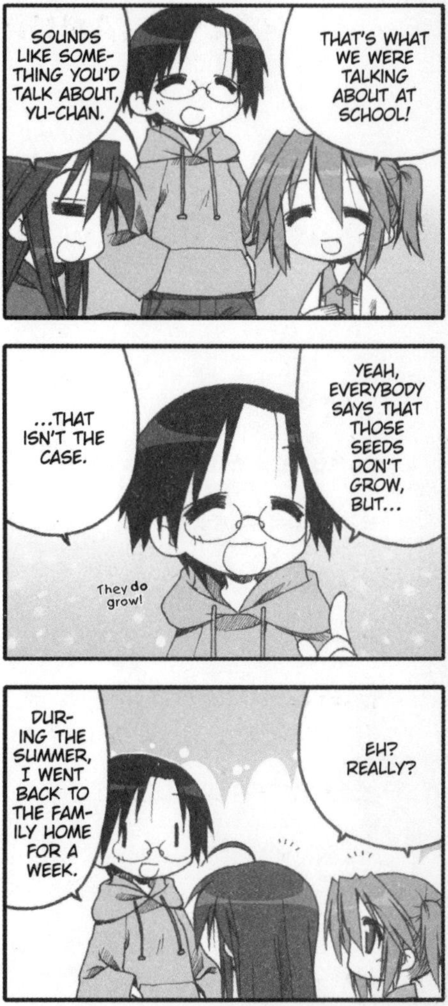

THAT'S WHAT WE WERE TALKING ABOUT AT SCHOOL!
SOUNDS LIKE SOME-THING YOU'D TALK ABOUT, YU-CHAN.
YEAH, EVERYBODY SAYS THAT THOSE SEEDS DON'T GROW, BUT...
...THAT ISN'T THE CASE.
They do grow!
EH? REALLY?
DUR-ING THE SUMMER, I WENT BACK TO THE FAM-ILY HOME FOR A WEEK.
About this big!
THERE WAS A WATERMELON STALK GROWING UP OUT OF THE KITCHEN SINK!
About 20 centimeters!
WAIT A MINUTE, NEE-SAN! THAT WAS ONLY BECAUSE THE STALK DIDN'T GET PROP-ERLY WASHED DOWN THE SINK!

perfectly healthy

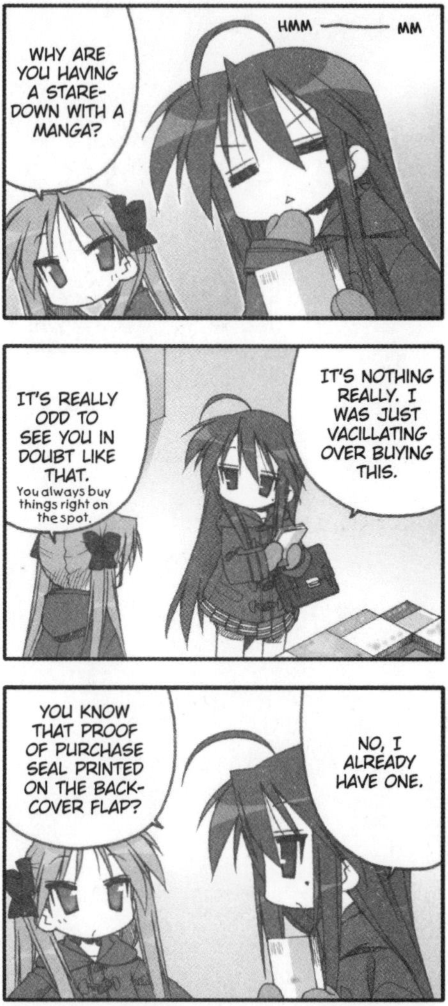

HMM —— MM
WHY ARE YOU HAVING A STARE-DOWN WITH A MANGA?
IT'S NOTHING REALLY. I WAS JUST VACILLATING OVER BUYING THIS.
IT'S REALLY ODD TO SEE YOU IN DOUBT LIKE THAT.
You always buy things right on the spot.
NO, I ALREADY HAVE ONE.
YOU KNOW THAT PROOF OF PURCHASE SEAL PRINTED ON THE BACK-COVER FLAP?
I WAS WONDERING IF I WANT TO KEEP ONE COPY IN PRISTINE CONDITION WITH THE PROOF OF PURCHASE STILL INTACT, LIKE I DO MY DVDS.
To use in my missionary work.
LOOK, I SEE WHERE YOU'RE COM-ING FROM, BUT COULD YOU TONE DOWN THE BOURGEOIS CONCEPTS?

HIYORI TAMURA'S HUMAN FILE

NAME: Minami Iwasaki

GENDER: ♀

PLACE OF BIRTH: Tokyo

BIRTHDAY: September 12th

BLOOD TYPE: A

STAR SIGN: Virgo

PRESENT RANK: Ryou-ou Academy, 1st Year, Class D

HANDEDNESS: Left Handed

BUST-SIZE RANK: Absent
*Actually, she seems self-conscious about it.

FAMILY & POSITION: Father, Mother, ☆ Eldest Daughter

HOBBIES: Reading, Keyboard Instruments
*That really suits her!

LIKES: Buckwheat Noodles, Quiet Places

DISLIKES: Carbonated Beverages, Her Body

FAVORITE COLORS: Green

SPECIAL SKILLS: Athletics
*She can do anything, can't she?

WEAK POINTS: None to speak of

CLUBS: None

CLASS REP: Health Committee

HIYORI'S MEMO

Ditto to Kobayakawa's note. (see above)
She's so expressionless that I find her a little scary, but according to Kobayakawa, she's really sweet.
She's amazingly good in study, sports and art.
Who cares that she doesn't have a bust size!

episode 99
cold transparency

● Comptiq, October 2006 issue

procurement

OH, HO! MIYUKI-SAN, YOU READ THE BEST-SELLERS TOO?
AH! YES. BUT I TEND TO READ EVERY BOOK I FIND.
I even read a few light novels.
IS THAT RIGHT?
I didn't expect that.
MOSTLY, THEY'RE THE BOOKS MY MOTHER BUYS BUT LEAVES UNTOUCHED.
OH! EVEN CHRONIC IMPULSE SHOPPERS DON'T DO THINGS THEY AREN'T USED TO DOING.

slip

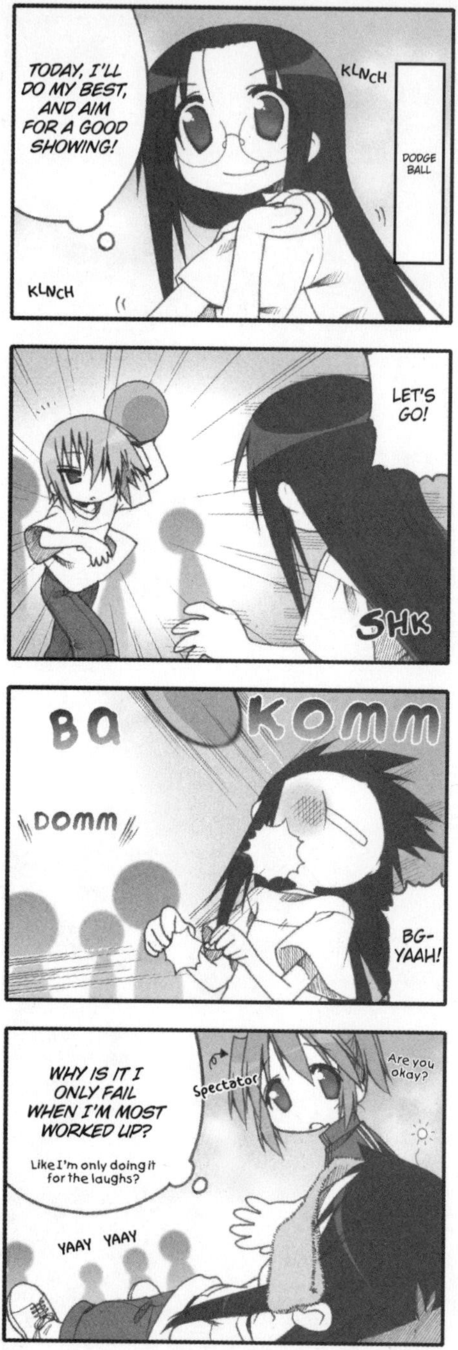
TODAY, I'LL DO MY BEST, AND AIM FOR A GOOD SHOWING!
KLNCH
DODGE BALL
KLNCH
LET'S GO!
SHK
BA KOMM
DOMM
BG-YAAH!
Are you okay?
Spectator
WHY IS IT I ONLY FAIL WHEN I'M MOST WORKED UP?
Like I'm only doing it for the laughs?
YAAY YAAY

could even fly through the sky

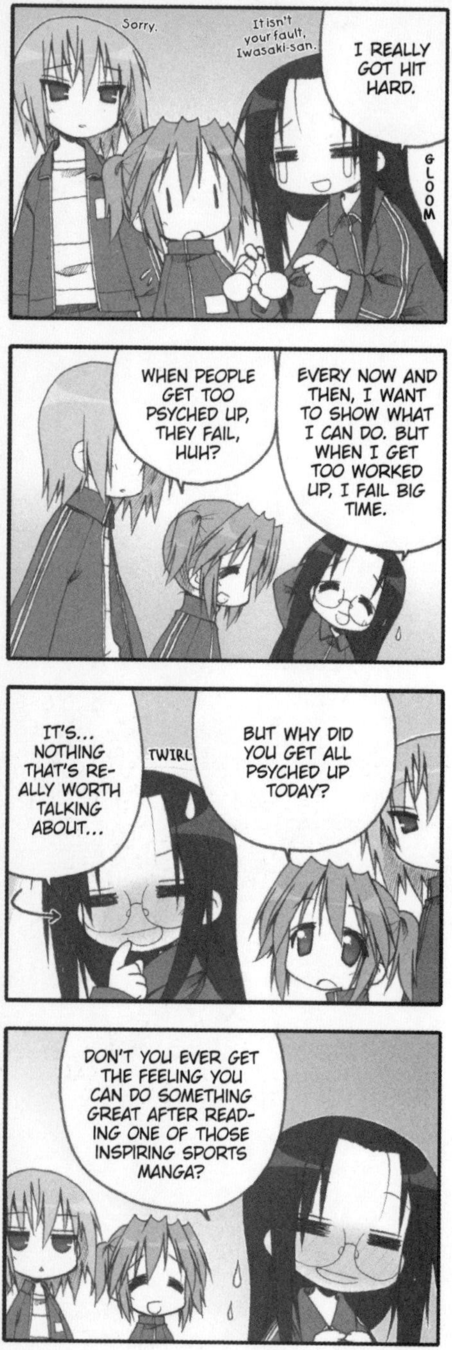
I REALLY GOT HIT HARD.
It isn't your fault, Iwasaki-san.
Sorry.
GLOOM
EVERY NOW AND THEN, I WANT TO SHOW WHAT I CAN DO. BUT WHEN I GET TOO WORKED UP, I FAIL BIG TIME.
WHEN PEOPLE GET TOO PSYCHED UP, THEY FAIL, HUH?
BUT WHY DID YOU GET ALL PSYCHED UP TODAY?
TWIRL
IT'S... NOTHING THAT'S RE-ALLY WORTH TALKING ABOUT...
DON'T YOU EVER GET THE FEELING YOU CAN DO SOMETHING GREAT AFTER READ-ING ONE OF THOSE INSPIRING SPORTS MANGA?

the seasons change

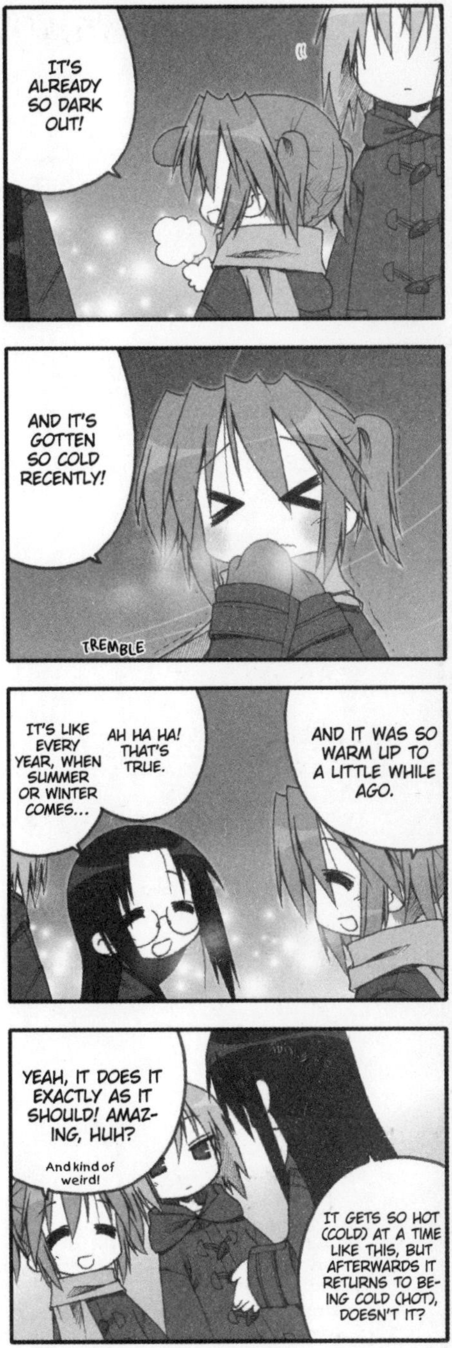
IT'S ALREADY SO DARK OUT!
AND IT'S GOTTEN SO COLD RECENTLY!
TREMBLE
AND IT WAS SO WARM UP TO A LITTLE WHILE AGO.
AH HA HA! THAT'S TRUE.
IT'S LIKE EVERY YEAR, WHEN SUMMER OR WINTER COMES...
IT GETS SO HOT (COLD) AT A TIME LIKE THIS, BUT AFTERWARDS IT RETURNS TO BEING COLD (HOT), DOESN'T IT?
YEAH, IT DOES IT EXACTLY AS IT SHOULD! AMAZING, HUH?
And kind of weird!

negligence is your worst enemy

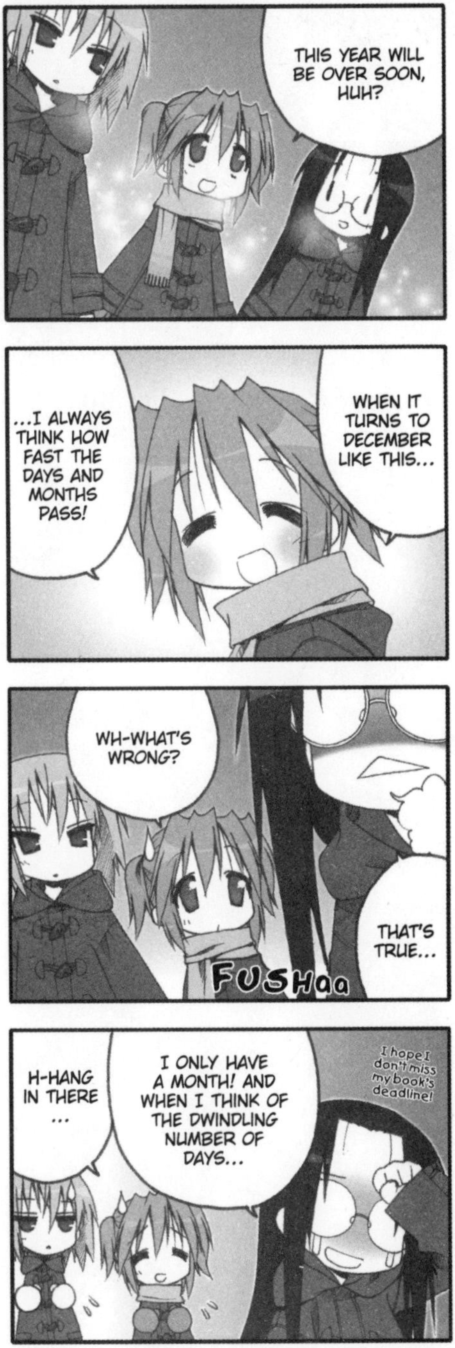
THIS YEAR WILL BE OVER SOON, HUH?
WHEN IT TURNS TO DECEMBER LIKE THIS...
...I ALWAYS THINK HOW FAST THE DAYS AND MONTHS PASS!
THAT'S TRUE...
FUSHaa
WH-WHAT'S WRONG?
I hope I don't miss my book's deadline!
I ONLY HAVE A MONTH! AND WHEN I THINK OF THE DWINDLING NUMBER OF DAYS...
H-HANG IN THERE ...

HIYORI TAMURA'S HUMAN FILE

NAME: Hiyori Tamura

GENDER: ♀

PLACE OF BIRTH: Saitama Prefecture

BIRTHDAY: May 24th

BLOOD TYPE: O

STAR SIGN: Gemini

PRESENT RANK: Ryou-ou Academy, 1st Year, Class D

HANDEDNESS: Left Handed

BUST-SIZE RANK: Small
*kind of small, but very cute! (Kou)

FAMILY & POSITION: Father, Mother, Eldest Brother, Second Brother, ☆ Eldest Daughter

HOBBIES: Reading, Doujinshi, Reading (manga & light novels), Flights of Fancy
*She's in a circle whose doujinshi I read. (Konata)

LIKES: Western Snacks, Milk, Art Tools

DISLIKES: Wasabi, Humidity

FAVORITE COLORS: Pink

SPECIAL SKILLS: Art

WEAK POINTS: Athletics

CLUBS: Animation Research Club
*Maybe I should have joined that. (Konata)

CLASS REP: No

HIYORI'S MEMO

A cute, cheeky kouhai in the Animation Research Club.
I don't mind you doing your doujin work, but you also have to do manga for the club too, you know! (Kou)
A classmate of Yu-chan, and an otaku like Kagami and me. (Konata)
I am not an otaku! (Kagami)

Lucky☆Star

episode 100
happy word

●Comp Ace, Vol. 010, February 2007
Extra Edition

a word's (mistaken) magic

GRR
GRR
SCRATCH
SCRATCH
GLANCE
注
意
100
MADE IN JAPAN
Ah... Maidin Japan...
BWAHH

power of love

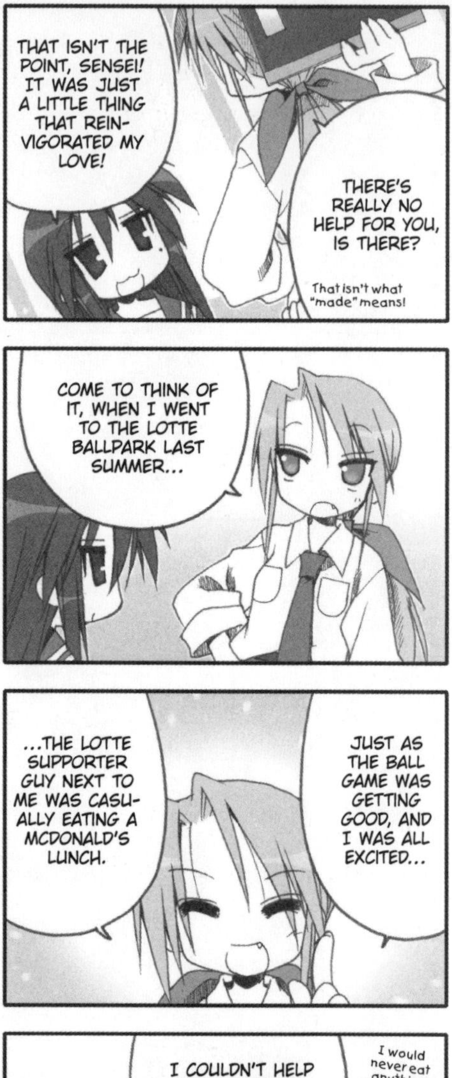
THERE'S REALLY NO HELP FOR YOU, IS THERE?
THAT ISN'T THE POINT, SENSEI! IT WAS JUST A LITTLE THING THAT REIN-VIGORATED MY LOVE!
That isn't what "made" means!
COME TO THINK OF IT, WHEN I WENT TO THE LOTTE BALLPARK LAST SUMMER...
JUST AS THE BALL GAME WAS GETTING GOOD, AND I WAS ALL EXCITED...
...THE LOTTE SUPPORTER GUY NEXT TO ME WAS CASU-ALLY EATING A MCDONALD'S LUNCH.
I would never eat anything but Lotteria Food!
I COULDN'T HELP BUT THINK TO MYSELF, THIS MAN'S LOVE OF LOTTE IS NOTHING COMPARED TO MINE!
WHAT'S THE GOOD OF TRASHING AN ALLY?

getting into it

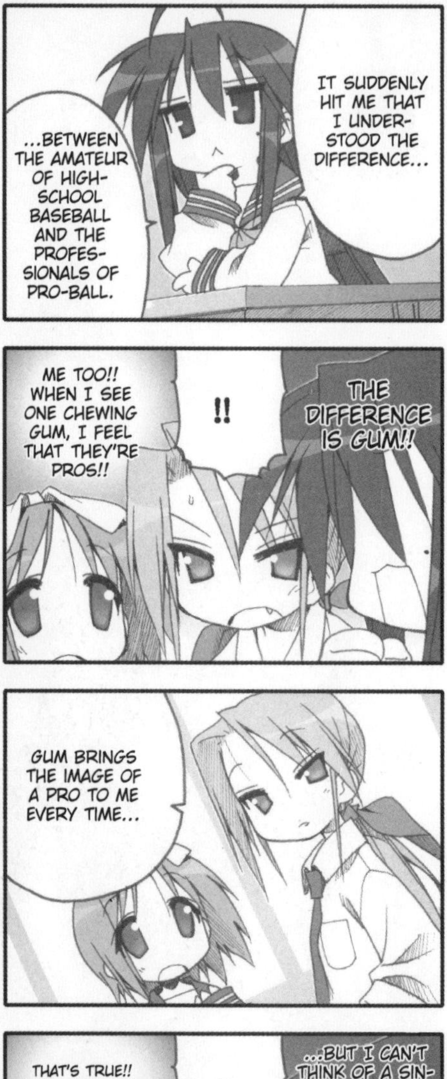
IT SUDDENLY HIT ME THAT I UNDER-STOOD THE DIFFERENCE...
...BETWEEN THE AMATEUR OF HIGH-SCHOOL BASEBALL AND THE PROFES-SIONALS OF PRO-BALL.
THE DIFFERENCE IS GUM!!
!!
ME TOO!! WHEN I SEE ONE CHEWING GUM, I FEEL THAT THEY'RE PROS!!
GUM BRINGS THE IMAGE OF A PRO TO ME EVERY TIME...
...BUT I CAN'T THINK OF A SIN-GLE OTHER PRO SPORT WHERE THE PLAYERS CHEW GUM!!
!!
THAT'S TRUE!! QUITE THE OPPO-SITE, I THINK IT'S FROWNED UPON OR BANNED IN OTHER SPORTS!!

leave out to dry

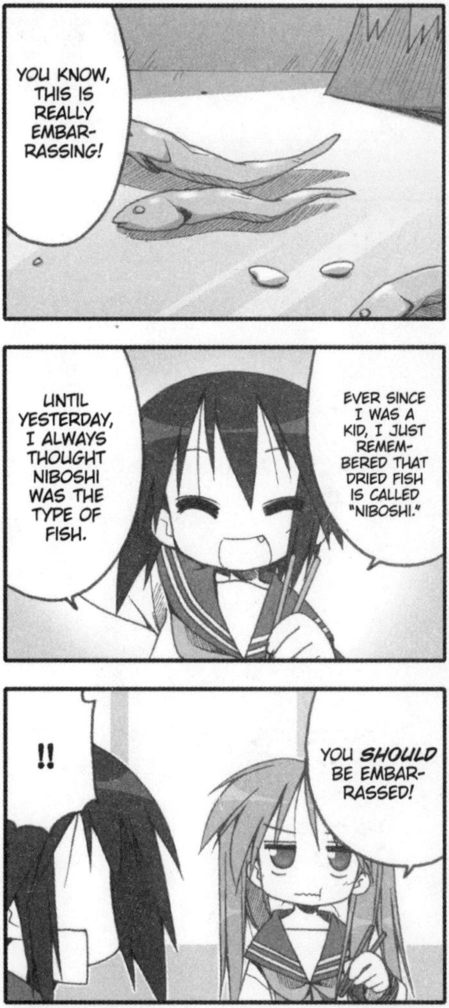

YOU KNOW, THIS IS REALLY EMBARRASSING!
EVER SINCE I WAS A KID, I JUST REMEMBERED THAT DRIED FISH IS CALLED "NIBOSHI."
UNTIL YESTERDAY, I ALWAYS THOUGHT NIBOSHI WAS THE TYPE OF FISH.
YOU *SHOULD* BE EMBARRASSED!
!!
! !
There, there...
MUNCH MUNCH

shout

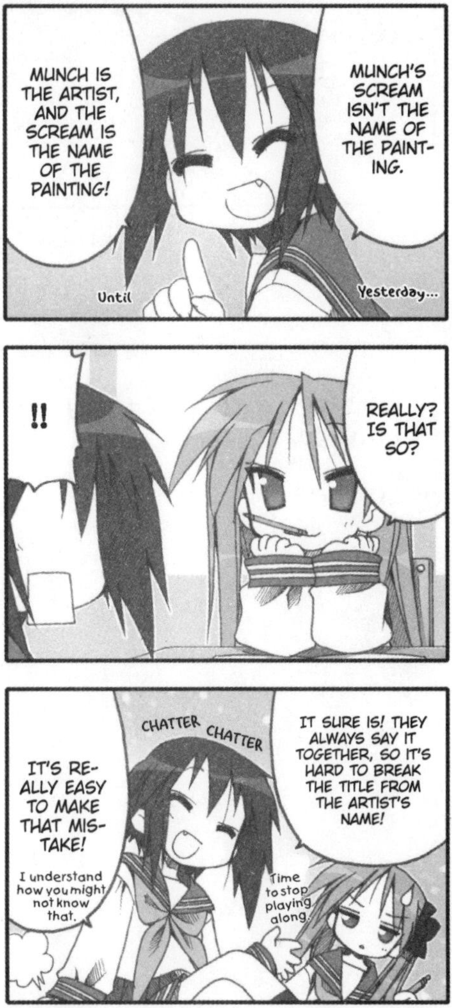

MUNCH'S SCREAM ISN'T THE NAME OF THE PAINTING.
Yesterday...
MUNCH IS THE ARTIST, AND THE SCREAM IS THE NAME OF THE PAINTING!
Until
REALLY? IS THAT SO?
!!
IT SURE IS! THEY ALWAYS SAY IT TOGETHER, SO IT'S HARD TO BREAK THE TITLE FROM THE ARTIST'S NAME!
CHATTER CHATTER
Time to stop playing along.
IT'S REALLY EASY TO MAKE THAT MISTAKE!
I understand how you might not know that.
I WAS JUST PLAYING WITH YOU A LITTLE.
BUT THE FACT THAT YOU GOT SO HAPPY TAKES ME ABACK A BIT.
AYANO!! THE DEVIL IS SITTING OVER THERE!! THE DEVIL!!
There, therrre!

HIYORI TAMURA'S HUMAN FILE

NAME: Patricia Martin

GENDER: ♀

PLACE OF BIRTH: United States of America

BIRTHDAY: April 16th

BLOOD TYPE: O

STAR SIGN: Aries

PRESENT RANK: Ryou-ou Academy, 1st Year, Class D

HANDEDNESS: Right Handed
*She's actually right-handed!

BUST-SIZE RANK: Large

FAMILY & POSITION:
Grandmother, Father, Mother,
☆ Eldest Daughter, Second Daughter

HOBBIES: Anime, Reading (manga)

LIKES: Mustard, Moe
*If I said that mustard went along with my image would you think me strange?

DISLIKES: Dried Foods, People Who Don't Speak Their Minds

FAVORITE COLORS: Red

SPECIAL SKILLS: English

WEAK POINTS: Japanese Class

CLUBS: None
*Please join the Animation Research Club!

CLASS REP: No

HIYORI'S MEMO

- She loves all Japanese anime and manga... Frankly, she's an outlaw, just like me. It seems she came on a student-exchange program because she wanted to learn Japanese culture.
She has an incredible amount of energy.

Lucky☆Star

episode 101
fighting the battle single-handedly

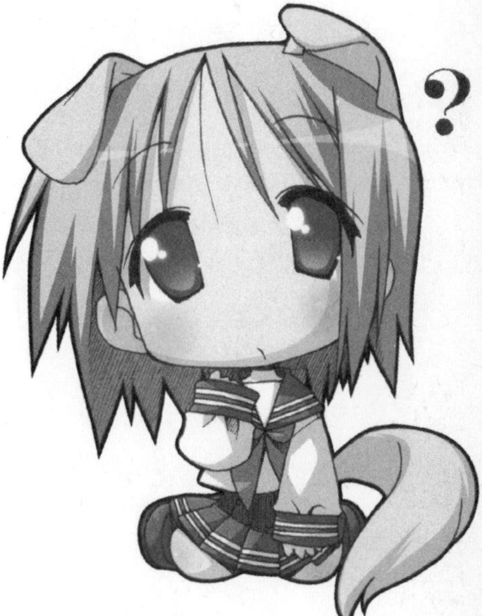
?

● Comptiq, November 2006 issue

same level

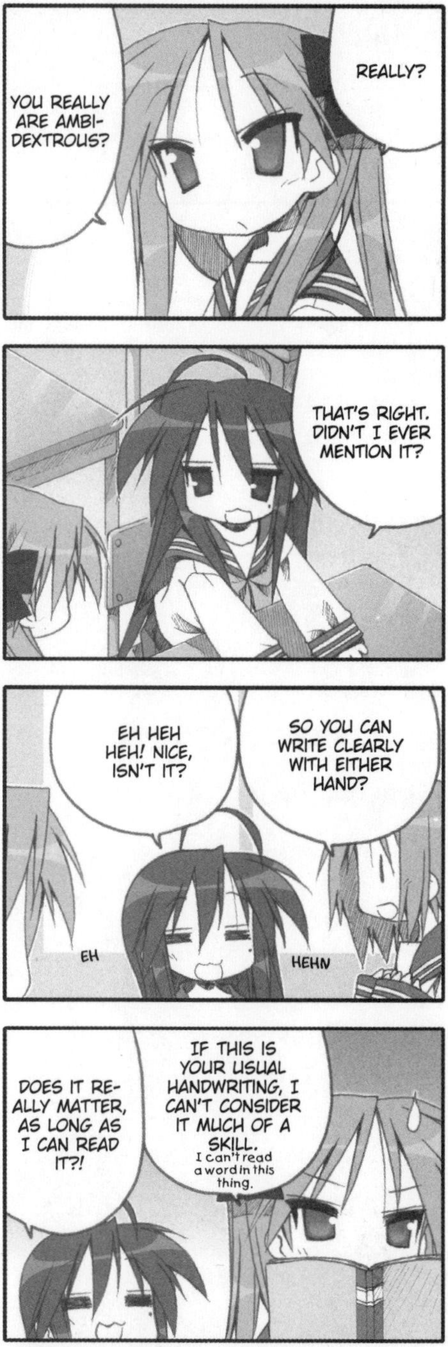
REALLY?
YOU REALLY ARE AMBI-DEXTROUS?
THAT'S RIGHT. DIDN'T I EVER MENTION IT?
SO YOU CAN WRITE CLEARLY WITH EITHER HAND?
EH HEH HEH! NICE, ISN'T IT?
HEHN
EH
IF THIS IS YOUR USUAL HANDWRITING, I CAN'T CONSIDER IT MUCH OF A SKILL.
I can't read a word in this thing.
DOES IT RE-ALLY MATTER, AS LONG AS I CAN READ IT?!

all alone

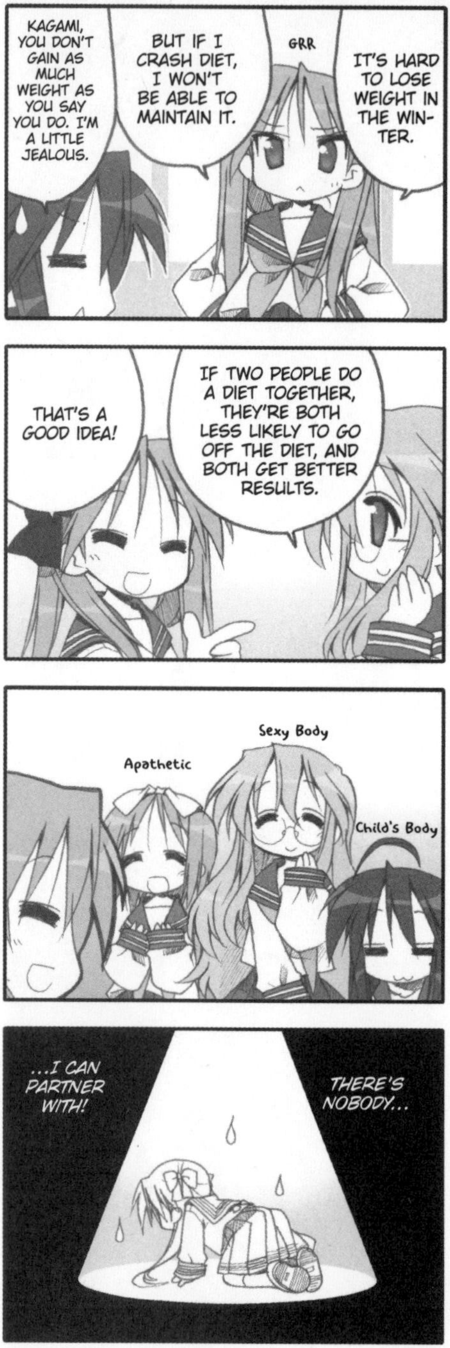
IT'S HARD TO LOSE WEIGHT IN THE WIN-TER.
GRR
BUT IF I CRASH DIET, I WON'T BE ABLE TO MAINTAIN IT.
KAGAMI, YOU DON'T GAIN AS MUCH WEIGHT AS YOU SAY YOU DO. I'M A LITTLE JEALOUS.
IF TWO PEOPLE DO A DIET TOGETHER, THEY'RE BOTH LESS LIKELY TO GO OFF THE DIET, AND BOTH GET BETTER RESULTS.
THAT'S A GOOD IDEA!
Sexy Body
Child's Body
Apathetic
THERE'S NOBODY...
...I CAN PARTNER WITH!

failing together

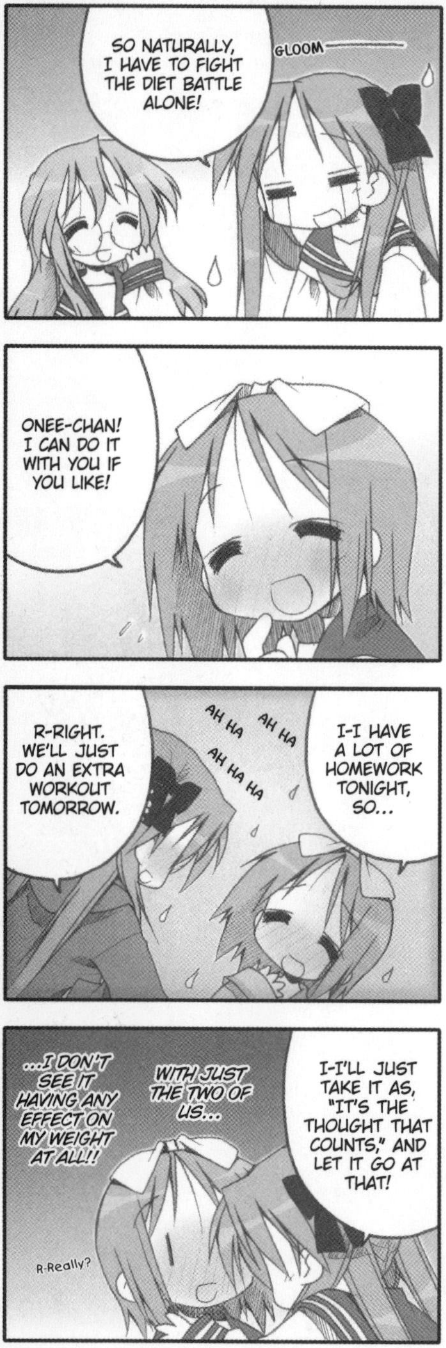
GLOOM
SO NATURALLY, I HAVE TO FIGHT THE DIET BATTLE ALONE!
ONEE-CHAN! I CAN DO IT WITH YOU IF YOU LIKE!
I-I HAVE A LOT OF HOMEWORK TONIGHT, SO...
AH HA AH HA AH HA HA
R-RIGHT. WE'LL JUST DO AN EXTRA WORKOUT TOMORROW.
I-I'LL JUST TAKE IT AS, "IT'S THE THOUGHT THAT COUNTS," AND LET IT GO AT THAT!
WITH JUST THE TWO OF US...
...I DON'T SEE IT HAVING ANY EFFECT ON MY WEIGHT AT ALL!!
R-Really?

how things go from now on

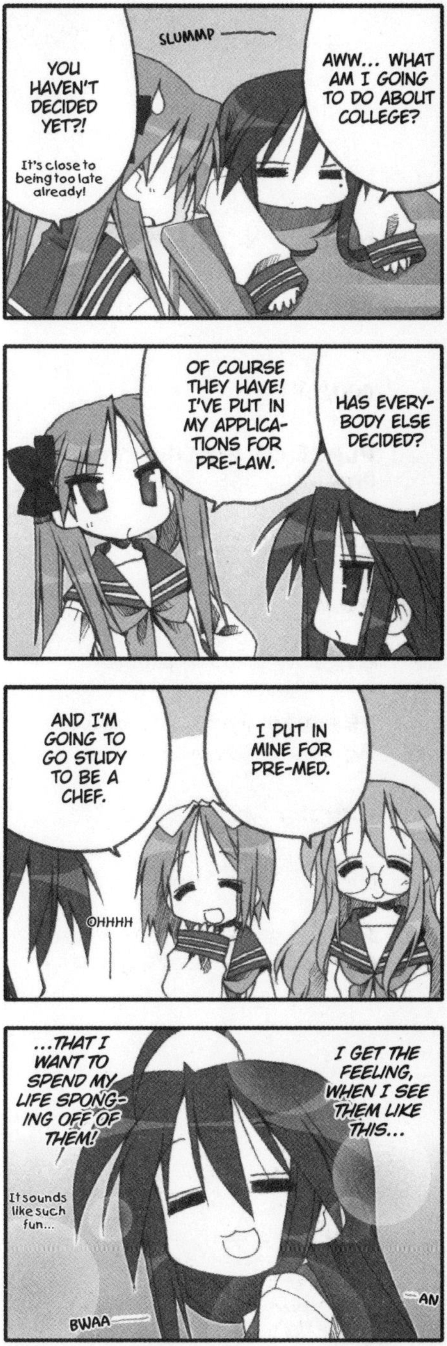
AWW... WHAT AM I GOING TO DO ABOUT COLLEGE?
SLUMMP
YOU HAVEN'T DECIDED YET?!
It's close to being too late already!
HAS EVERY-BODY ELSE DECIDED?
OF COURSE THEY HAVE! I'VE PUT IN MY APPLICA-TIONS FOR PRE-LAW.
I PUT IN MINE FOR PRE-MED.
AND I'M GOING TO GO STUDY TO BE A CHEF.
OHHHH
I GET THE FEELING, WHEN I SEE THEM LIKE THIS...
...THAT I WANT TO SPEND MY LIFE SPONG-ING OFF OF THEM!
—AN
It sounds like such fun...
BWAA—

preparations for the future

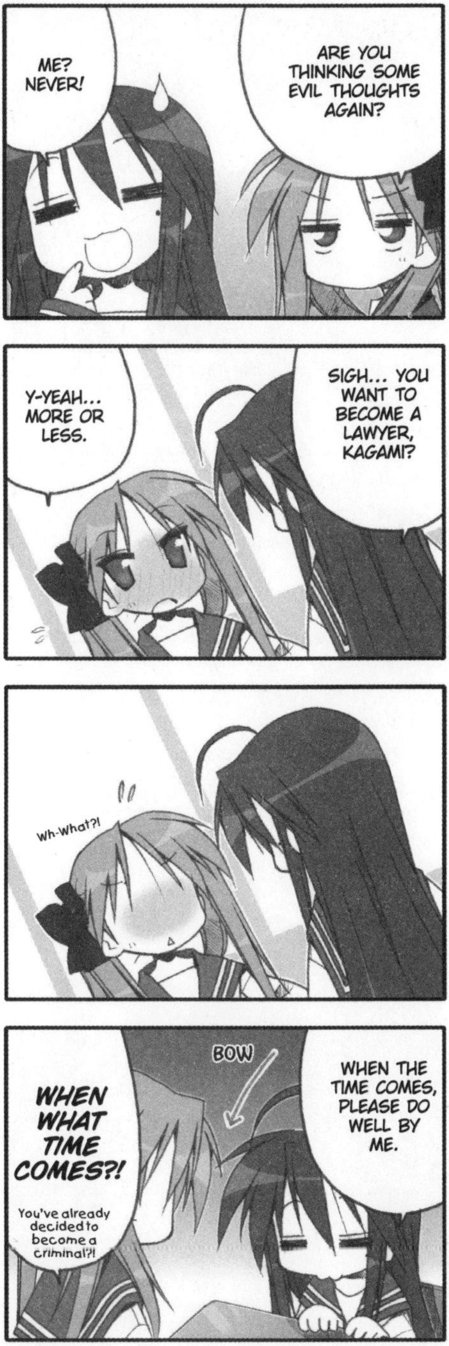
ARE YOU THINKING SOME EVIL THOUGHTS AGAIN?
ME? NEVER!
SIGH... YOU WANT TO BECOME A LAWYER, KAGAMI?
Y-YEAH... MORE OR LESS.
Wh-What?!
WHEN THE TIME COMES, PLEASE DO WELL BY ME.
BOW
WHEN WHAT TIME COMES?!
You've already decided to become a criminal?!

HIYORI TAMURA'S HUMAN FILE

NAME: Nanako Kuroi

GENDER: ♀

PLACE OF BIRTH: Kanagawa Prefecture

BIRTHDAY: February 8th

BLOOD TYPE: O

STAR SIGN: Aquarius

PRESENT RANK: Ryou-ou Academy, World History Teacher

HANDEDNESS: Left Handed

BUST-SIZE RANK: Large

FAMILY & POSITION: Father, Mother, ☆ Eldest daughter

HOBBIES: Watching Sports with a Beer in Hand, Video Games
*I'll bet she watches while playing her games

LIKES: Nattou, Lotte
*Nattou, so manly!

DISLIKES: Shiitake Mushrooms, TV Sports that Cut Off Before the End, People Not Keeping to Schedule
*People who don't keep to schedule are her natural enemies.

FAVORITE COLORS: White

SPECIAL SKILLS: World History (Teaches it)

WEAK POINTS: English

CLUBS: Does Not Sponsor Any

CLASS REP: Does Not Sponsor Any

HIYORI'S MEMO

The Home-Room Teacher of Class 3-B, and World History Teacher.
Apparently she plays Net Games with Izumi-sempai.
She seems to perform corporal punishment on Izumi-sempai, but she's otherwise a very popular teacher.
I love her affected Kansai accent! It's so cute!

Lucky☆Star

episode 102
do your best! do your best!

● Comptiq, November 2006 issue

spinning your wheels

HMM ——— MM
WHAT'S WRONG?
MM? OH, NOTHING. THE STORY PLOT I SENT ARRIVED THERE, BUT...
OH, THAT'S GOOD NEWS, RIGHT?
I DID SEVER-AL DIFFERENT VARIATIONS ON IT, YOU KNOW?
AND AT THE VERY END, I JUST TACKED ON A HALF-BAKED IDEA THAT HAD JUST OCCURRED TO ME.
AND IT MADE ME KIND OF SAD.
Up to that moment, I was all revved up and hard working.
TH- THOSE THINGS HAPPEN, I GUESS.

three thousand worlds

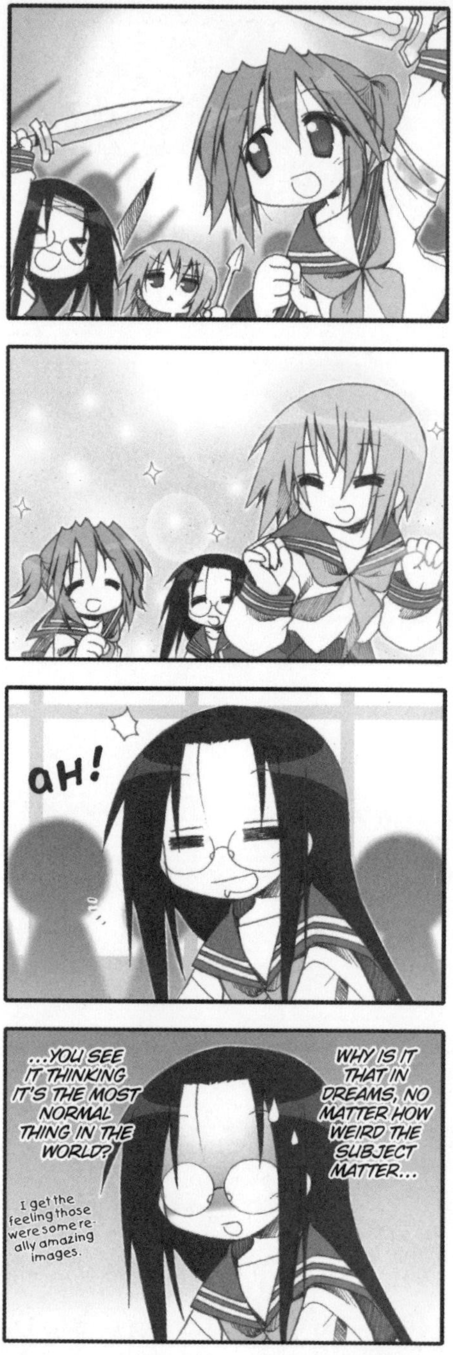
aH!
WHY IS IT THAT IN DREAMS, NO MATTER HOW WEIRD THE SUBJECT MATTER...
...YOU SEE IT THINKING IT'S THE MOST NORMAL THING IN THE WORLD?
I get the feeling those were some really amazing images.

kagami-sama

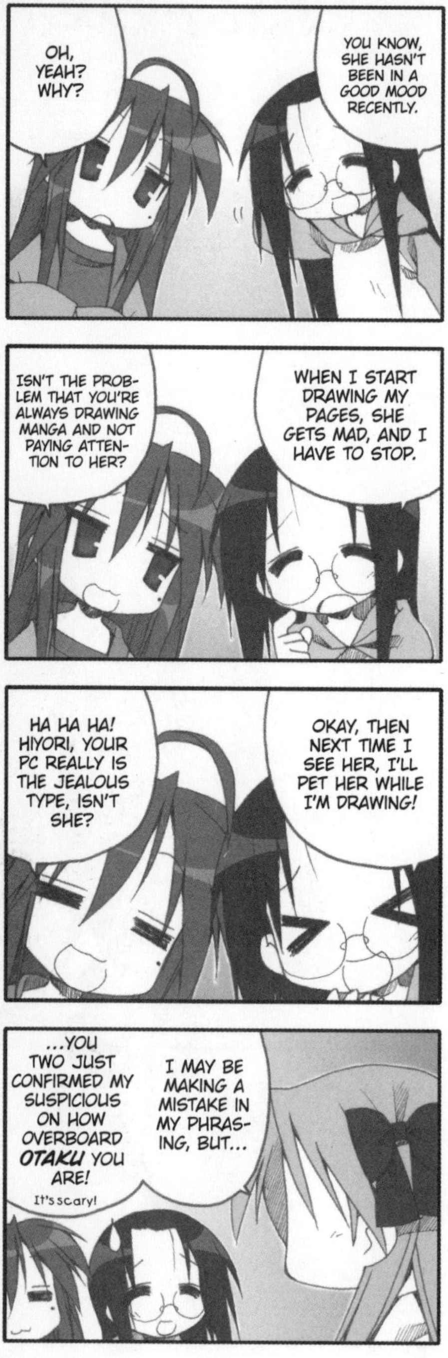
YOU KNOW, SHE HASN'T BEEN IN A GOOD MOOD RECENTLY.
OH, YEAH? WHY?
WHEN I START DRAWING MY PAGES, SHE GETS MAD, AND I HAVE TO STOP.
ISN'T THE PROBLEM THAT YOU'RE ALWAYS DRAWING MANGA AND NOT PAYING ATTENTION TO HER?
OKAY, THEN NEXT TIME I SEE HER, I'LL PET HER WHILE I'M DRAWING!
HA HA HA! HIYORI, YOUR PC REALLY IS THE JEALOUS TYPE, ISN'T SHE?
I MAY BE MAKING A MISTAKE IN MY PHRASING, BUT...
...YOU TWO JUST CONFIRMED MY SUSPICIOUS ON HOW OVERBOARD **OTAKU** YOU ARE!
It's scary!

meeting place

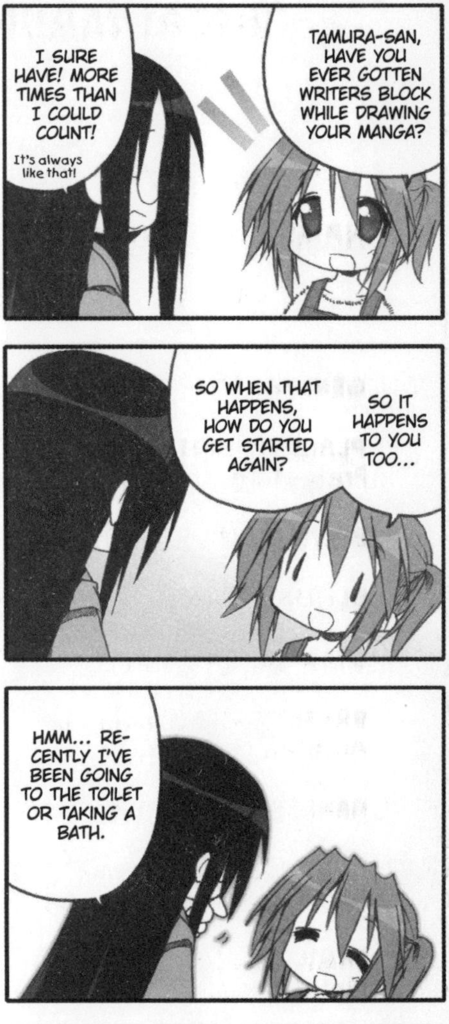
TAMURA-SAN, HAVE YOU EVER GOTTEN WRITERS BLOCK WHILE DRAWING YOUR MANGA?
I SURE HAVE! MORE TIMES THAN I COULD COUNT!
It's always like that!
SO IT HAPPENS TO YOU TOO...
SO WHEN THAT HAPPENS, HOW DO YOU GET STARTED AGAIN?
HMM... RE-CENTLY I'VE BEEN GOING TO THE TOILET OR TAKING A BATH.
THE TOILET OR A BATH...?
YES! THE TOILET OR A BATH!
That seems to unblock the ideas.

yes, i am ambitious

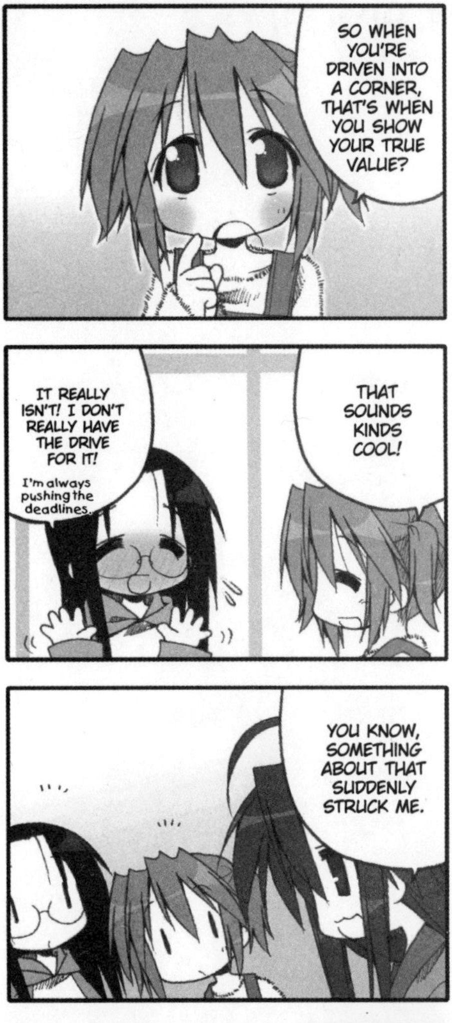
SO WHEN YOU'RE DRIVEN INTO A CORNER, THAT'S WHEN YOU SHOW YOUR TRUE VALUE?
THAT SOUNDS KINDS COOL!
IT REALLY ISN'T! I DON'T REALLY HAVE THE DRIVE FOR IT!
I'm always pushing the deadlines.
YOU KNOW, SOMETHING ABOUT THAT SUDDENLY STRUCK ME.
AREN'T YOU JUST PROCRAS-TINATING?
Like those people who could suc-ceed if they only tried?
NO, REALLY! I WORK AT IT EVERY-DAY! BUT ONLY A LITTLE AT A TIME!

HIYORI TAMURA'S HUMAN FILE

NAME: Hikaru Sakuraba

GENDER: ♀

PLACE OF BIRTH: Saitama Prefecture

BIRTHDAY: January 25th

BLOOD TYPE: O

STAR SIGN: Aquarius

PRESENT RANK: Ryou-ou Academy, Biology Teacher

HANDEDNESS: Left Handed

BUST-SIZE RANK: Minimal
*Sensei is also short.

FAMILY & POSITION: Father, Mother, ☆ Eldest daughter

HOBBIES: Motocross GP, Reading BL Literature
*She doesn't look like she'd like that, but...

LIKES: Calorie Mate, Sleeping
*Calorie Mate! ...w

DISLIKES: Vegetables, People with the Wrong Idea

FAVORITE COLORS: Purple

SPECIAL SKILLS: Biology (Teaches it)

WEAK POINTS: Home Economics

CLUBS: Biology Club (Faculty Advisor), Animation Research Club (Faculty Advisor)

CLASS REP: Does Not Sponsor Any

HIYORI'S MEMO

Our minimalist, pretty Animation Research Club Advisor.
She's the homeroom teacher for Class 3-C and teaches Biology.
She's easy to talk to, but sometimes her blunt statements will stab you in the heart.
She is a childhood friend (as the male of the two) of Amahara-sensei.

episode 103
a strong-person's theory

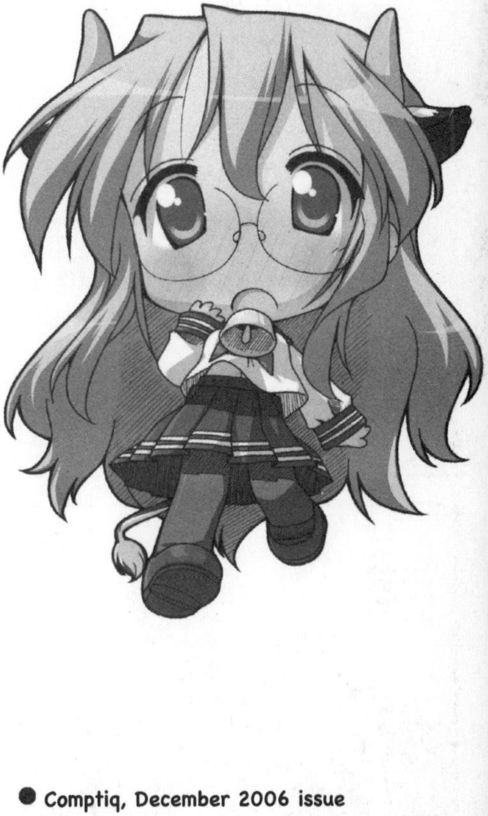

● Comptiq, December 2006 issue

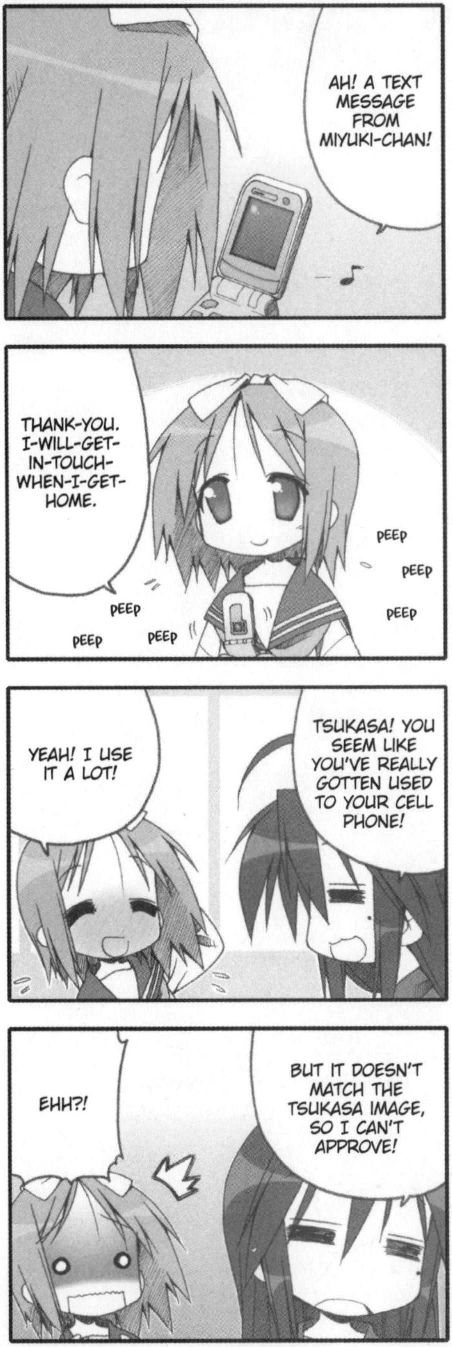
AH! A TEXT MESSAGE FROM MIYUKI-CHAN!
THANK-YOU. I-WILL-GET-IN-TOUCH-WHEN-I-GET-HOME.
PEEP PEEP PEEP PEEP PEEP PEEP
TSUKASA! YOU SEEM LIKE YOU'VE REALLY GOTTEN USED TO YOUR CELL PHONE!
YEAH! I USE IT A LOT!
BUT IT DOESN'T MATCH THE TSUKASA IMAGE, SO I CAN'T APPROVE!
EHH?!

too late

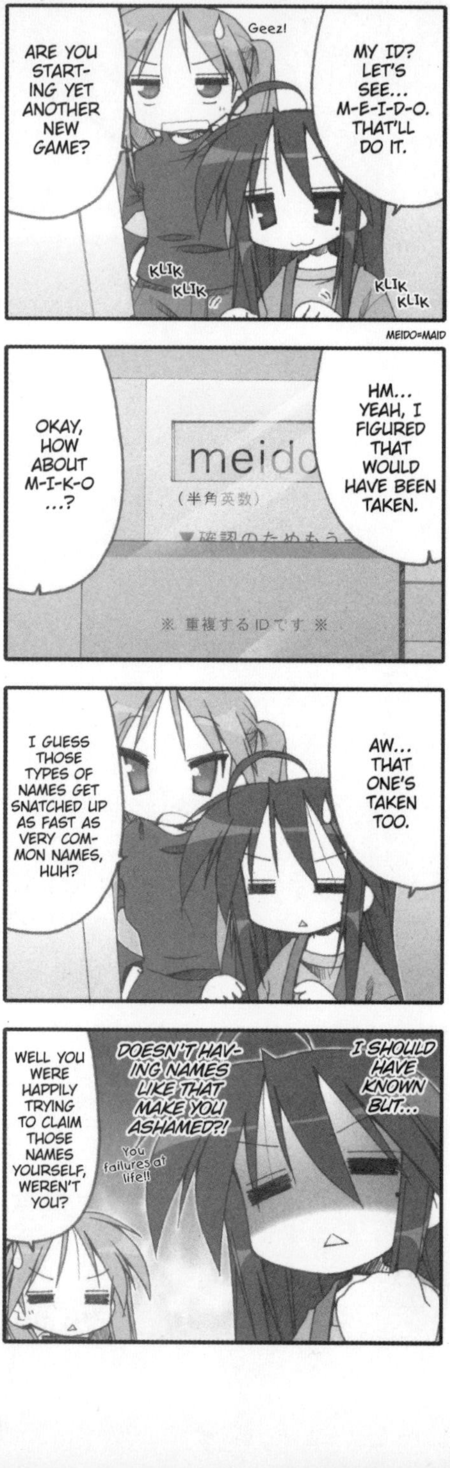
MY ID? LET'S SEE... M-E-I-D-O. THAT'LL DO IT.
Geez!
ARE YOU START-ING YET ANOTHER NEW GAME?
KLIK KLIK
KLIK KLIK
HM... YEAH, I FIGURED THAT WOULD HAVE BEEN TAKEN.
meido
(半角英数)
OKAY, HOW ABOUT M-I-K-O ...?
※ 重複するIDです ※
AW... THAT ONE'S TAKEN TOO.
I GUESS THOSE TYPES OF NAMES GET SNATCHED UP AS FAST AS VERY COM-MON NAMES, HUH?
I SHOULD HAVE KNOWN BUT...
DOESN'T HAV-ING NAMES LIKE THAT MAKE YOU ASHAMED?!
You failures at life!!
WELL YOU WERE HAPPILY TRYING TO CLAIM THOSE NAMES YOURSELF, WEREN'T YOU?

MEIDO=MAID

determined

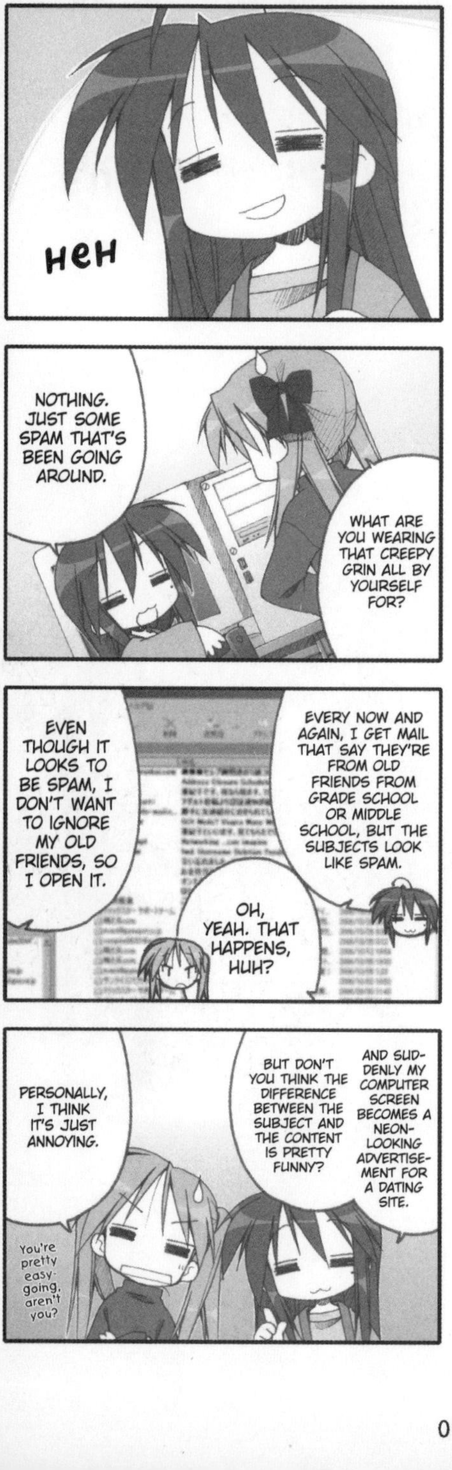
HEH
WHAT ARE YOU WEARING THAT CREEPY GRIN ALL BY YOURSELF FOR?
NOTHING. JUST SOME SPAM THAT'S BEEN GOING AROUND.
EVERY NOW AND AGAIN, I GET MAIL THAT SAY THEY'RE FROM OLD FRIENDS FROM GRADE SCHOOL OR MIDDLE SCHOOL, BUT THE SUBJECTS LOOK LIKE SPAM.
EVEN THOUGH IT LOOKS TO BE SPAM, I DON'T WANT TO IGNORE MY OLD FRIENDS, SO I OPEN IT.
OH, YEAH. THAT HAPPENS, HUH?
AND SUD-DENLY MY COMPUTER SCREEN BECOMES A NEON-LOOKING ADVERTISE-MENT FOR A DATING SITE.
BUT DON'T YOU THINK THE DIFFERENCE BETWEEN THE SUBJECT AND THE CONTENT IS PRETTY FUNNY?
PERSONALLY, I THINK IT'S JUST ANNOYING.
You're pretty easy-going, aren't you?

missing in action

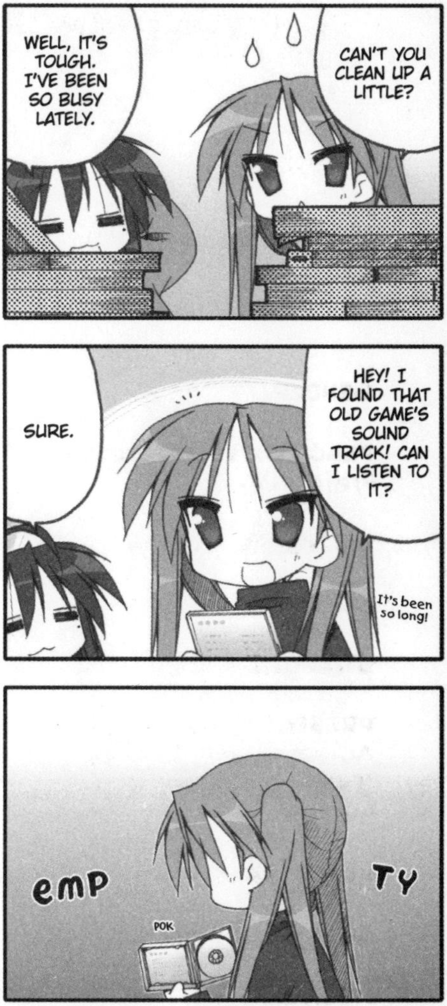
CAN'T YOU CLEAN UP A LITTLE?
WELL, IT'S TOUGH. I'VE BEEN SO BUSY LATELY.
HEY! I FOUND THAT OLD GAME'S SOUND TRACK! CAN I LISTEN TO IT?
It's been so long!
SURE.
TY
emp
POK
UM... KONATA...
IF IT ISN'T IN THERE, THEN IT WILL TAKE SOME TIME BEFORE I CAN LOCATE IT.
That hap-pens a lot to me.

missing in action 2

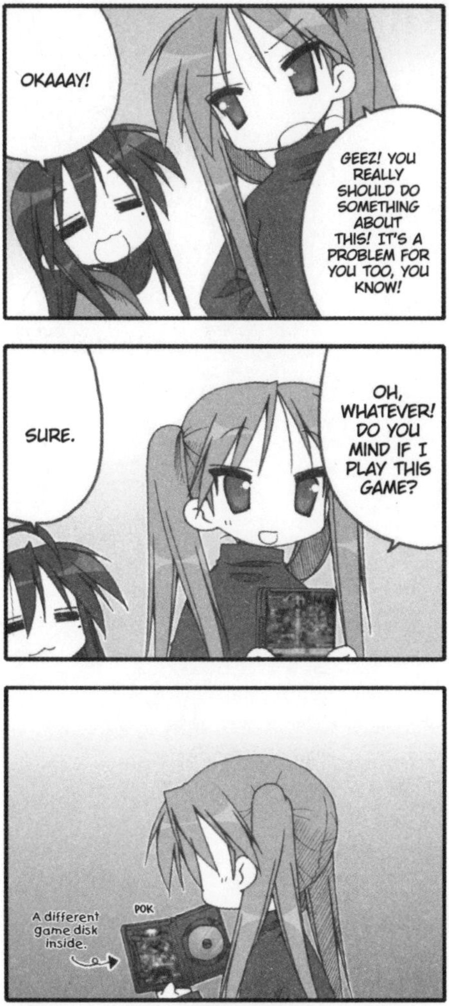
GEEZ! YOU REALLY SHOULD DO SOMETHING ABOUT THIS! IT'S A PROBLEM FOR YOU TOO, YOU KNOW!
OKAAAY!
OH, WHATEVER! DO YOU MIND IF I PLAY THIS GAME?
SURE.
POK
A different game disk inside.
UM... KONATA...
Listen you...
IN A LITTLE WHILE, I'LL DO A GAME RELAY, SO COULD YOU PUT THAT DISK IN THE RIGHT BOX, KAGAMI?
That hap-pens a lot to me.

HIYORI TAMURA'S HUMAN FILE

NAME: Fuyuki Amahara

GENDER: ♀

PLACE OF BIRTH: Kanagawa Prefecture

BIRTHDAY: September 17th

BLOOD TYPE: A

STAR SIGN: Virgo

PRESENT RANK: Ryou-ou Academy, Health Office Chief
*Everybody loves that she's the nurse in the Health Office

HANDEDNESS: Left Handed

BUST-SIZE RANK: Medium

FAMILY & POSITION: Father,
☆ Eldest daughter

HOBBIES: Taking Walks, Reading

LIKES: Tea, Ancient Art, Occult, Horror
*Behind that smile are those hobbies?

DISLIKES: Boats (can't swim)
*What a great quality!

FAVORITE COLORS: White

SPECIAL SKILLS: Japanese Class, English

WEAK POINTS: None to speak of

CLUBS: Tea Club (Faculty Advisor)

CLASS REP: Does Not Sponsor Any

HIYORI'S MEMO

Teaches health and fitness at our school and is the school nurse.
She is childhood friends (as the female of the two) with Sakruaba-sensei.
Knows Kobayakawa-san and Iwasaki-san very well.
Pretty and gentle, and popular with the whole school.
Rumors are that she is actually very rich...

Lucky☆Star

episode 104
that is justice

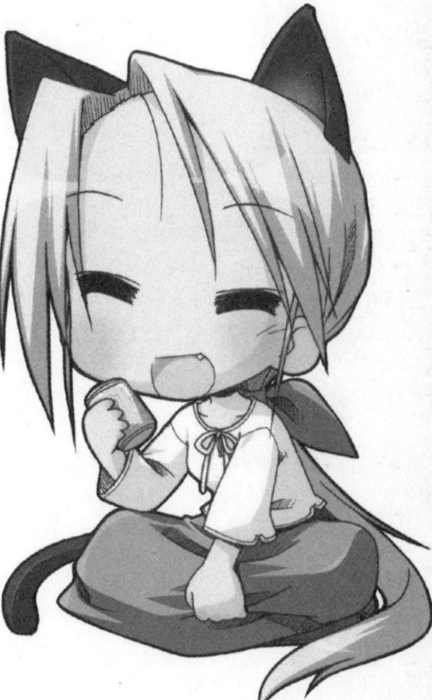

● Comptiq, December 2006 issue

Paradise

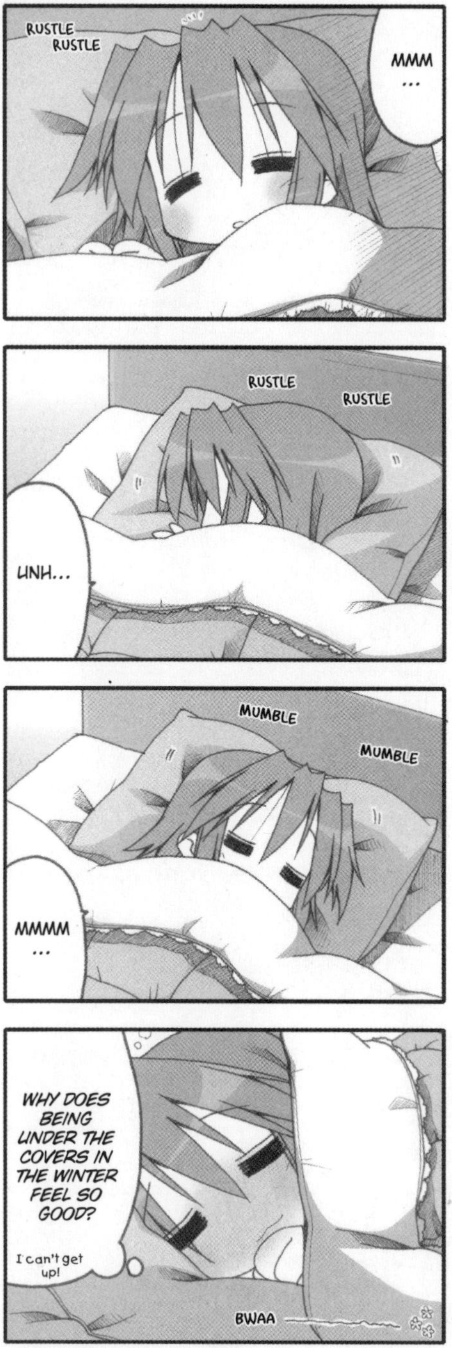
MMM ...
RUSTLE RUSTLE
RUSTLE RUSTLE
UNH...
MUMBLE MUMBLE
MMMM ...
WHY DOES BEING UNDER THE COVERS IN THE WINTER FEEL SO GOOD?
I can't get up!
BWAA

evolution

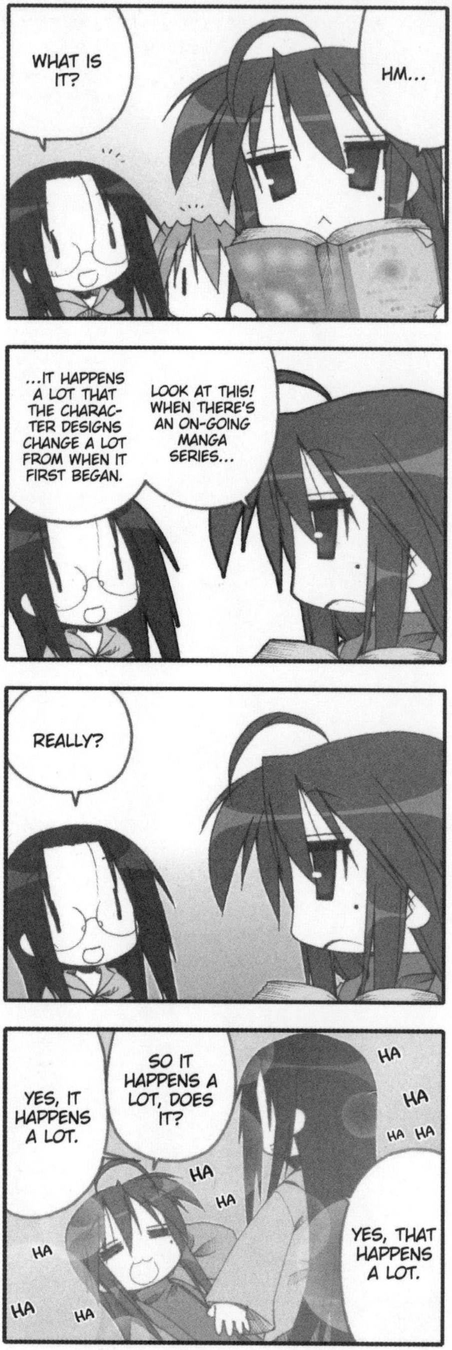
HM...
WHAT IS IT?
LOOK AT THIS! WHEN THERE'S AN ON-GOING MANGA SERIES...
...IT HAPPENS A LOT THAT THE CHARACTER DESIGNS CHANGE A LOT FROM WHEN IT FIRST BEGAN.
REALLY?
HA
HA
HA HA
SO IT HAPPENS A LOT, DOES IT?
YES, IT HAPPENS A LOT.
HA
HA
YES, THAT HAPPENS A LOT.
HA
HA
HA

evolved

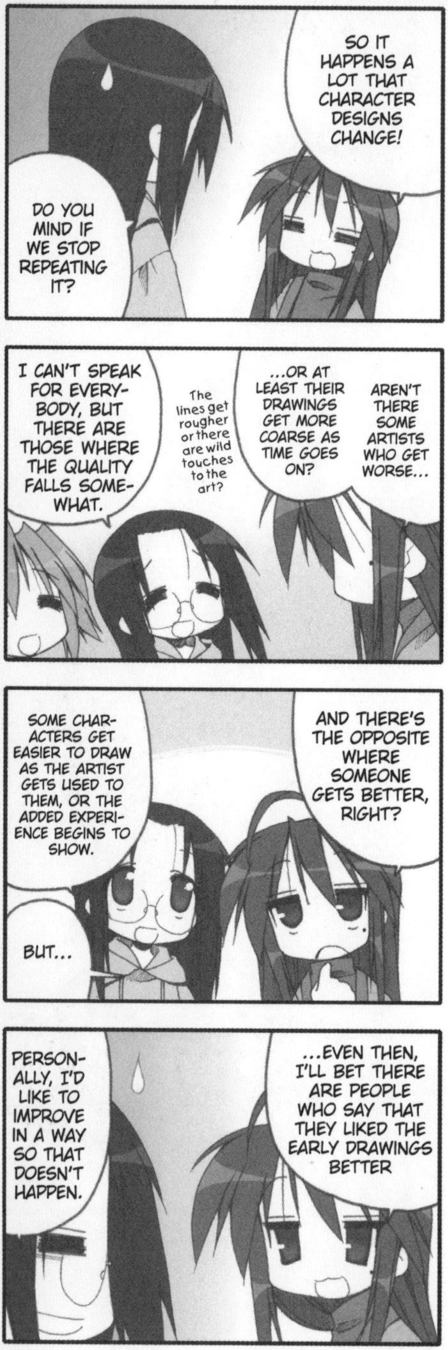
SO IT HAPPENS A LOT THAT CHARACTER DESIGNS CHANGE!
DO YOU MIND IF WE STOP REPEATING IT?
AREN'T THERE SOME ARTISTS WHO GET WORSE...
...OR AT LEAST THEIR DRAWINGS GET MORE COARSE AS TIME GOES ON?
The lines get rougher or there are wild touches to the art?
I CAN'T SPEAK FOR EVERYBODY, BUT THERE ARE THOSE WHERE THE QUALITY FALLS SOMEWHAT.
AND THERE'S THE OPPOSITE WHERE SOMEONE GETS BETTER, RIGHT?
SOME CHARACTERS GET EASIER TO DRAW AS THE ARTIST GETS USED TO THEM, OR THE ADDED EXPERIENCE BEGINS TO SHOW.
BUT...
...EVEN THEN, I'LL BET THERE ARE PEOPLE WHO SAY THAT THEY LIKED THE EARLY DRAWINGS BETTER
PERSONALLY, I'D LIKE TO IMPROVE IN A WAY SO THAT DOESN'T HAPPEN.

comrades

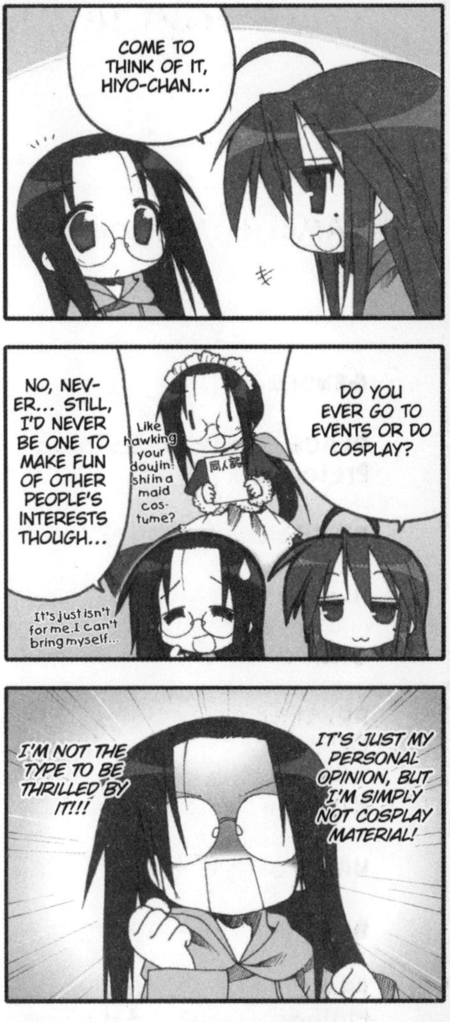
COME TO THINK OF IT, HIYO-CHAN...
DO YOU EVER GO TO EVENTS OR DO COSPLAY?
Like hawking your doujinshi in a maid costume?
NO, NEVER... STILL, I'D NEVER BE ONE TO MAKE FUN OF OTHER PEOPLE'S INTERESTS THOUGH...
It's just isn't for me. I can't bring myself...
IT'S JUST MY PERSONAL OPINION, BUT I'M SIMPLY NOT COSPLAY MATERIAL!
I'M NOT THE TYPE TO BE THRILLED BY IT!!!
VWIP
GOOD!

enemy

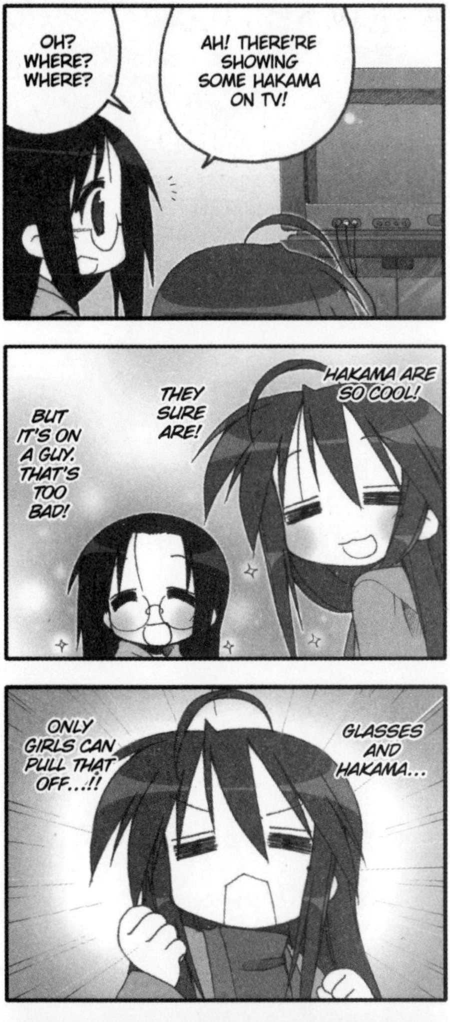
AH! THERE'RE SHOWING SOME HAKAMA ON TV!
OH? WHERE? WHERE?
HAKAMA ARE SO COOL!
THEY SURE ARE!
BUT IT'S ON A GUY. THAT'S TOO BAD!
GLASSES AND HAKAMA...
ONLY GIRLS CAN PULL THAT OFF...!!
PERSONALLY, I THINK THAT GUYS CAN DO IT TOO.
Boooo!!
EHHH?!

HIYORI TAMURA'S HUMAN FILE

NAME: Yui Narumi

GENDER: ♀

PLACE OF BIRTH: Saitama Prefecture

BIRTHDAY: October 7th

BLOOD TYPE: A

STAR SIGN: Libra

PRESENT RANK: Saitama Police Officer
*I'll do my best not to meet her as a part of her line of work.

HANDEDNESS: Right Handed

BUST-SIZE RANK: Large

FAMILY & POSITION: Father, Mother, ☆ Eldest daughter, Second Daughter, Husband

HOBBIES: Driving
*From what I hear, she's really something.

LIKES: Senbei, Stir-fry Veggies, Old Games, Her Husband

DISLIKES: Certain Vegetables (especially Tomato-style), When Members of the Family Live Far Away
*Feels it keenly.

FAVORITE COLORS: Blue

SPECIAL SKILLS: Ethics Class

WEAK POINTS: Math

CLUBS (CIRCLES): None

CLASS REP: ******

HIYORI'S MEMO

Kobayakawa-san's older sister.
And both sisters are cousins with Izumi-sempai.
Lots of energy, and so presents a contrast to Kobayakawa-san's personality.
She's married, but her husband has to live far away on business, so she spends a lot of time at Sempai's place.

Lucky☆Star

episode 105
goddess

● Comptiq, December 2006 issue

what do they intend?

STAAARE
CON-VEYER BELT SU-SHI...
WHAT IS IT, ONEE-CHAN?
IS THERE SOMETHING SPECIAL YOU'RE WAITING FOR?
NOT ESPE-CIALLY. IT'S JUST THAT I CAN'T FIGURE IT OUT...
no waSABI!
I DON'T REALLY THINK THEY NEED THE SIGN FOR TAMAGO-YAKI.

TAMAGO-YAKI=FRIED EGG

Limited Time Only

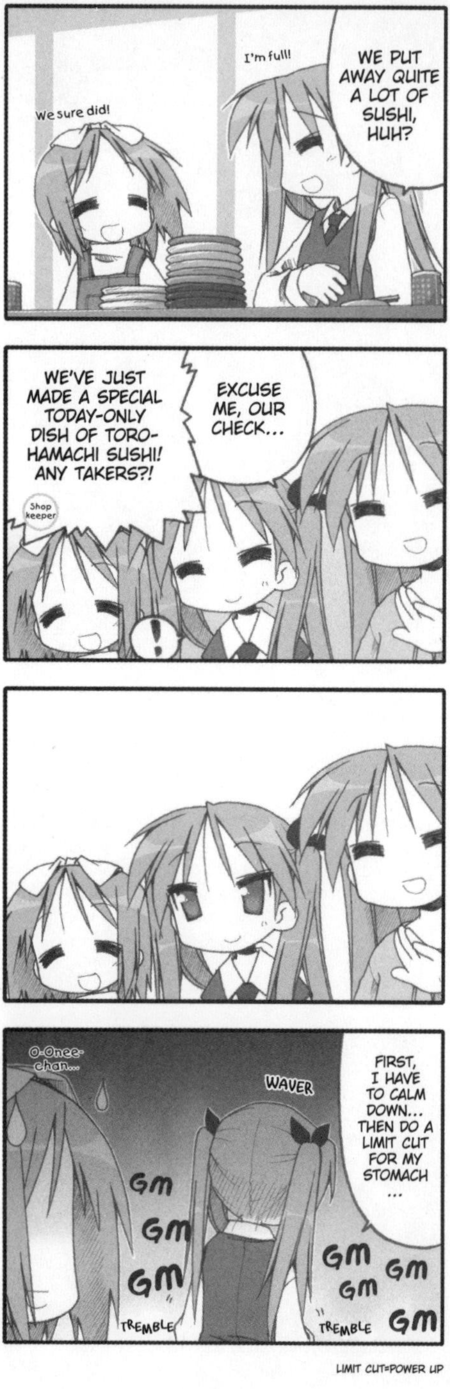
WE PUT AWAY QUITE A LOT OF SUSHI, HUH?
I'm full!
We sure did!
EXCUSE ME, OUR CHECK...
WE'VE JUST MADE A SPECIAL TODAY-ONLY DISH OF TORO-HAMACHI SUSHI! ANY TAKERS?!
Shop keeper
FIRST, I HAVE TO CALM DOWN... THEN DO A LIMIT CUT FOR MY STOMACH ...
WAVER
O-Onee-chan...
GM GM GM
GM GM GM GM
TREMBLE
TREMBLE

LIMIT CUT=POWER UP

her

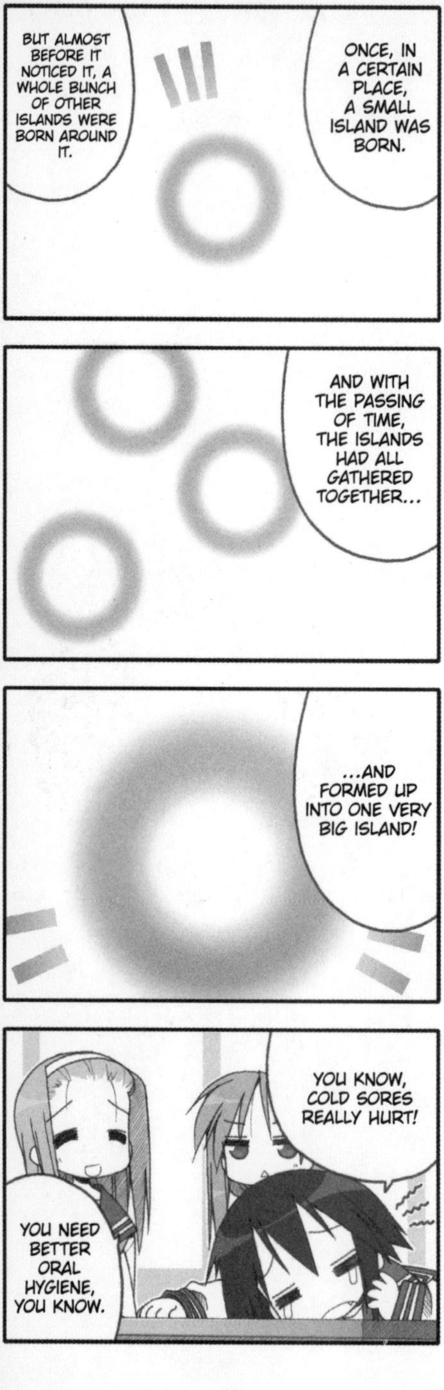
ONCE, IN A CERTAIN PLACE, A SMALL ISLAND WAS BORN.
BUT ALMOST BEFORE IT NOTICED IT, A WHOLE BUNCH OF OTHER ISLANDS WERE BORN AROUND IT.
AND WITH THE PASSING OF TIME, THE ISLANDS HAD ALL GATHERED TOGETHER...
...AND FORMED UP INTO ONE VERY BIG ISLAND!
YOU KNOW, COLD SORES REALLY HURT!
YOU NEED BETTER ORAL HYGIENE, YOU KNOW.

dying so many times

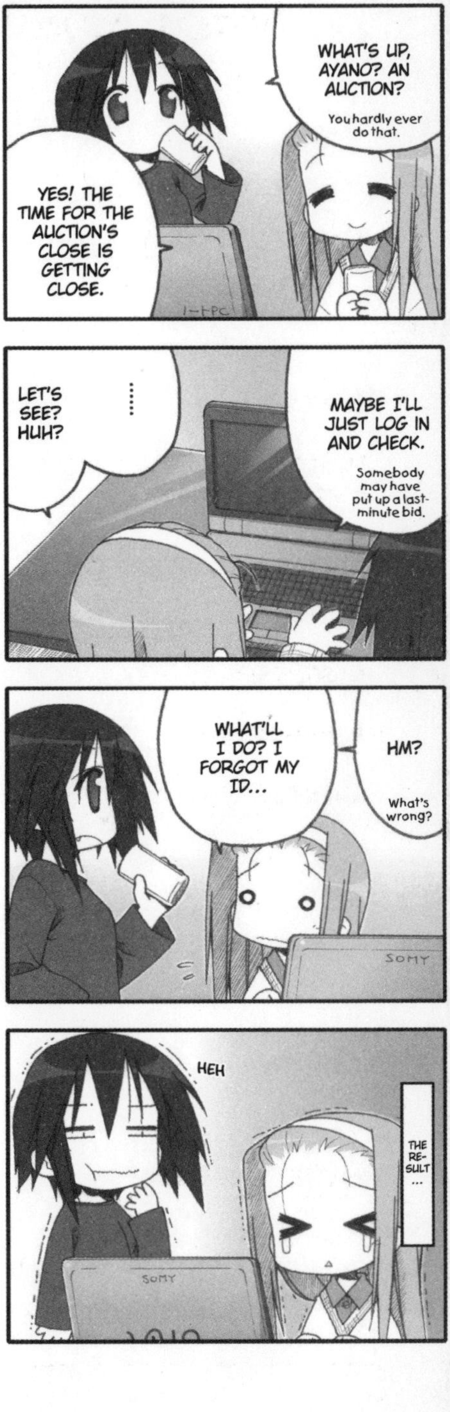
WHAT'S UP, AYANO? AN AUCTION?
You hardly ever do that.
YES! THE TIME FOR THE AUCTION'S CLOSE IS GETTING CLOSE.
MAYBE I'LL JUST LOG IN AND CHECK.
Somebody may have put up a last-minute bid.
......
LET'S SEE? HUH?
HM?
What's wrong?
WHAT'LL I DO? I FORGOT MY ID...
THE RESULT...
HEH

you're that kind of person

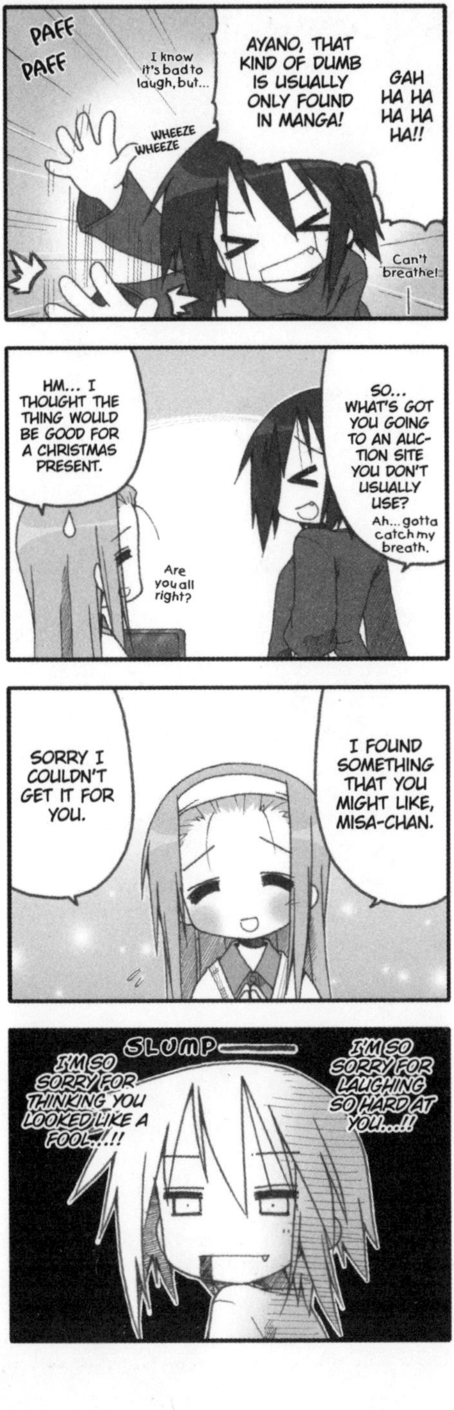
GAH HA HA HA HA HA!!
AYANO, THAT KIND OF DUMB IS USUALLY ONLY FOUND IN MANGA!
I know it's bad to laugh, but...
PAFF PAFF
WHEEZE WHEEZE
Can't breathe!
SO... WHAT'S GOT YOU GOING TO AN AUCTION SITE YOU DON'T USUALLY USE?
Ah... gotta catch my breath.
HM... I THOUGHT THE THING WOULD BE GOOD FOR A CHRISTMAS PRESENT.
Are you all right?
I FOUND SOMETHING THAT YOU MIGHT LIKE, MISA-CHAN.
SORRY I COULDN'T GET IT FOR YOU.
I'M SO SORRY FOR LAUGHING SO HARD AT YOU...!!
SLUMP——
I'M SO SORRY FOR THINKING YOU LOOKED LIKE A FOOL...!!

HIYORI TAMURA'S HUMAN FILE

NAME: Soujirou Izumi

GENDER: ♂

PLACE OF BIRTH: Ishikawa Prefecture

BIRTHDAY: August 21st

BLOOD TYPE: O

STAR SIGN: LEO

PRESENT RANK: ******

HANDEDNESS: Ambidextrous

BUST-SIZE RANK: ******

FAMILY & POSITION: ☆ Father, Eldest daughter

HOBBIES: Games, Anime, Reading
*He's upfront about his hobbies.

LIKES: Sushi, Moe
*A nice father to have in that respect.

DISLIKES: Deadlines, Delays in Publishing
*In some ways, rather like myself.

FAVORITE COLORS: Blue, White

SPECIAL SKILLS: None to speak of

WEAK POINTS: None to speak of

CLUBS: ******

CLASS REP: ******

HIYORI'S MEMO

One look at him and Izumi-sempai, and you can tell they are father and daughter.
He's a very understanding (because of his otaku-ism) and good father in my opinion.
Think of him as Izumi-sempai reaching her potential.
They say he's an author.

Lucky☆Star

episode 106
just no good

●Comptiq, January 2007 issue

a world of convenience

KONATA'S LATE AGAIN!
BRRRRRnng
HELLO? HUH?! OKAY, WHAT HAPPENED NOW?
AW, GEEZ! ENOUGH WITH THE EXCUSES! JUST GET HERE!
I CAN'T BELIEVE HER!
For pity's sake!
......
BUT EVEN WITH ALL THAT...
PACHIK
THESE CELL PHONES ARE SO CONVENIENT, I CAN'T IMAGINE NOW HOW I GOT ALONG WITHOUT ONE!
Staaare
THAT'S SO TRUE!

value

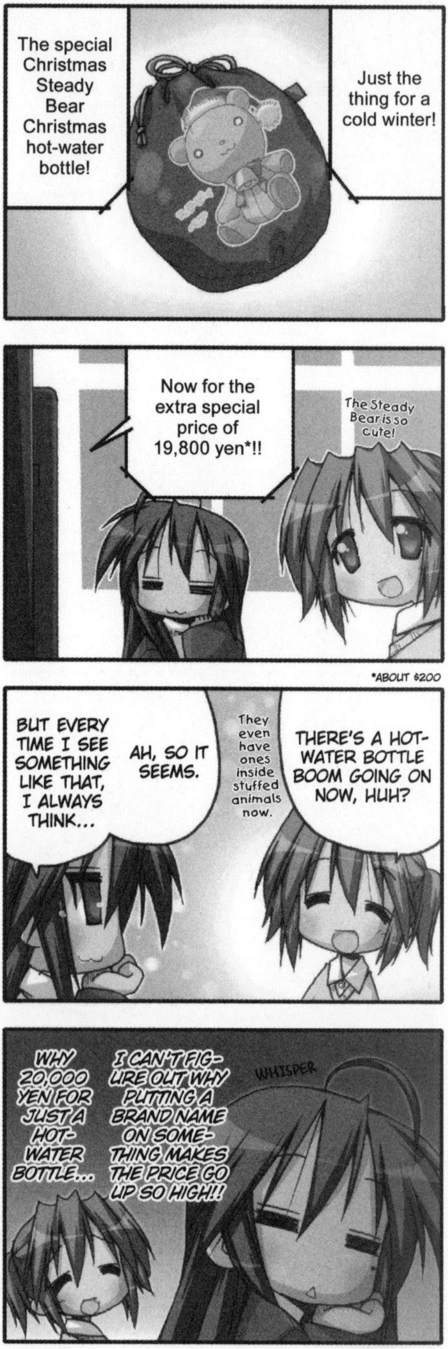
Just the thing for a cold winter!
The special Christmas Steady Bear Christmas hot-water bottle!
The Steady Bear is so cute!
Now for the extra special price of 19,800 yen*!!
THERE'S A HOT-WATER BOTTLE BOOM GOING ON NOW, HUH?
They even have ones inside stuffed animals now.
AH, SO IT SEEMS.
BUT EVERY TIME I SEE SOMETHING LIKE THAT, I ALWAYS THINK...
WHISPER
I CAN'T FIGURE OUT WHY PUTTING A BRAND NAME ON SOMETHING MAKES THE PRICE GO UP SO HIGH!!
WHY 20,000 YEN FOR JUST A HOT-WATER BOTTLE...

*ABOUT $200

the hard-to-understand people

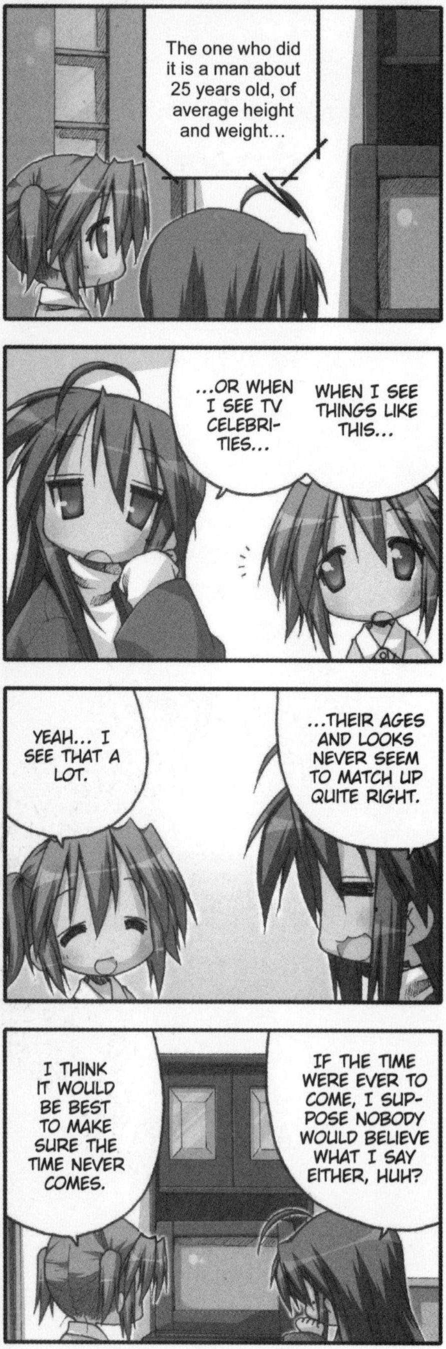
The one who did it is a man about 25 years old, of average height and weight…
WHEN I SEE THINGS LIKE THIS...
...OR WHEN I SEE TV CELEBRITIES...
...THEIR AGES AND LOOKS NEVER SEEM TO MATCH UP QUITE RIGHT.
YEAH... I SEE THAT A LOT.
IF THE TIME WERE EVER TO COME, I SUPPOSE NOBODY WOULD BELIEVE WHAT I SAY EITHER, HUH?
I THINK IT WOULD BE BEST TO MAKE SURE THE TIME NEVER COMES.

that kind of girl

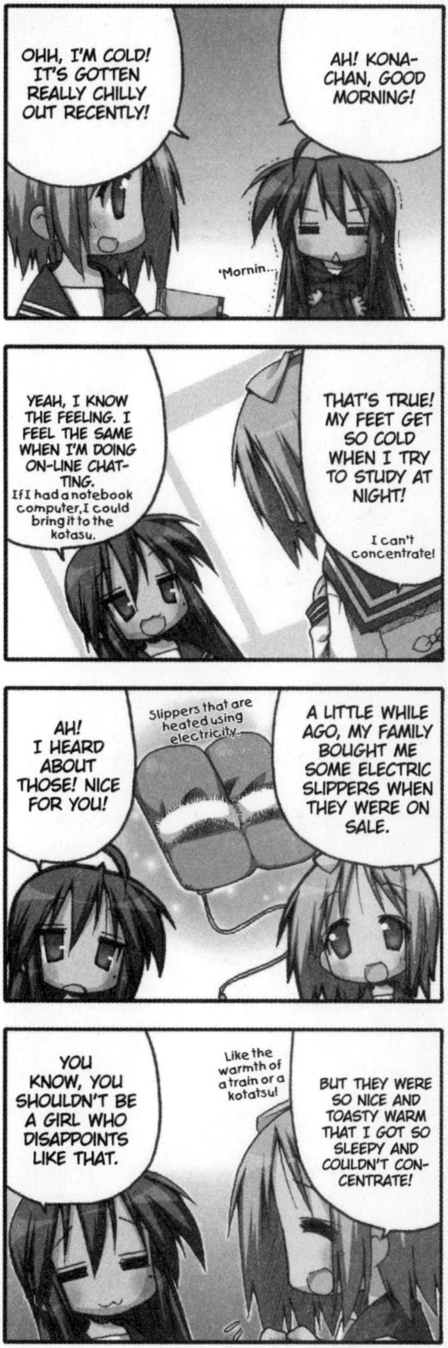
AH! KONA-CHAN, GOOD MORNING!
OHH, I'M COLD! IT'S GOTTEN REALLY CHILLY OUT RECENTLY!
'Mornin...
THAT'S TRUE! MY FEET GET SO COLD WHEN I TRY TO STUDY AT NIGHT!
I can't concentrate!
YEAH, I KNOW THE FEELING. I FEEL THE SAME WHEN I'M DOING ON-LINE CHAT-TING.
If I had a notebook computer, I could bring it to the kotatsu.
A LITTLE WHILE AGO, MY FAMILY BOUGHT ME SOME ELECTRIC SLIPPERS WHEN THEY WERE ON SALE.
Slippers that are heated using electricity.
AH! I HEARD ABOUT THOSE! NICE FOR YOU!
BUT THEY WERE SO NICE AND TOASTY WARM THAT I GOT SO SLEEPY AND COULDN'T CON-CENTRATE!
Like the warmth of a train or a kotatsu!
YOU KNOW, YOU SHOULDN'T BE A GIRL WHO DISAPPOINTS LIKE THAT.

girl of her times

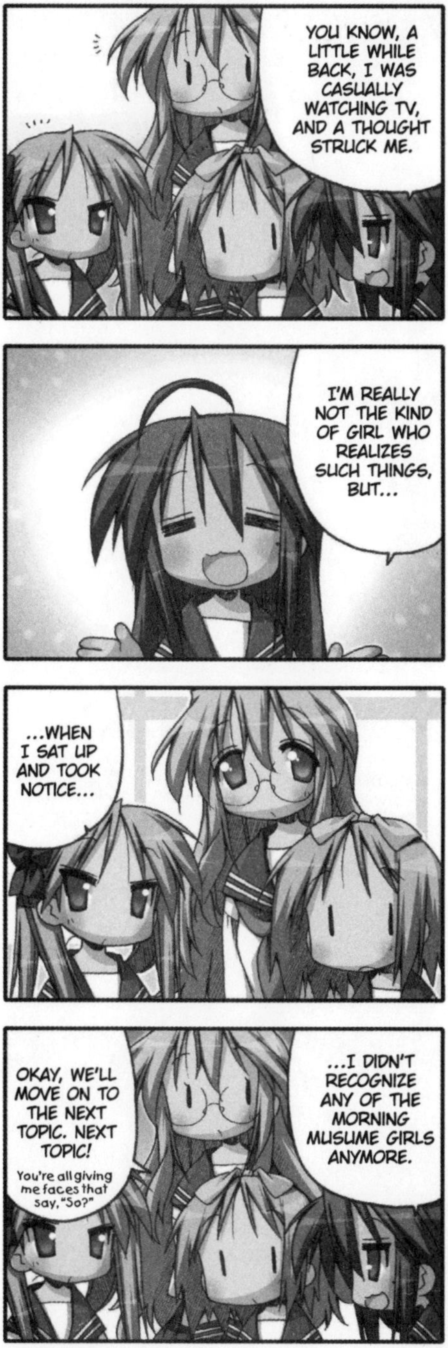
YOU KNOW, A LITTLE WHILE BACK, I WAS CASUALLY WATCHING TV, AND A THOUGHT STRUCK ME.
I'M REALLY NOT THE KIND OF GIRL WHO REALIZES SUCH THINGS, BUT...
...WHEN I SAT UP AND TOOK NOTICE...
...I DIDN'T RECOGNIZE ANY OF THE MORNING MUSUME GIRLS ANYMORE.
OKAY, WE'LL MOVE ON TO THE NEXT TOPIC. NEXT TOPIC!
You're all giving me faces that say, "So?"

HIYORI TAMURA'S HUMAN FILE

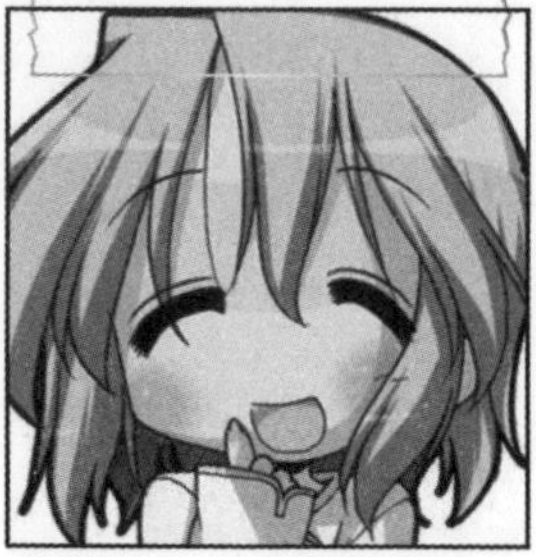

NAME: Yukari Takara

GENDER: ♀

PLACE OF BIRTH: Tokyo

BIRTHDAY: March 6th

BLOOD TYPE: O

STAR SIGN: Pisces

PRESENT RANK: ******

HANDEDNESS: Left Handed

BUST-SIZE RANK: Average

FAMILY & POSITION: Father, ☆ Mother, Eldest daughter
*Although she looks more like an older sister than a mother

HOBBIES: Shopping, Talking
*She really loves to talk.

LIKES: Boiled Tofu, Curry

DISLIKES: Vegetables with a Pale Color, Nattou

FAVORITE COLORS: Cherry Blossom Pink

SPECIAL SKILLS: None!

WEAK POINTS: Loads and Loads.

CLUBS: ******

CLASS REP: ******

HIYORI'S MEMO

One look at her and Takara-sempai, and you can tell they are mother and daughter.
Or rather, judging by her looks and personality, she seems more like Takara-sempai's sister.
She's that type you always see. The type who could never survive without someone to help her, but she always seems to find somebody.
Really cute!

Lucky☆Star

episode 107
fighting girls

● Comptiq, January 2007 issue

a rule

STAAARE
......
AH!
AW, MAN! I'M DEAD!
Went off the line.
WH- WHY?!

the model effect

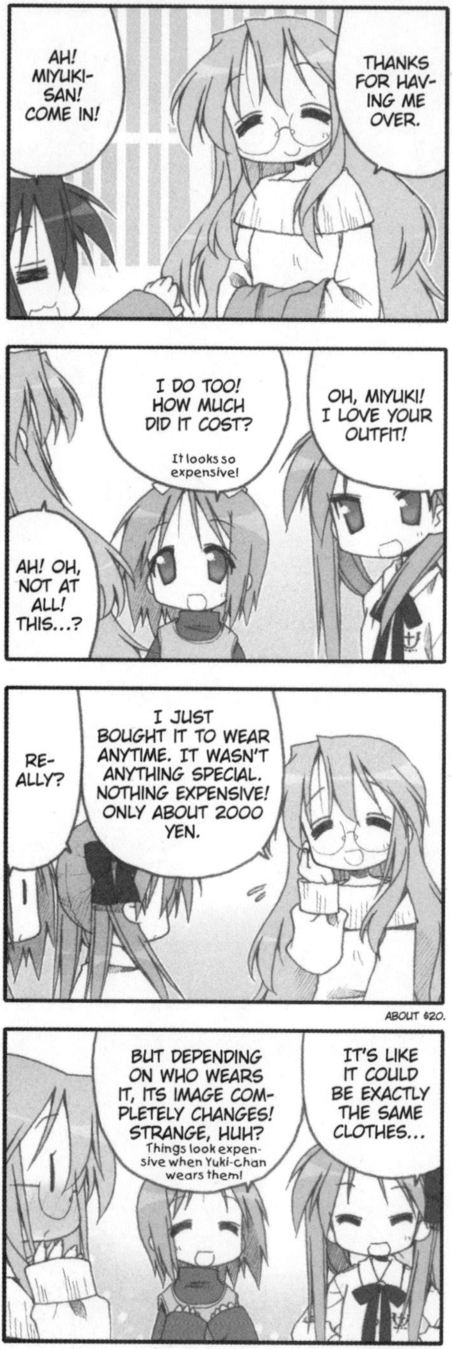
THANKS FOR HAV-ING ME OVER.
AH! MIYUKI-SAN! COME IN!
OH, MIYUKI! I LOVE YOUR OUTFIT!
I DO TOO! HOW MUCH DID IT COST?
It looks so expensive!
AH! OH, NOT AT ALL! THIS...?
I JUST BOUGHT IT TO WEAR ANYTIME. IT WASN'T ANYTHING SPECIAL. NOTHING EXPENSIVE! ONLY ABOUT 2000 YEN.
RE-ALLY?
ABOUT $20.
IT'S LIKE IT COULD BE EXACTLY THE SAME CLOTHES...
BUT DEPENDING ON WHO WEARS IT, ITS IMAGE COM-PLETELY CHANGES! STRANGE, HUH?
Things look expen-sive when Yuki-chan wears them!

first impression

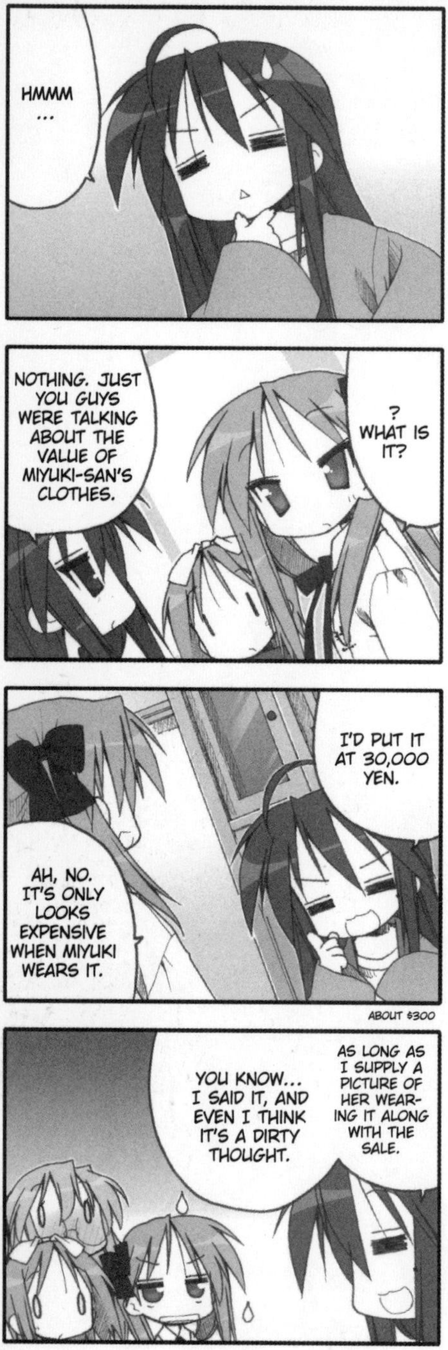
HMMM ...
? WHAT IS IT?
NOTHING. JUST YOU GUYS WERE TALKING ABOUT THE VALUE OF MIYUKI-SAN'S CLOTHES.
I'D PUT IT AT 30,000 YEN.
AH, NO. IT'S ONLY LOOKS EXPENSIVE WHEN MIYUKI WEARS IT.
ABOUT $300
AS LONG AS I SUPPLY A PICTURE OF HER WEAR-ING IT ALONG WITH THE SALE.
YOU KNOW... I SAID IT, AND EVEN I THINK IT'S A DIRTY THOUGHT.

party night

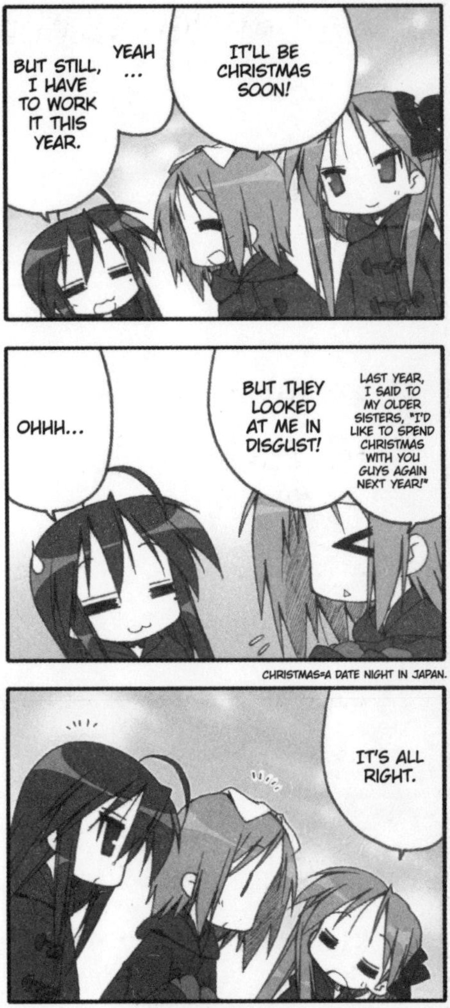

IT'LL BE CHRISTMAS SOON!
YEAH ...
BUT STILL, I HAVE TO WORK IT THIS YEAR.
LAST YEAR, I SAID TO MY OLDER SISTERS, "I'D LIKE TO SPEND CHRISTMAS WITH YOU GUYS AGAIN NEXT YEAR!"
BUT THEY LOOKED AT ME IN DISGUST!
OHHH...
CHRISTMAS=A DATE NIGHT IN JAPAN.
IT'S ALL RIGHT.
OUR WHOLE FAMILY WILL BE TOGETHER AGAIN THIS YEAR.
YEAH...
So they never stood a chance.

a look of envy

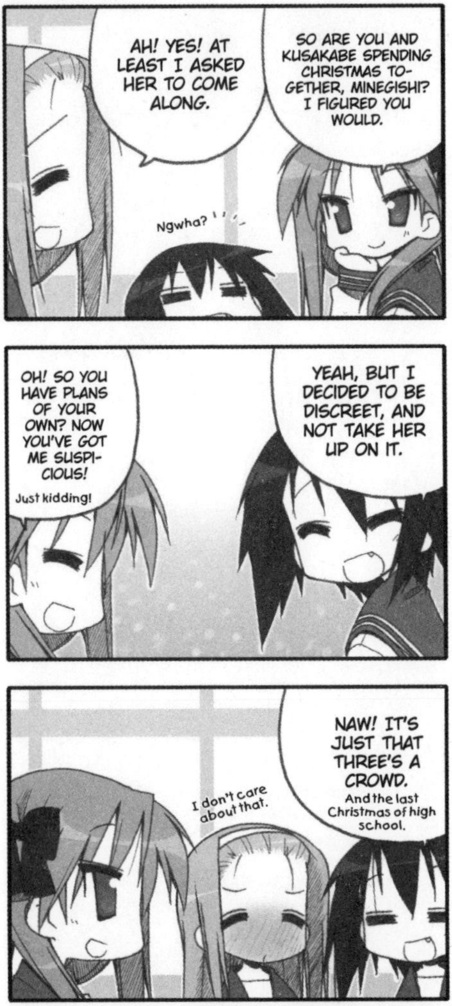

SO ARE YOU AND KUSAKABE SPENDING CHRISTMAS TO-GETHER, MINEGISHI? I FIGURED YOU WOULD.
AH! YES! AT LEAST I ASKED HER TO COME ALONG.
Ngwha?
YEAH, BUT I DECIDED TO BE DISCREET, AND NOT TAKE HER UP ON IT.
OH! SO YOU HAVE PLANS OF YOUR OWN? NOW YOU'VE GOT ME SUSPI-CIOUS!
Just kidding!
NAW! IT'S JUST THAT THREE'S A CROWD.
And the last Christmas of high school.
I don't care about that.
Have fun, you two!
Oh, you!
YOU MEAN THE ONE WHO JUST DOESN'T GET IT IS...
...me...?

HIYORI TAMURA'S HUMAN FILE

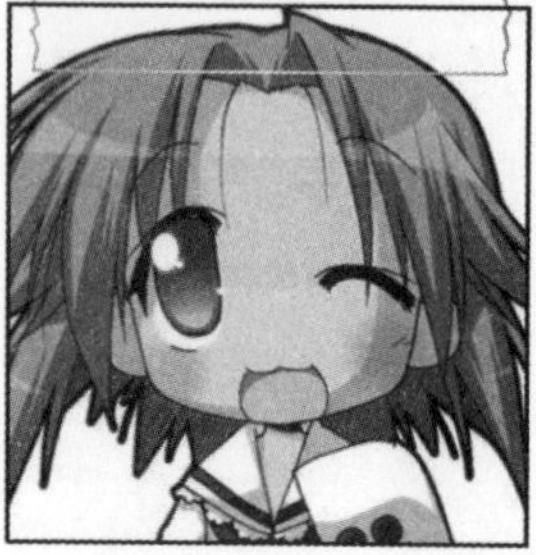

NAME: Akira Kogami

GENDER: ♀

PLACE OF BIRTH: Tokyo

BIRTHDAY: February 14th

BLOOD TYPE: O

STAR SIGN: Aquarius

PRESENT RANK: Mashiro Private Middle School, 3rd Year, Class A
*Ah, so she's still in middle school.

HANDEDNESS: Right Handed

BUST-SIZE RANK: Minimum

FAMILY & POSITION: Father, Mother, ☆ Eldest daughter, Second Daughter

HOBBIES: Games

LIKES: Skewered Liver Dishes
*What you'd expect from cool older guys, though.

DISLIKES: Nothing to speak of

FAVORITE COLORS: Blue
*But listening to her on the radio, black suits her better.

SPECIAL SKILLS: None to speak of

WEAK POINTS: None to speak of

CLUBS: None

CLASS REP: No

HIYORI'S MEMO

An idol who appears on TV and radio.
She seems like a grade-school student, and she is a perfect match the recent moe boom.
Maybe she is an airhead or just pretending to be one, but she gives the impression of being pretty dumb.

Lucky☆Star

episode 108
a reason to smile

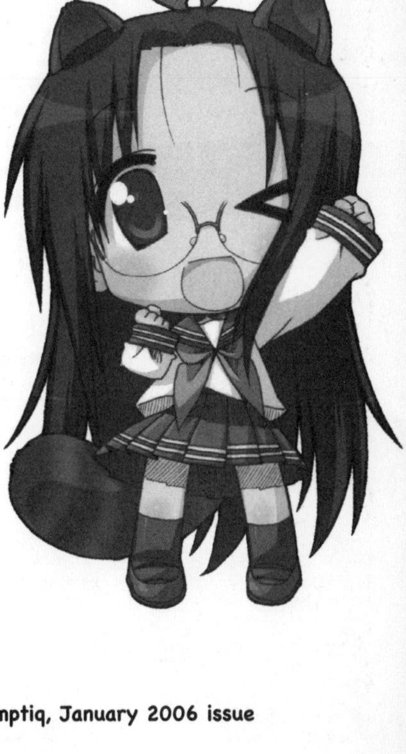

●Comptiq, January 2006 issue

wall of ice

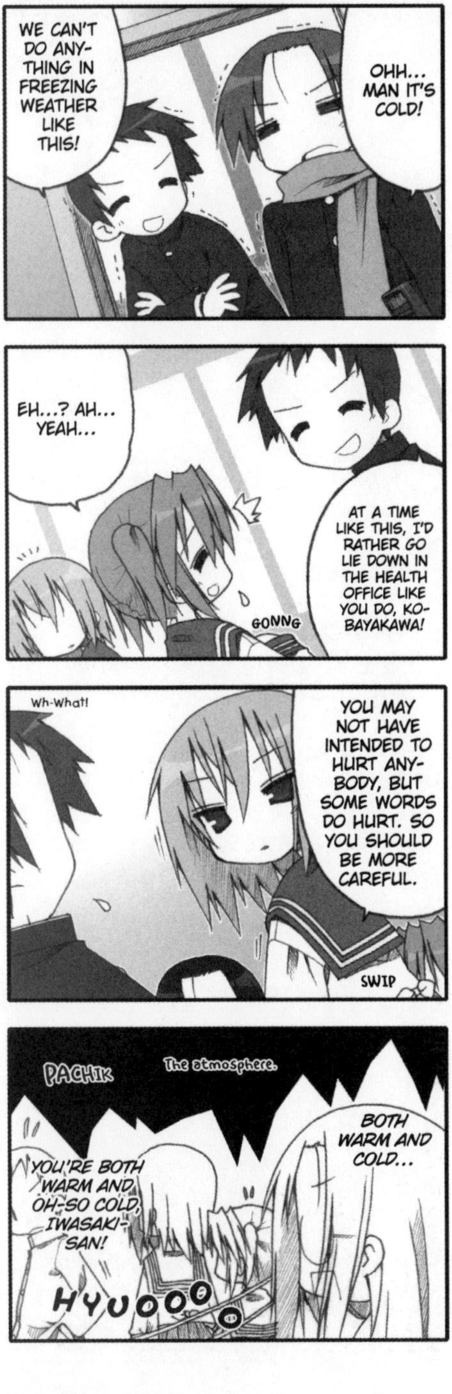

OHH... MAN IT'S COLD!
WE CAN'T DO ANYTHING IN FREEZING WEATHER LIKE THIS!
AT A TIME LIKE THIS, I'D RATHER GO LIE DOWN IN THE HEALTH OFFICE LIKE YOU DO, KOBAYAKAWA!
EH...? AH... YEAH...
GONNG
YOU MAY NOT HAVE INTENDED TO HURT ANYBODY, BUT SOME WORDS DO HURT. SO YOU SHOULD BE MORE CAREFUL.
Wh-What!
SWIP
PACHIK
The atmosphere.
BOTH WARM AND COLD...
YOU'RE BOTH WARM AND OH-SO COLD, IWASAKI-SAN!
HYUOOOO

serious talk

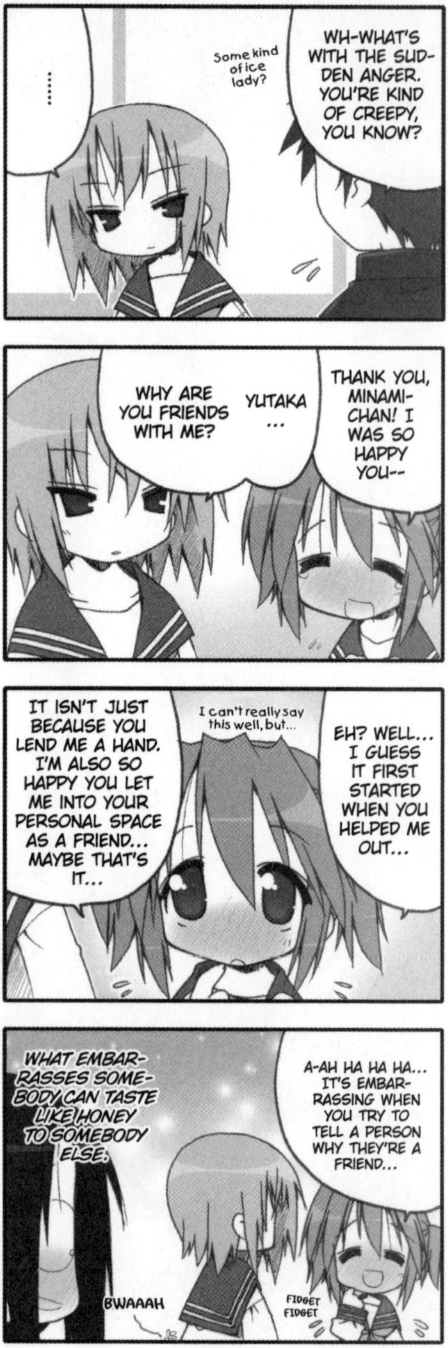
WH-WHAT'S WITH THE SUD-DEN ANGER. YOU'RE KIND OF CREEPY, YOU KNOW?
Some kind of ice lady?
......
THANK YOU, MINAMI-CHAN! I WAS SO HAPPY YOU--
YUTAKA ...
WHY ARE YOU FRIENDS WITH ME?
EH? WELL... I GUESS IT FIRST STARTED WHEN YOU HELPED ME OUT...
I can't really say this well, but...
IT ISN'T JUST BECAUSE YOU LEND ME A HAND. I'M ALSO SO HAPPY YOU LET ME INTO YOUR PERSONAL SPACE AS A FRIEND... MAYBE THAT'S IT...
A-AH HA HA HA... IT'S EMBAR-RASSING WHEN YOU TRY TO TELL A PERSON WHY THEY'RE A FRIEND...
WHAT EMBAR-RASSES SOME-BODY CAN TASTE LIKE HONEY TO SOMEBODY ELSE.
FIDGET FIDGET
BWAAAH

wheel

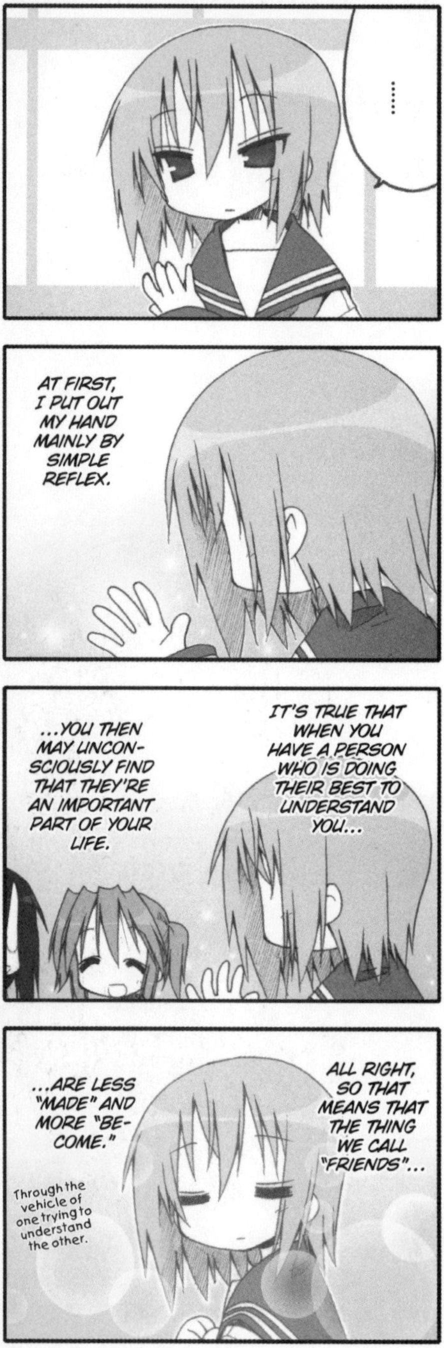
......
AT FIRST, I PUT OUT MY HAND MAINLY BY SIMPLE REFLEX.
IT'S TRUE THAT WHEN YOU HAVE A PERSON WHO IS DOING THEIR BEST TO UNDERSTAND YOU...
...YOU THEN MAY UNCON-SCIOUSLY FIND THAT THEY'RE AN IMPORTANT PART OF YOUR LIFE.
ALL RIGHT, SO THAT MEANS THAT THE THING WE CALL "FRIENDS"...
...ARE LESS "MADE" AND MORE "BE-COME."
Through the vehicle of one trying to understand the other.

a tiny thing

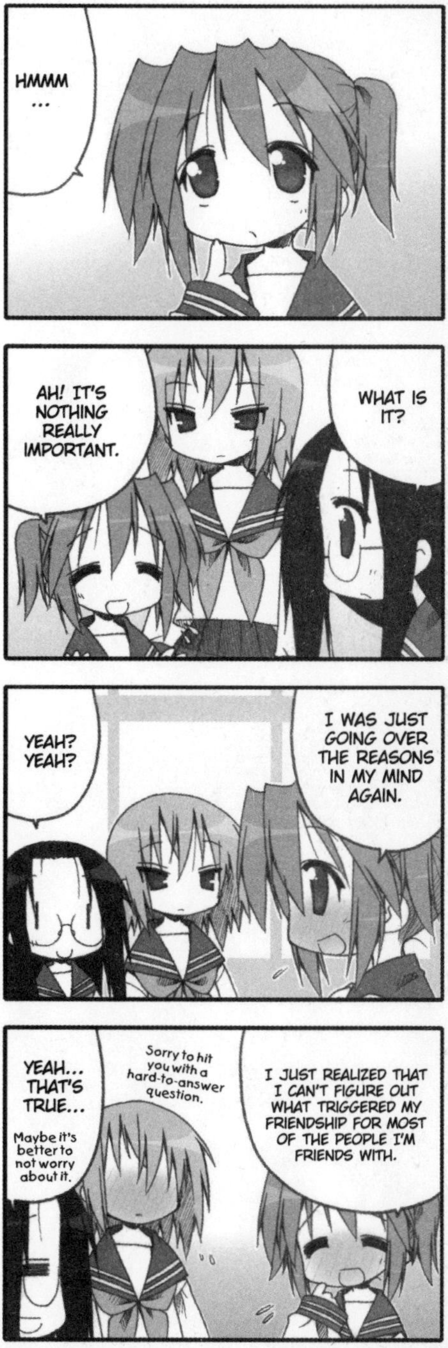
HMMM ...
WHAT IS IT?
AH! IT'S NOTHING REALLY IMPORTANT.
I WAS JUST GOING OVER THE REASONS IN MY MIND AGAIN.
YEAH? YEAH?
I JUST REALIZED THAT I CAN'T FIGURE OUT WHAT TRIGGERED MY FRIENDSHIP FOR MOST OF THE PEOPLE I'M FRIENDS WITH.
Sorry to hit you with a hard-to-answer question.
YEAH... THAT'S TRUE...
Maybe it's better to not worry about it.

target

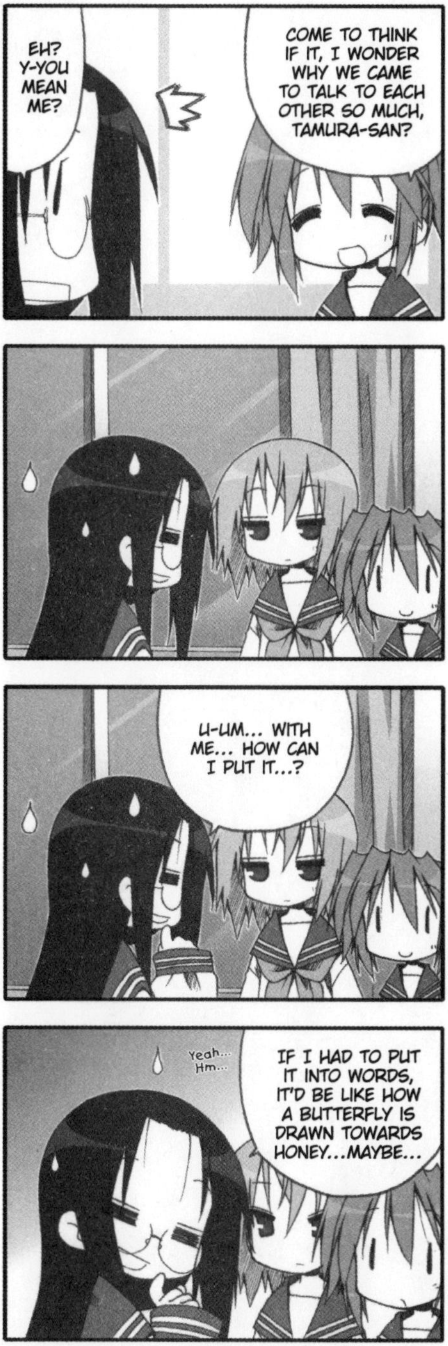
COME TO THINK IF IT, I WONDER WHY WE CAME TO TALK TO EACH OTHER SO MUCH, TAMURA-SAN?
EH? Y-YOU MEAN ME?
U-UM... WITH ME... HOW CAN I PUT IT...?
IF I HAD TO PUT IT INTO WORDS, IT'D BE LIKE HOW A BUTTERFLY IS DRAWN TOWARDS HONEY...MAYBE...
Yeah... Hm...

happy time

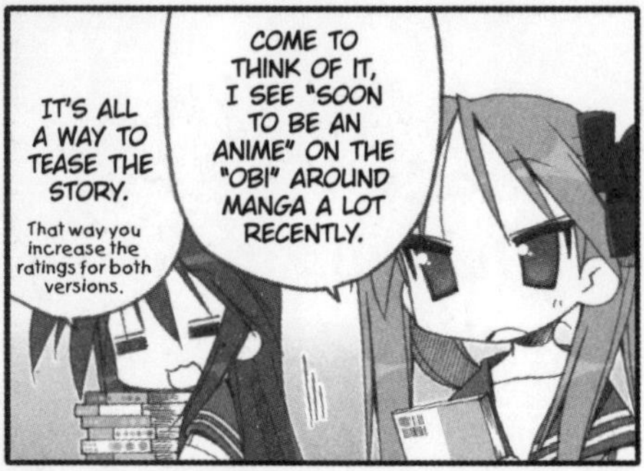
COME TO THINK OF IT, I SEE "SOON TO BE AN ANIME" ON THE "OBI" AROUND MANGA A LOT RECENTLY.
IT'S ALL A WAY TO TEASE THE STORY.
That way you increase the ratings for both versions.

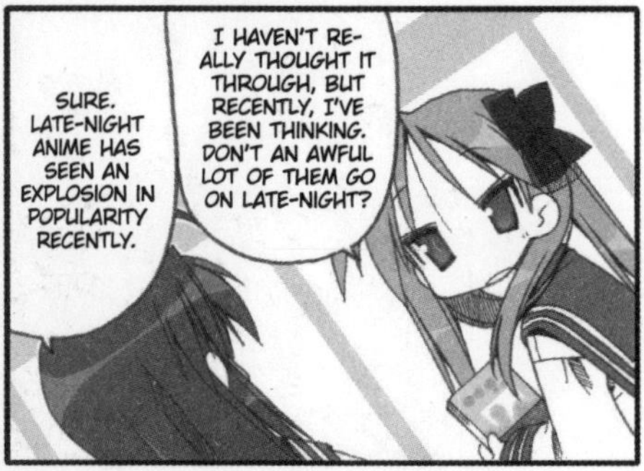
I HAVEN'T REALLY THOUGHT IT THROUGH, BUT RECENTLY, I'VE BEEN THINKING. DON'T AN AWFUL LOT OF THEM GO ON LATE-NIGHT?
SURE. LATE-NIGHT ANIME HAS SEEN AN EXPLOSION IN POPULARITY RECENTLY.

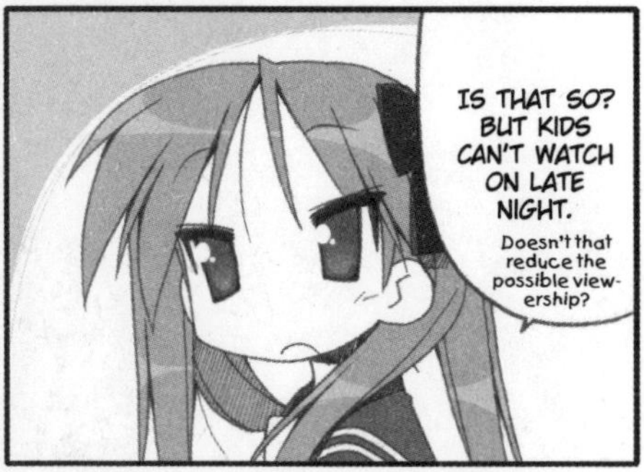
IS THAT SO? BUT KIDS CAN'T WATCH ON LATE NIGHT.
Doesn't that reduce the possible viewership?

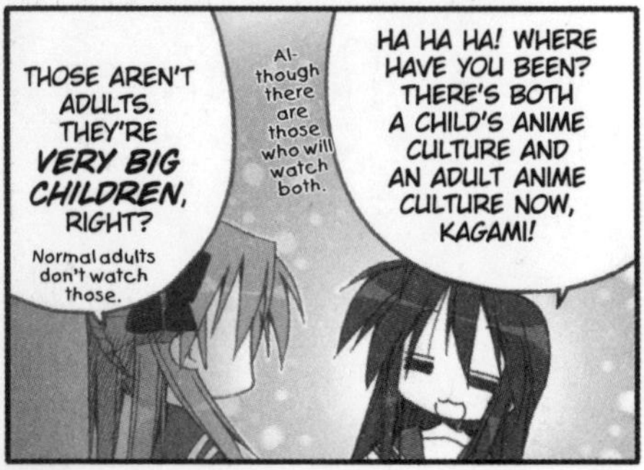
HA HA HA! WHERE HAVE YOU BEEN? THERE'S BOTH A CHILD'S ANIME CULTURE AND AN ADULT ANIME CULTURE NOW, KAGAMI!
Although there are those who will watch both.
THOSE AREN'T ADULTS. THEY'RE VERY BIG CHILDREN, RIGHT?
Normal adults don't watch those.

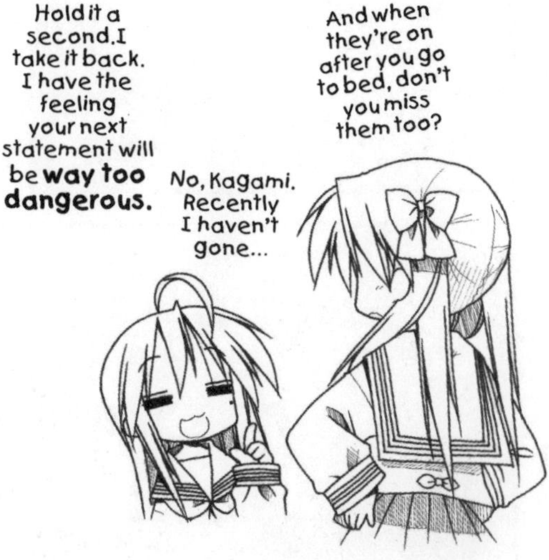
And when they're on after you go to bed, don't you miss them too?
No, Kagami. Recently I haven't gone...
Hold it a second. I take it back. I have the feeling your next statement will be way too dangerous.

● **Drawn for this volume.**

Lucky☆Star

episode 109
digital junkie

●Comptiq, February 2007 issue

unusual circumstances

REALLY! I COULDN'T STOP LAUGHING!
CHATTER
CHATTER
Don't talk with food in your mouth.
AND THE, RIGHT AFTER THAT--
URK!
RUNCH
GU
DID YOU BITE THE INSIDE OF YOUR CHEEK? ARE YOU ALL RIGHT?
YEAH, I'M FINE... I'M LESS WORRIED ABOUT NOW, AND MORE ABOUT AFTER-WARDS.
ISN'T BITING YOUR CHEEK RELATED TO COLD SORES?
It's got me feeling blue!
DIDN'T I TELL YOU NOT TO TALK WITH FOOD IN YOUR MOUTH?
This is your punishment.
AYANO!! HIIRAGI IS COLDER THAN A WIN-TER WIND!
AAH
WAA

only slightly sticky

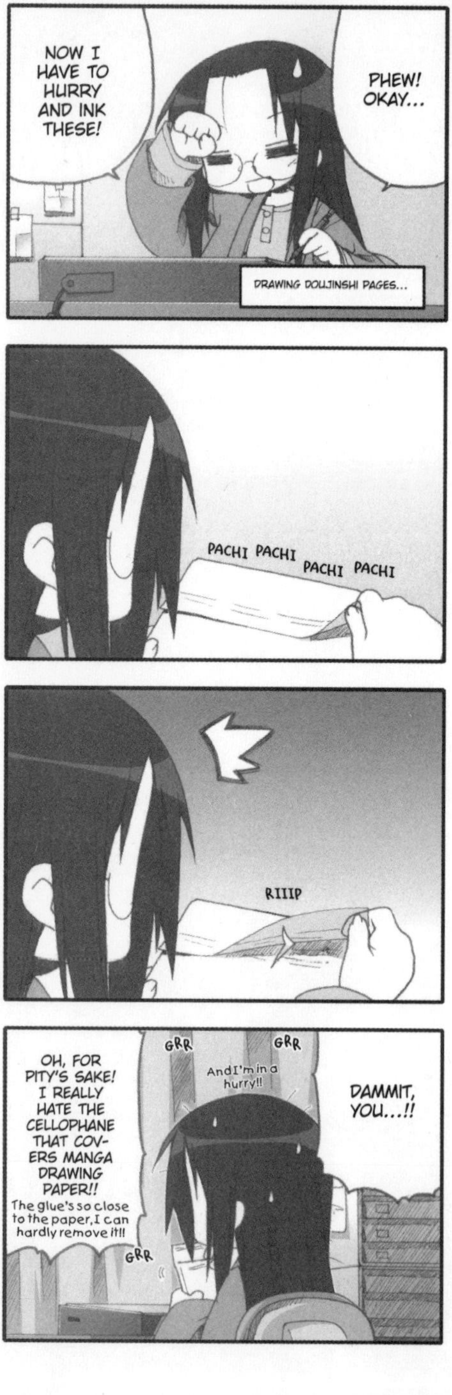
PHEW! OKAY...
NOW I HAVE TO HURRY AND INK THESE!
DRAWING DOUJINSHI PAGES...
PACHI PACHI PACHI PACHI
RIIIP
DAMMIT, YOU...!!
GRR
And I'm in a hurry!!
GRR
OH, FOR PITY'S SAKE! I REALLY HATE THE CELLOPHANE THAT COVERS MANGA DRAWING PAPER!!
The glue's so close to the paper, I can hardly remove it!!
GRR

first action

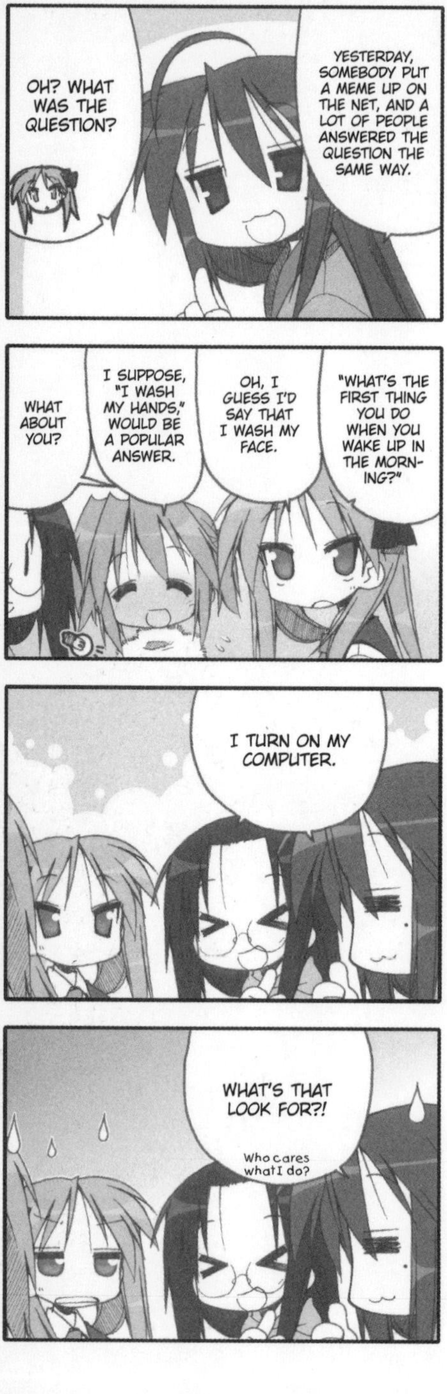
YESTERDAY, SOMEBODY PUT A MEME UP ON THE NET, AND A LOT OF PEOPLE ANSWERED THE QUESTION THE SAME WAY.
OH? WHAT WAS THE QUESTION?
"WHAT'S THE FIRST THING YOU DO WHEN YOU WAKE UP IN THE MORNING?"
OH, I GUESS I'D SAY THAT I WASH MY FACE.
I SUPPOSE, "I WASH MY HANDS," WOULD BE A POPULAR ANSWER.
WHAT ABOUT YOU?
I TURN ON MY COMPUTER.
WHAT'S THAT LOOK FOR?!
Who cares what I do?

fate

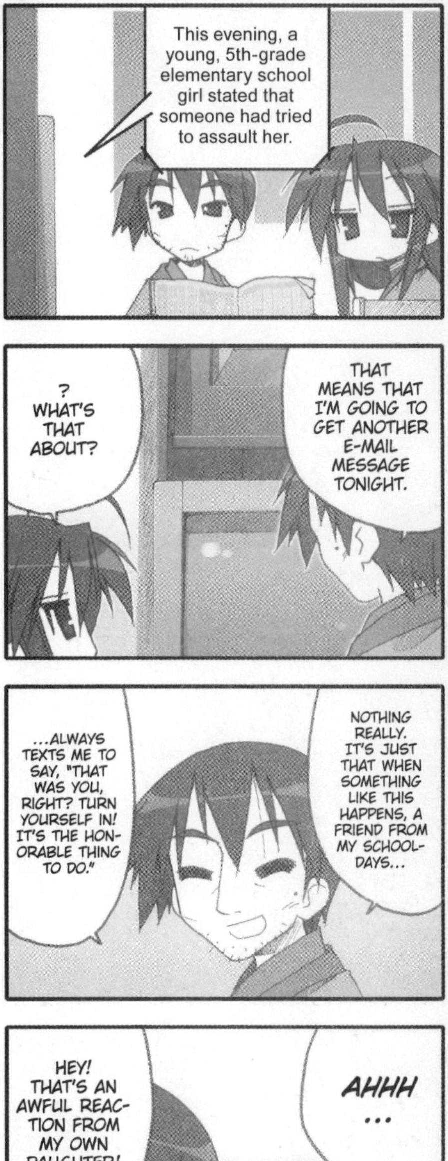
This evening, a young, 5th-grade elementary school girl stated that someone had tried to assault her.
THAT MEANS THAT I'M GOING TO GET ANOTHER E-MAIL MESSAGE TONIGHT.
? WHAT'S THAT ABOUT?
NOTHING REALLY. IT'S JUST THAT WHEN SOMETHING LIKE THIS HAPPENS, A FRIEND FROM MY SCHOOL-DAYS...
...ALWAYS TEXTS ME TO SAY, "THAT WAS YOU, RIGHT? TURN YOURSELF IN! IT'S THE HON-ORABLE THING TO DO."
AHHH ...
HEY! THAT'S AN AWFUL REAC-TION FROM MY OWN DAUGHTER!
You completely agree with the guy, don't you?!

unredeemable

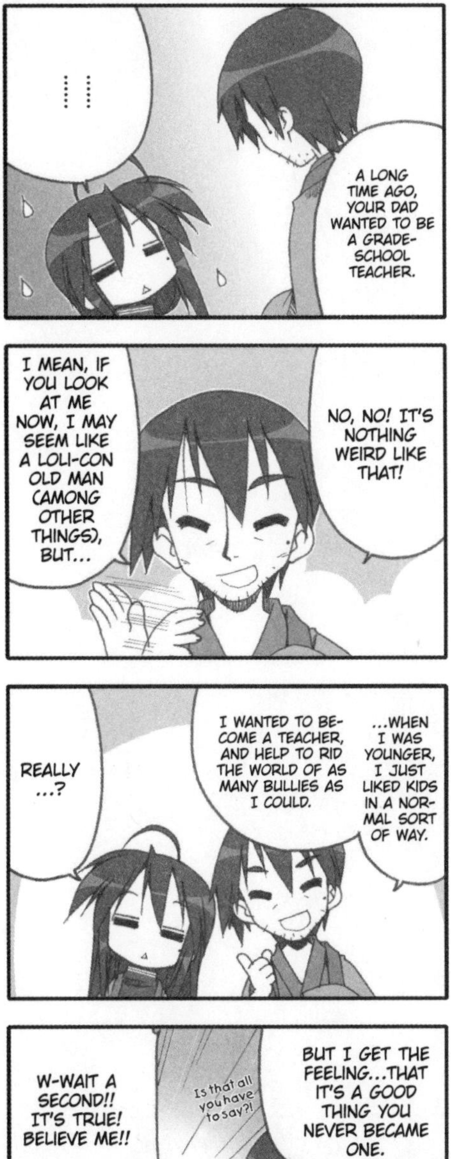
A LONG TIME AGO, YOUR DAD WANTED TO BE A GRADE-SCHOOL TEACHER.
......
NO, NO! IT'S NOTHING WEIRD LIKE THAT!
I MEAN, IF YOU LOOK AT ME NOW, I MAY SEEM LIKE A LOLI-CON OLD MAN (AMONG OTHER THINGS), BUT...
...WHEN I WAS YOUNGER, I JUST LIKED KIDS IN A NOR-MAL SORT OF WAY.
I WANTED TO BE-COME A TEACHER, AND HELP TO RID THE WORLD OF AS MANY BULLIES AS I COULD.
REALLY ...?
BUT I GET THE FEELING...THAT IT'S A GOOD THING YOU NEVER BECAME ONE.
For the kids' sake.
Is that all you have to say?!
W-WAIT A SECOND!! IT'S TRUE! BELIEVE ME!!

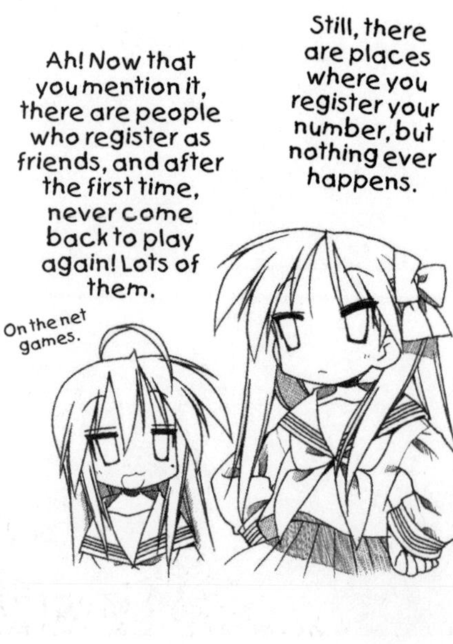
Still, there are places where you register your number, but nothing ever happens.
Ah! Now that you mention it, there are people who register as friends, and after the first time, never come back to play again! Lots of them.
On the net games.

self awareness

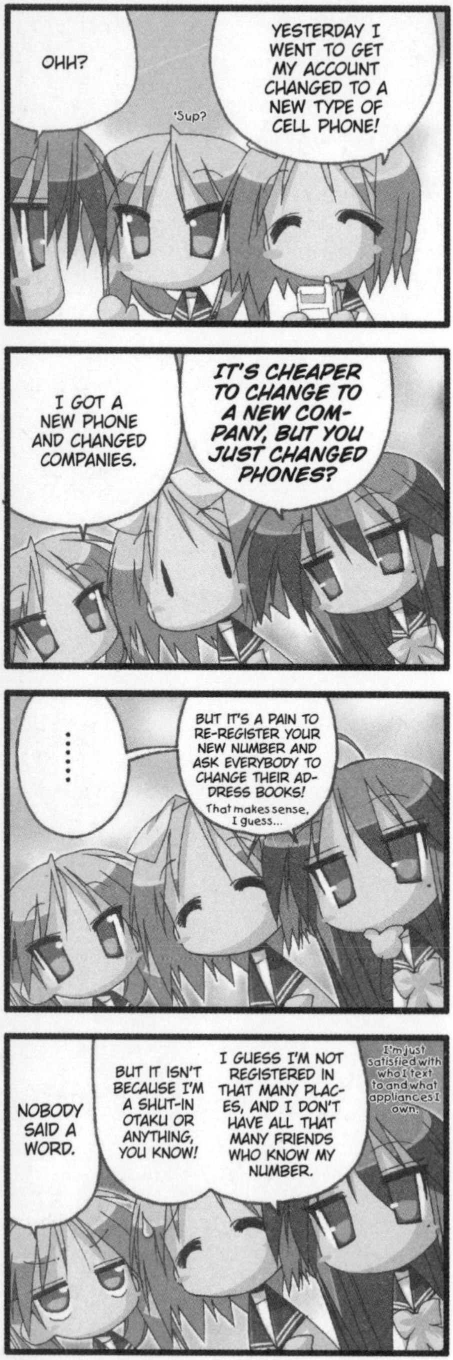
YESTERDAY I WENT TO GET MY ACCOUNT CHANGED TO A NEW TYPE OF CELL PHONE!
'Sup?
OHH?
IT'S CHEAPER TO CHANGE TO A NEW COMPANY, BUT YOU JUST CHANGED PHONES?
I GOT A NEW PHONE AND CHANGED COMPANIES.
BUT IT'S A PAIN TO RE-REGISTER YOUR NEW NUMBER AND ASK EVERYBODY TO CHANGE THEIR ADDRESS BOOKS!
That makes sense, I guess...
......
I'm just satisfied with who I text to and what appliances I own.
I GUESS I'M NOT REGISTERED IN THAT MANY PLACES, AND I DON'T HAVE ALL THAT MANY FRIENDS WHO KNOW MY NUMBER.
BUT IT ISN'T BECAUSE I'M A SHUT-IN OTAKU OR ANYTHING, YOU KNOW!
NOBODY SAID A WORD.

● Mobile Newtype, August 2005 issue

Lucky☆Star

episode 110
an actual idol

●Comptiq, February 2007 issue

calling

KLIK
KLIK
WAIT! WAIT!
YOU KNOW THAT'S THE WRONG THING TO DO, DON'T YOU?
COME ON! WHY DO YOU DO THIS TO ME?!
HEEY! HOW MANY TIMES DO I HAVE TO TELL YOU?!
KAGAMI, UM...
You realize that it isn't listening to you, right?
It's just a game.
S-SURE, I KNOW! I JUST...CAN'T HELP MYSELF. SEE...?

just looking at what you eat

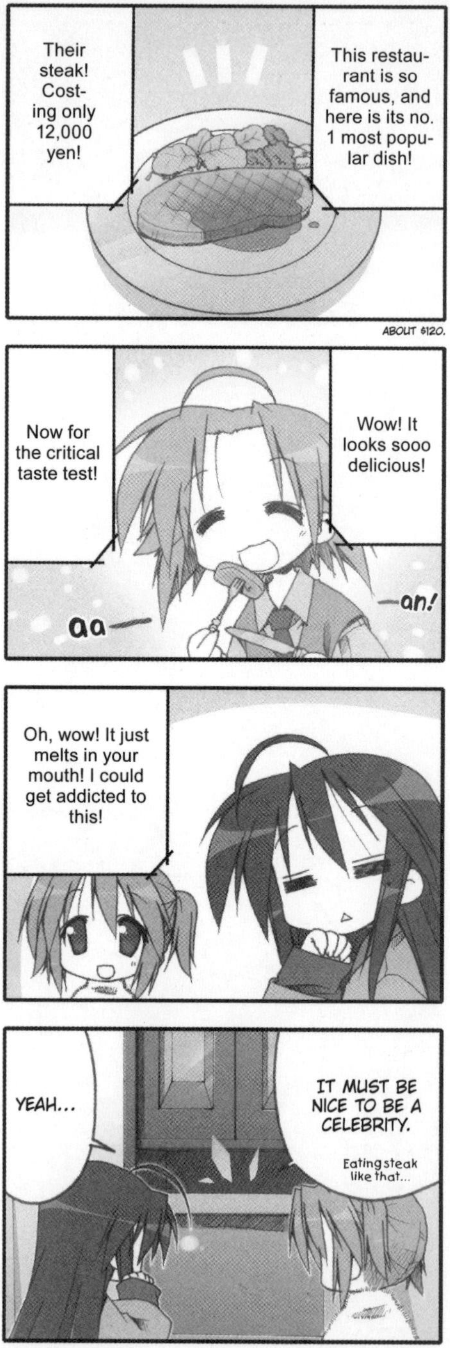
This restaurant is so famous, and here is its no. 1 most popular dish!
Their steak! Costing only 12,000 yen!
ABOUT $120.
Wow! It looks sooo delicious!
Now for the critical taste test!
aa— —an!
Oh, wow! It just melts in your mouth! I could get addicted to this!
IT MUST BE NICE TO BE A CELEBRITY.
Eating steak like that...
YEAH...

just watching you bathe

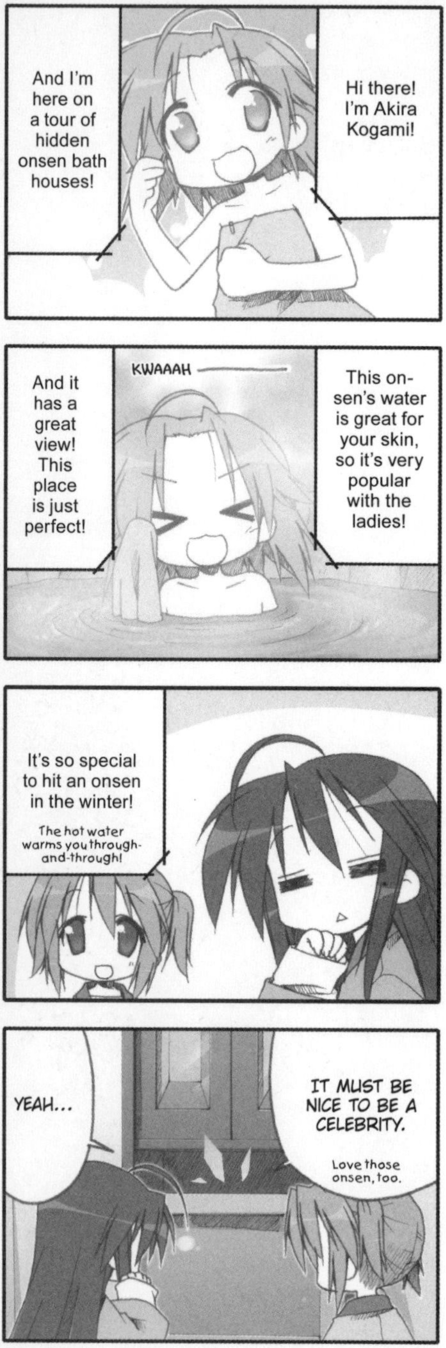
Hi there! I'm Akira Kogami!
And I'm here on a tour of hidden onsen bath houses!
This onsen's water is great for your skin, so it's very popular with the ladies!
KWAAAH
And it has a great view! This place is just perfect!
It's so special to hit an onsen in the winter!
The hot water warms you through-and-through!
IT MUST BE NICE TO BE A CELEBRITY.
Love those onsen, too.
YEAH...

lack of transparency

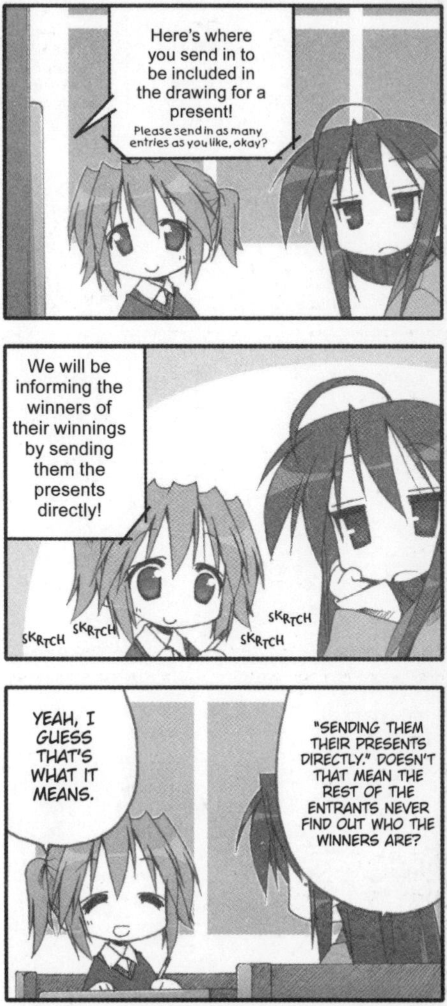
Here's where you send in to be included in the drawing for a present!
Please send in as many entries as you like, okay?
We will be informing the winners of their winnings by sending them the presents directly!
SKRTCH
SKRTCH
SKRTCH
SKRTCH
"SENDING THEM THEIR PRESENTS DIRECTLY." DOESN'T THAT MEAN THE REST OF THE ENTRANTS NEVER FIND OUT WHO THE WINNERS ARE?
YEAH, I GUESS THAT'S WHAT IT MEANS.
FOR SOME REASON, I FIND SUCH CONTESTS VERRRRY SUSPICIOUS!
DOOM

wrong number

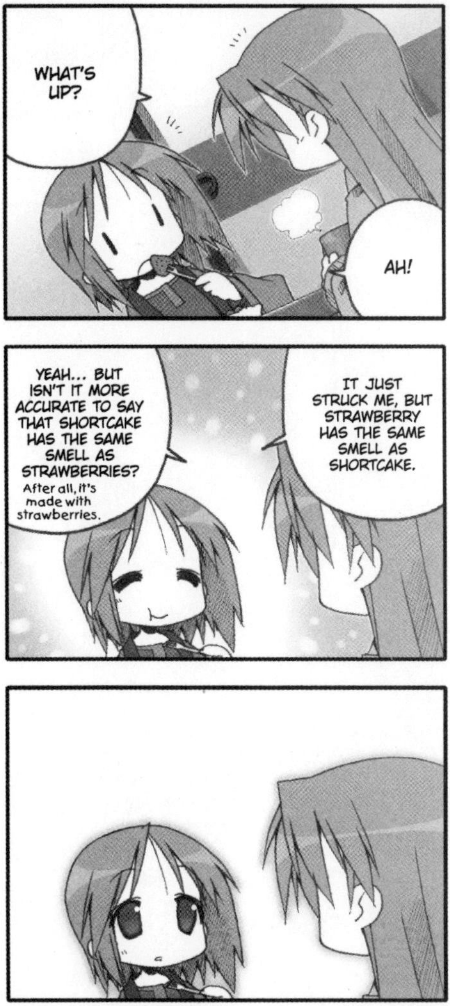
AH!
WHAT'S UP?
IT JUST STRUCK ME, BUT STRAWBERRY HAS THE SAME SMELL AS SHORTCAKE.
YEAH... BUT ISN'T IT MORE ACCURATE TO SAY THAT SHORTCAKE HAS THE SAME SMELL AS STRAWBERRIES?
After all, it's made with strawberries.
UM... IS IT REALLY...?
YEAH, SURE, PEOPLE HAVE THOSE ILLUSIONS EVERY NOW AND AGAIN.

a coded yes

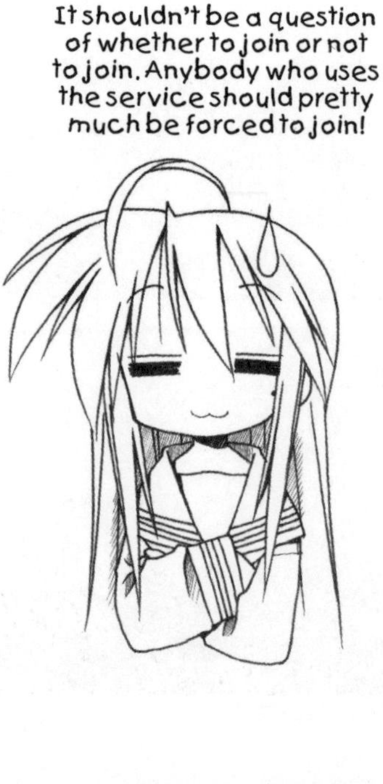
It shouldn't be a question of whether to join or not to join. Anybody who uses the service should pretty much be forced to join!

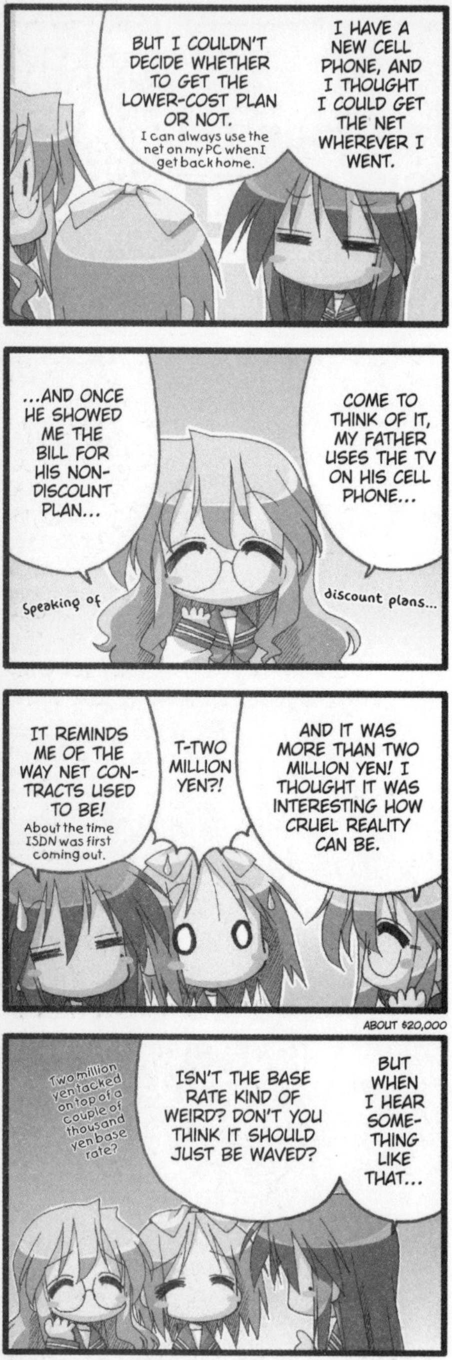
I HAVE A NEW CELL PHONE, AND I THOUGHT I COULD GET THE NET WHEREVER I WENT.
BUT I COULDN'T DECIDE WHETHER TO GET THE LOWER-COST PLAN OR NOT.
I can always use the net on my PC when I get back home.
COME TO THINK OF IT, MY FATHER USES THE TV ON HIS CELL PHONE...
...AND ONCE HE SHOWED ME THE BILL FOR HIS NON-DISCOUNT PLAN...
Speaking of
discount plans...
AND IT WAS MORE THAN TWO MILLION YEN! I THOUGHT IT WAS INTERESTING HOW CRUEL REALITY CAN BE.
T-TWO MILLION YEN?!
IT REMINDS ME OF THE WAY NET CONTRACTS USED TO BE!
About the time ISDN was first coming out.
ABOUT $20,000
BUT WHEN I HEAR SOMETHING LIKE THAT...
ISN'T THE BASE RATE KIND OF WEIRD? DON'T YOU THINK IT SHOULD JUST BE WAVED?
Two million yen tacked on top of a couple of thousand yen base rate?

● **Mobile Newtype, September 2005 issue**

Lucky☆Star

episode 111
suspect

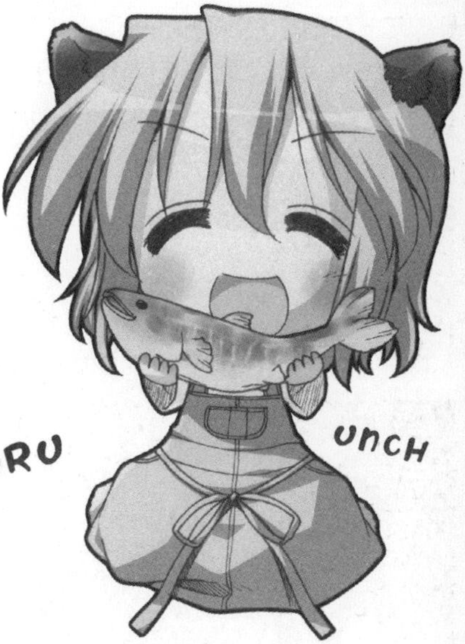
GRU
UNCH

● Comptiq, February 2007 issue

space saving

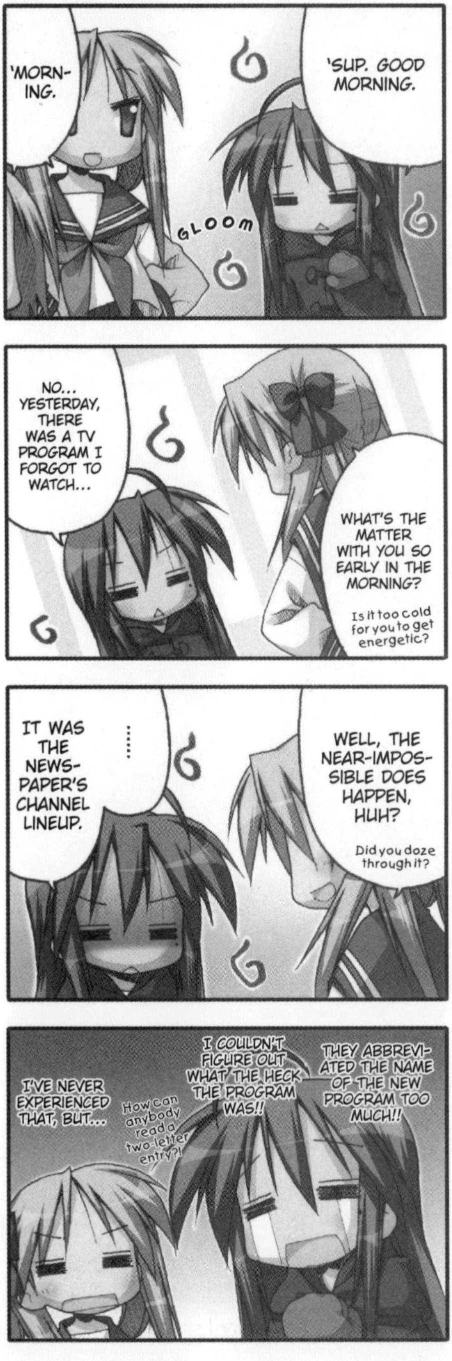
'SUP. GOOD MORNING.
'MORNING.
GLOOM
WHAT'S THE MATTER WITH YOU SO EARLY IN THE MORNING?
Is it too cold for you to get energetic?
NO... YESTERDAY, THERE WAS A TV PROGRAM I FORGOT TO WATCH...
WELL, THE NEAR-IMPOSSIBLE DOES HAPPEN, HUH?
Did you doze through it?
......
IT WAS THE NEWS-PAPER'S CHANNEL LINEUP.
THEY ABBREVIATED THE NAME OF THE NEW PROGRAM TOO MUCH!!
I COULDN'T FIGURE OUT WHAT THE HECK THE PROGRAM WAS!!
How can anybody read a two-letter entry?!
I'VE NEVER EXPERIENCED THAT, BUT...

high strung

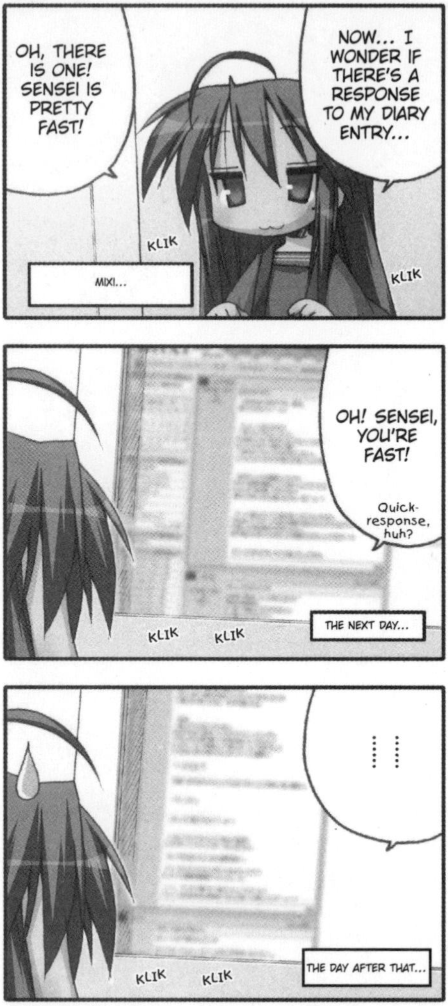
NOW... I WONDER IF THERE'S A RESPONSE TO MY DIARY ENTRY...
OH, THERE IS ONE! SENSEI IS PRETTY FAST!
KLIK
KLIK
MIXI...
OH! SENSEI, YOU'RE FAST!
Quick-response, huh?
THE NEXT DAY...
KLIK
KLIK
......
......
THE DAY AFTER THAT...
KLIK
KLIK
SENSEI...
Do you have too much time on your hands?
NO... IT'S JUST LIKE I'M ADDICTED... OR BEFORE I NOTICE IT, I'M CHECKING MY UPDATES...
YEAH... WELL, I UNDER-STAND, BUT...

above the clouds

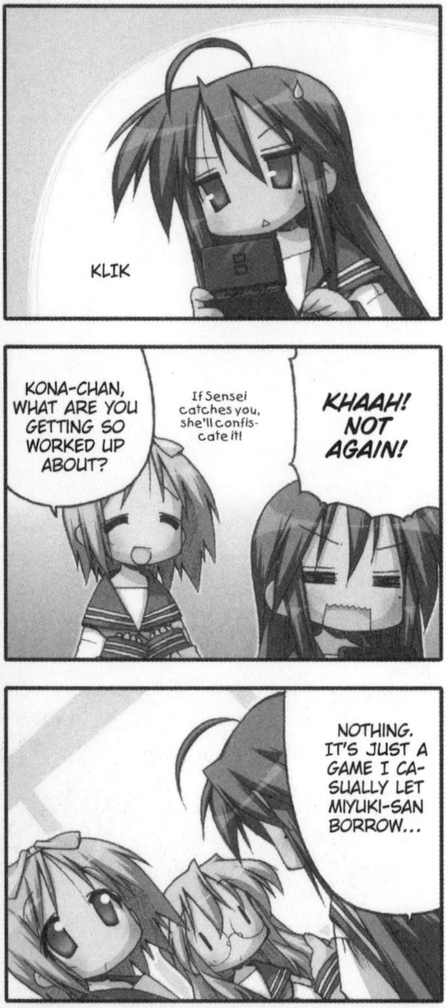
KLIK
KHAAH! NOT AGAIN!
If Sensei catches you, she'll confis-cate it!
KONA-CHAN, WHAT ARE YOU GETTING SO WORKED UP ABOUT?
NOTHING. IT'S JUST A GAME I CA-SUALLY LET MIYUKI-SAN BORROW...
NOW, EVER SINCE I GOT IT BACK, I CAN'T EVEN COME CLOSE TO THE LEVEL REACHED!
DON'T YOU THINK THAT'S UNFORGIV-ABLE?!
Now I can't put my name in the top-ten scores list of my own game!
I-I'M SO SORRY!!

white world

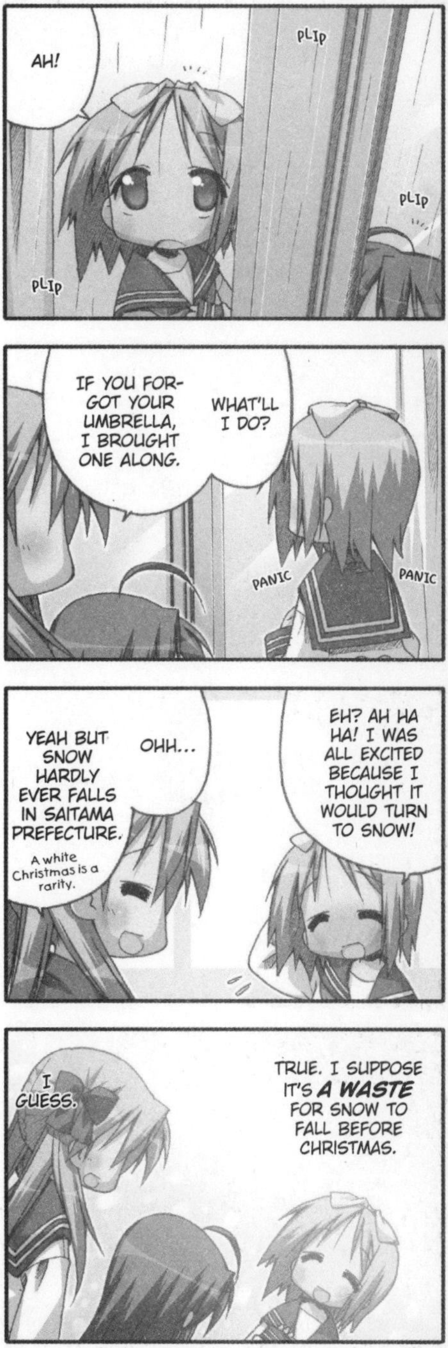
PLIP
AH!
PLIP
PLIP
WHAT'LL I DO?
IF YOU FOR-GOT YOUR UMBRELLA, I BROUGHT ONE ALONG.
PANIC
PANIC
EH? AH HA HA! I WAS ALL EXCITED BECAUSE I THOUGHT IT WOULD TURN TO SNOW!
OHH...
YEAH BUT SNOW HARDLY EVER FALLS IN SAITAMA PREFECTURE.
A white Christmas is a rarity.
TRUE. I SUPPOSE IT'S **A WASTE** FOR SNOW TO FALL BEFORE CHRISTMAS.
I GUESS.

happy life

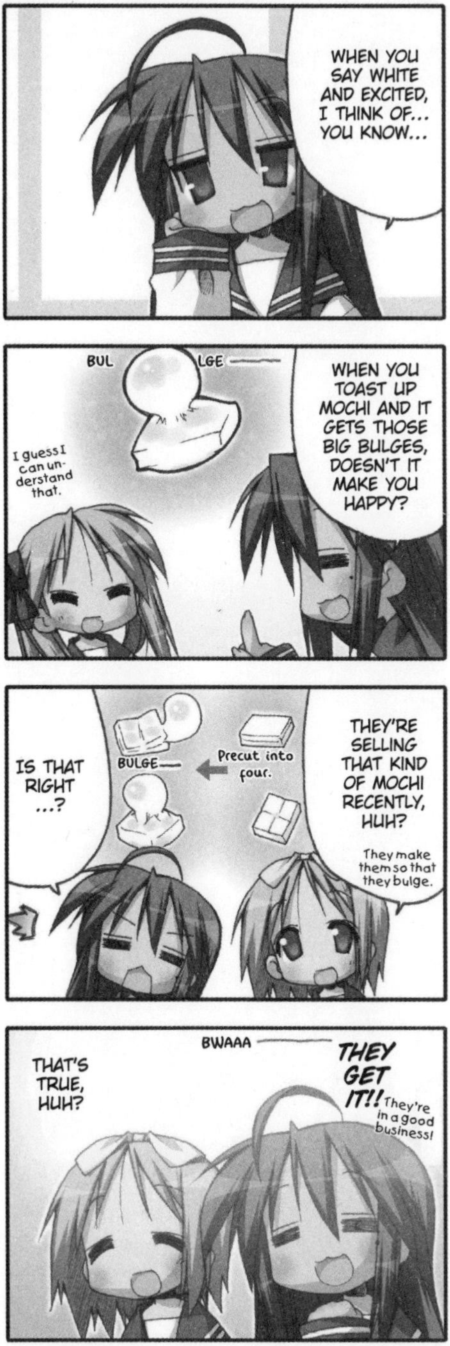
WHEN YOU SAY WHITE AND EXCITED, I THINK OF... YOU KNOW...
WHEN YOU TOAST UP MOCHI AND IT GETS THOSE BIG BULGES, DOESN'T IT MAKE YOU HAPPY?
BUL LGE ——
I guess I can un-derstand that.
THEY'RE SELLING THAT KIND OF MOCHI RECENTLY, HUH?
Precut into four.
BULGE——
IS THAT RIGHT ...?
They make them so that they bulge.
THEY GET IT!!
They're in a good business!
BWAAA ——
THAT'S TRUE, HUH?

It's hard to live in this new world!
Still, it isn't the tool's fault. It's the human using the tool.
SHUUUU
POFF

things you can do and things you don't do

SINCE I WENT TO THE TROUBLE OF GETTING A NEW CELL PHONE, I'D BETTER LEARN HOW TO USE THE CAMERA!
I CAN TAKE ALL KINDS OF PICTURES WITH THIS THING!
OHHH
SORRY. PHOTOS AREN'T ALLOWED INSIDE THE STORE.
AH! IS THAT RIGHT? SORRY.
PLEASE NO TALKING ON THE CELL PHONE OR PHOTOGRAPHY IN THE RESTAURANT.
SHUUUU
PLUNK

● Mobile Newtype, October 2005 issue

Lucky☆Star

episode 112
first i want a hug

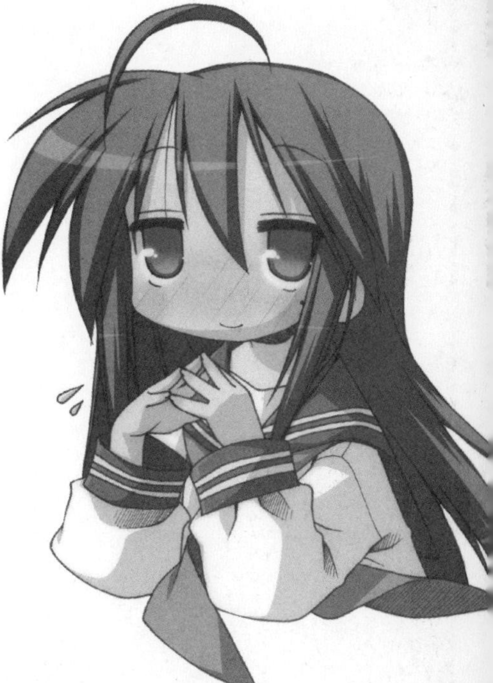

● Comptiq, March 2007 issue

usual suspects

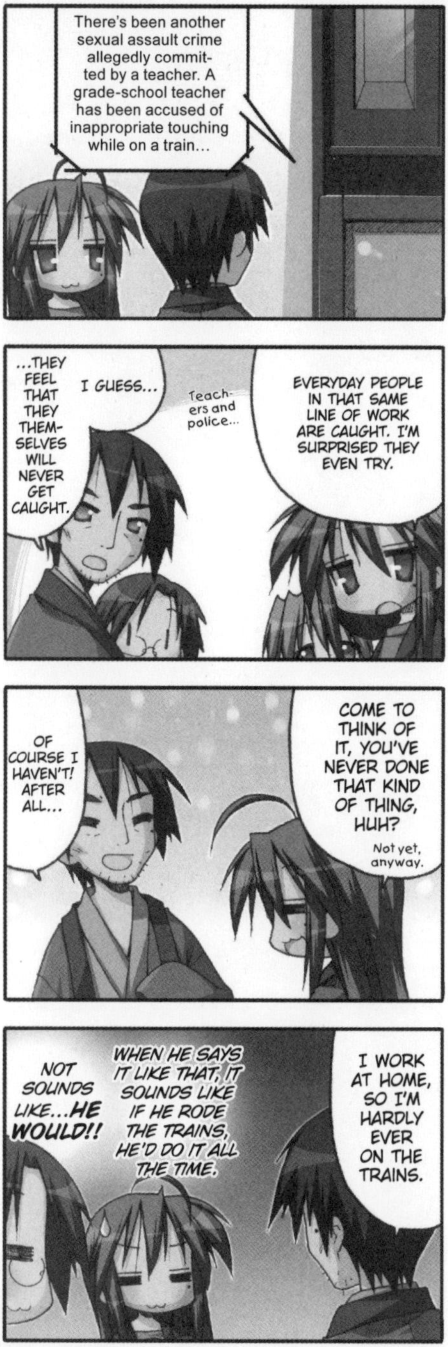
There's been another sexual assault crime allegedly commit-ted by a teacher. A grade-school teacher has been accused of inappropriate touching while on a train...
EVERYDAY PEOPLE IN THAT SAME LINE OF WORK ARE CAUGHT. I'M SURPRISED THEY EVEN TRY.
Teach-ers and police...
I GUESS...
...THEY FEEL THAT THEY THEM-SELVES WILL NEVER GET CAUGHT.
COME TO THINK OF IT, YOU'VE NEVER DONE THAT KIND OF THING, HUH?
Not yet, anyway.
OF COURSE I HAVEN'T! AFTER ALL...
I WORK AT HOME, SO I'M HARDLY EVER ON THE TRAINS.
WHEN HE SAYS IT LIKE THAT, IT SOUNDS LIKE IF HE RODE THE TRAINS, HE'D DO IT ALL THE TIME.
NOT SOUNDS LIKE...**HE WOULD!!**

a fair cop

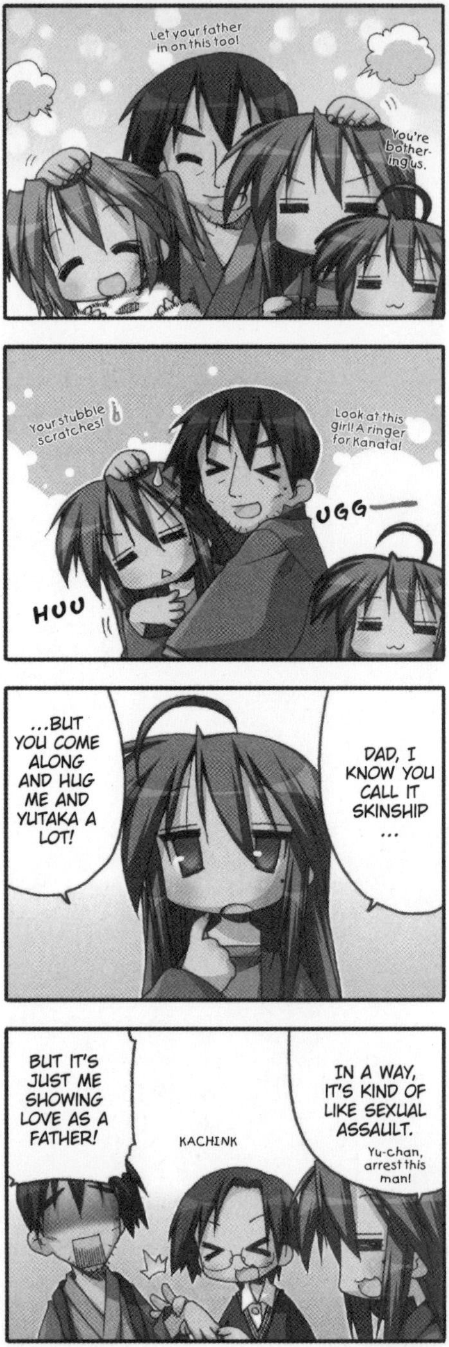
Let your father in on this too!
You're bothering us.
Look at this girl! A ringer for Kanata!
Your stubble scratches!
UGG—
HUU
DAD, I KNOW YOU CALL IT SKINSHIP ...
...BUT YOU COME ALONG AND HUG ME AND YUTAKA A LOT!
IN A WAY, IT'S KIND OF LIKE SEXUAL ASSAULT.
Yu-chan, arrest this man!
KACHINK
BUT IT'S JUST ME SHOWING LOVE AS A FATHER!

precautionary measures

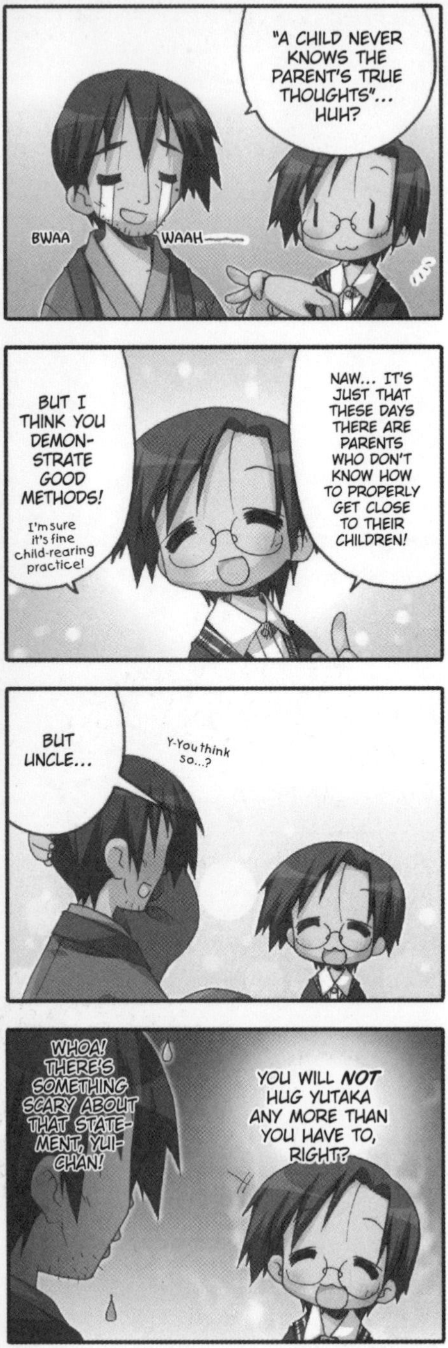
"A CHILD NEVER KNOWS THE PARENT'S TRUE THOUGHTS"... HUH?
WAAH—
BWAA
NAW... IT'S JUST THAT THESE DAYS THERE ARE PARENTS WHO DON'T KNOW HOW TO PROPERLY GET CLOSE TO THEIR CHILDREN!
BUT I THINK YOU DEMONSTRATE GOOD METHODS!
I'm sure it's fine child-rearing practice!
Y-You think so...?
BUT UNCLE...
YOU WILL *NOT* HUG YUTAKA ANY MORE THAN YOU HAVE TO, RIGHT?
WHOA! THERE'S SOMETHING SCARY ABOUT THAT STATEMENT, YUI-CHAN!

sleep spell

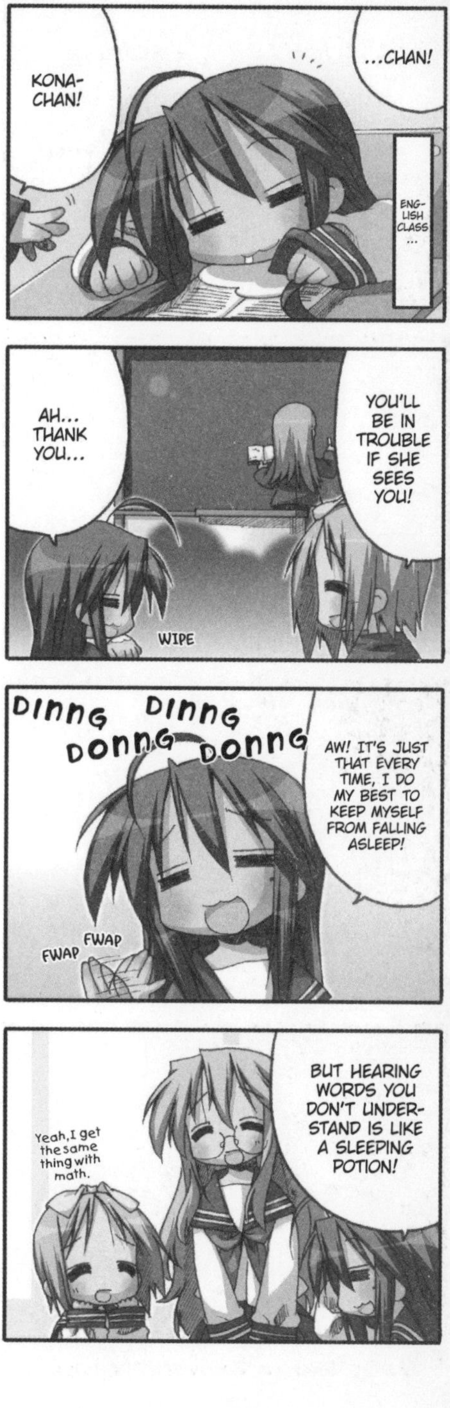

...CHAN!
ENG-LISH CLASS ...
KONA-CHAN!
YOU'LL BE IN TROUBLE IF SHE SEES YOU!
AH... THANK YOU...
WIPE
AW! IT'S JUST THAT EVERY TIME, I DO MY BEST TO KEEP MYSELF FROM FALLING ASLEEP!
DINNG DINNG DONNG DONNG
FWAP FWAP
BUT HEARING WORDS YOU DON'T UNDER-STAND IS LIKE A SLEEPING POTION!
Yeah, I get the same thing with math.

broken record

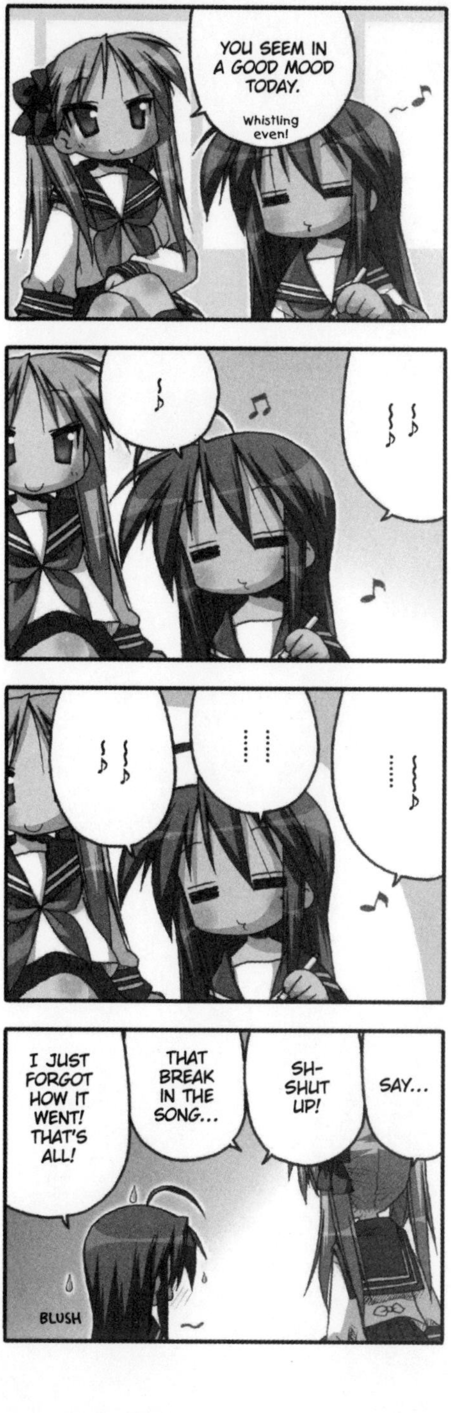

YOU SEEM IN A GOOD MOOD TODAY.
Whistling even!
SAY...
SH-SHUT UP!
THAT BREAK IN THE SONG...
I JUST FORGOT HOW IT WENT! THAT'S ALL!
BLUSH

The way that policeman looked at me was... creepily warm!
You're just imagining it!
Shut up!!
You have no right to say anything!

please, god

O-OH, NO! I DON'T HAVE MY CELL PHONE!
MAYBE I SHOULD CALL MYSELF AND FIND IT BY THE RINGS?
URK! I HOPE SOMEBODY FINDS IT AND SENDS IT BACK TO ME!
Some nice person...
HEY. LISTEN...
SEARCH
SEARCH
I'M SORRY, KAGAMI. I JUST THOUGHT I'D SURPRISE YOU A LITTLE.
BACK WHEN WE WERE IN THE BATHROOM, I WENT INTO YOUR BAG, AND I CHANGED YOUR RING TONE TO AN ANIME RING TONE I LIKED.
Changed it on your phone.
!?
I'M GLAD IT NEVER RANG!
You didn't have to hit me with a closed fist!
OH, PLEASE MAKE IT NOT RING! PLEASE MAKE IT NOT RING!
They'll think I'm an otaku!

● Mobile Newtype, January 2006 issue

Lucky☆Star

episode 113
welcome back

● Comptiq, March 2007 issue

the real thing

YO! GOOD MORN-ING!
OH! GOOD MORNING, SENSEI!
BY THE WAY, IZUMI! YOU SHOULD ANSWER YOUR E-MAIL QUICKER!
It's not like it takes much effort!
HUH? I NEVER GOT ANY E-MAIL FROM YOU YESTERDAY, SENSEI.
NO! I SENT YOU ONE. I THINK THE TITLE SAID, "CHANGE OF ADDRESS" OR SOME-THING.
AH...
I MAY HAVE *TRASHED* IT.
DON'T YOU TEND TO THINK ANYTHING FROM AN UNUSUAL ADDRESS IS SPAM?
No matter what title it has.
I UNDER-STAND WHERE YOU'RE COMING FROM, BUT CHECK THEM FIRST!

waiting

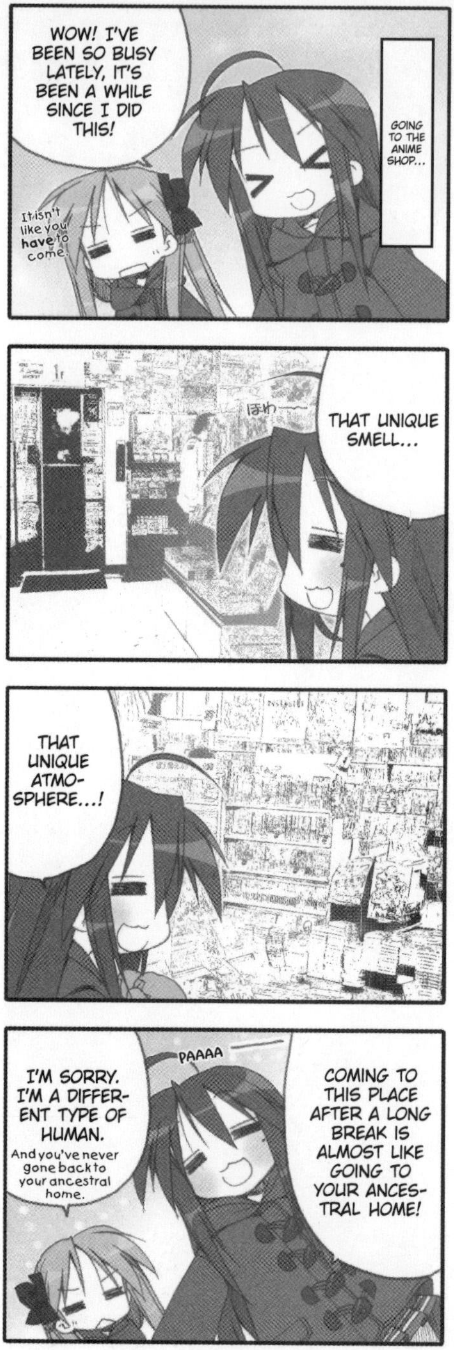
GOING TO THE ANIME SHOP...
WOW! I'VE BEEN SO BUSY LATELY, IT'S BEEN A WHILE SINCE I DID THIS!
It isn't like you **have** to come.
THAT UNIQUE SMELL...
ほわ〜〜
THAT UNIQUE ATMO-SPHERE...!
COMING TO THIS PLACE AFTER A LONG BREAK IS ALMOST LIKE GOING TO YOUR ANCES-TRAL HOME!
PAAAA
I'M SORRY. I'M A DIFFER-ENT TYPE OF HUMAN.
And you've never gone back to your ancestral home.

110% mega-shock

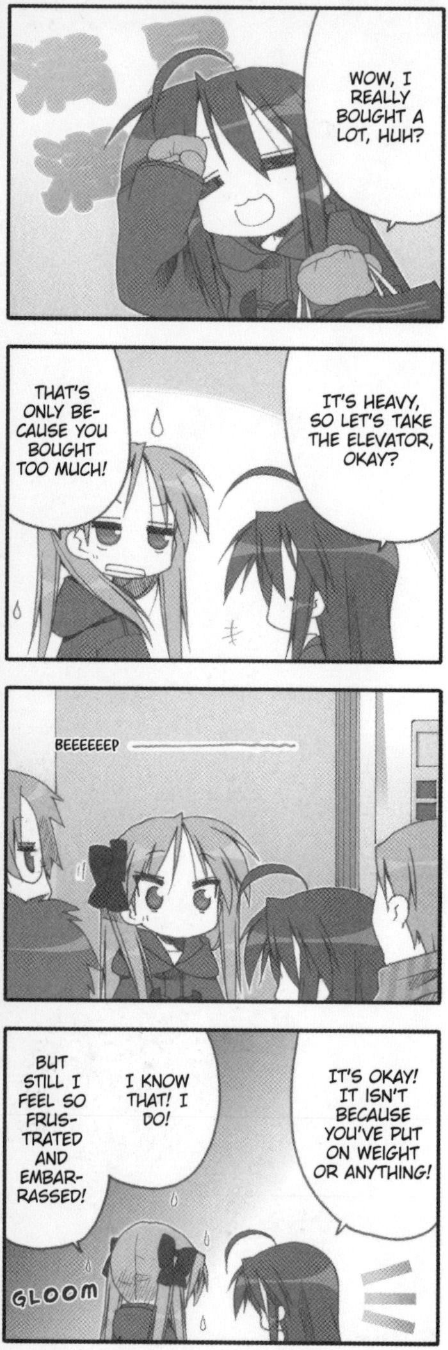
WOW, I REALLY BOUGHT A LOT, HUH?
IT'S HEAVY, SO LET'S TAKE THE ELEVATOR, OKAY?
THAT'S ONLY BE-CAUSE YOU BOUGHT TOO MUCH!
BEEEEEEP
IT'S OKAY! IT ISN'T BECAUSE YOU'VE PUT ON WEIGHT OR ANYTHING!
I KNOW THAT! I DO!
BUT STILL I FEEL SO FRUS-TRATED AND EMBAR-RASSED!
GLOOM

complex city

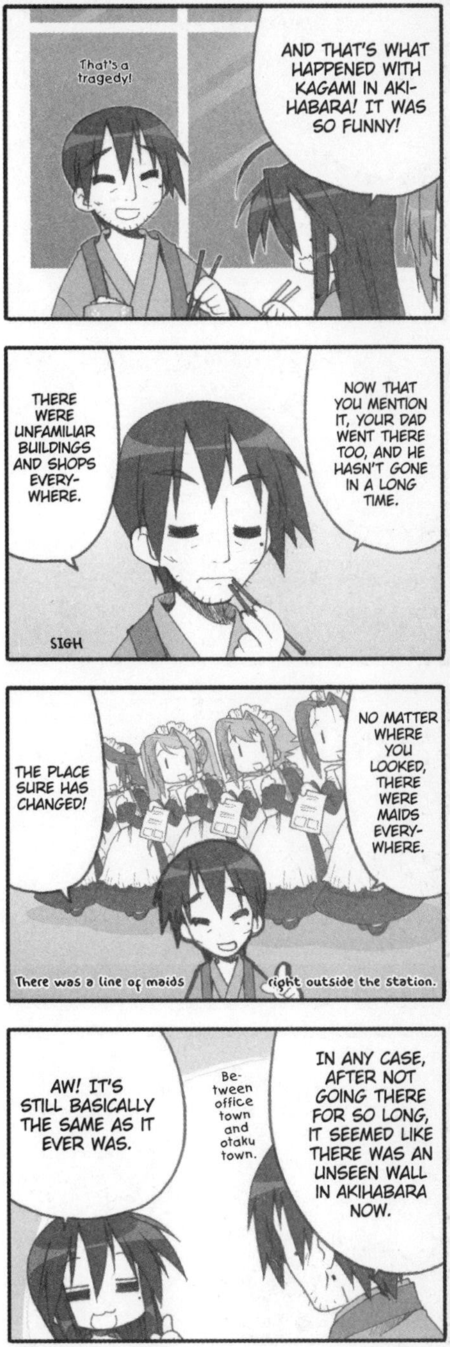
AND THAT'S WHAT HAPPENED WITH KAGAMI IN AKI-HABARA! IT WAS SO FUNNY!
That's a tragedy!
NOW THAT YOU MENTION IT, YOUR DAD WENT THERE TOO, AND HE HASN'T GONE IN A LONG TIME.
THERE WERE UNFAMILIAR BUILDINGS AND SHOPS EVERY-WHERE.
SIGH
NO MATTER WHERE YOU LOOKED, THERE WERE MAIDS EVERY-WHERE.
THE PLACE SURE HAS CHANGED!
There was a line of maids right outside the station.
IN ANY CASE, AFTER NOT GOING THERE FOR SO LONG, IT SEEMED LIKE THERE WAS AN UNSEEN WALL IN AKIHABARA NOW.
Be-tween office town and otaku town.
AW! IT'S STILL BASICALLY THE SAME AS IT EVER WAS.

follow up attack

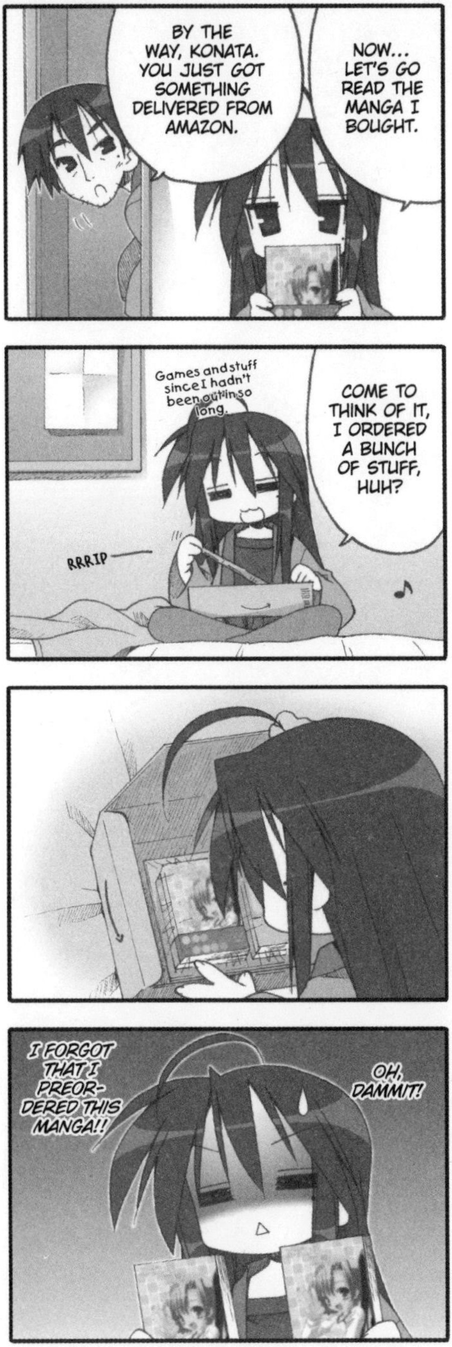
NOW... LET'S GO READ THE MANGA I BOUGHT.
BY THE WAY, KONATA. YOU JUST GOT SOMETHING DELIVERED FROM AMAZON.
COME TO THINK OF IT, I ORDERED A BUNCH OF STUFF, HUH?
Games and stuff since I hadn't been out in so long.
RRRIP
OH, DAMMIT!
I FORGOT THAT I PREOR-DERED THIS MANGA!!

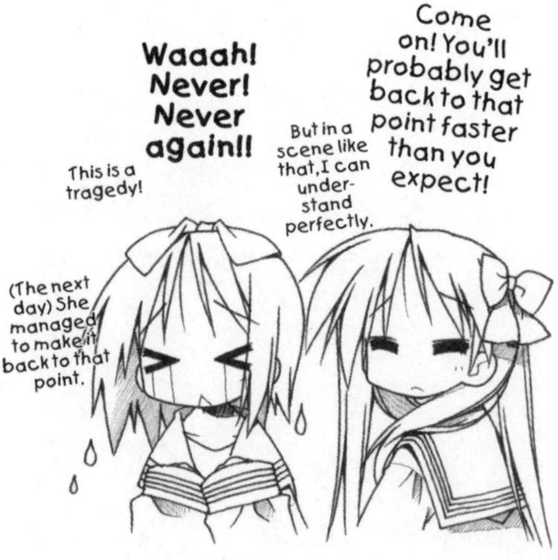
Come on! You'll probably get back to that point faster than you expect!
But in a scene like that, I can understand perfectly.
Waaah! Never! Never again!!
This is a tragedy!
(The next day) She managed to make it back to that point.

no good

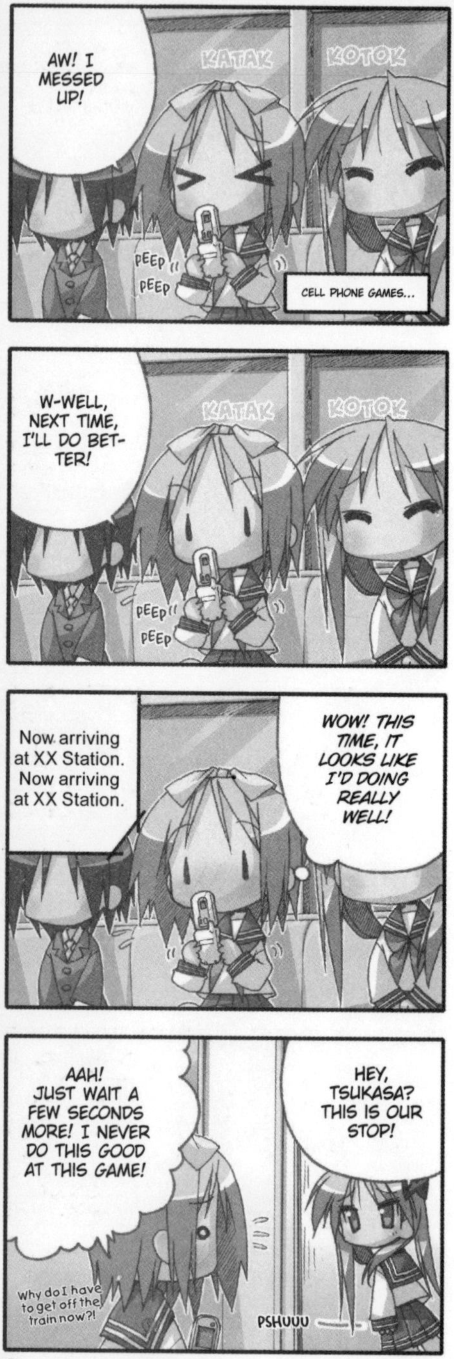
KOTOK
KATAK
AW! I MESSED UP!
PEEP PEEP
CELL PHONE GAMES...
KOTOK
KATAK
W-WELL, NEXT TIME, I'LL DO BET-TER!
PEEP PEEP
WOW! THIS TIME, IT LOOKS LIKE I'D DOING REALLY WELL!
Now arriving at XX Station. Now arriving at XX Station.
HEY, TSUKASA? THIS IS OUR STOP!
AAH! JUST WAIT A FEW SECONDS MORE! I NEVER DO THIS GOOD AT THIS GAME!
Why do I have to get off the train now?!
PSHUUU

● Mobile Newtype, March 2006 issue

Lucky☆Star

episode 114
loved ones

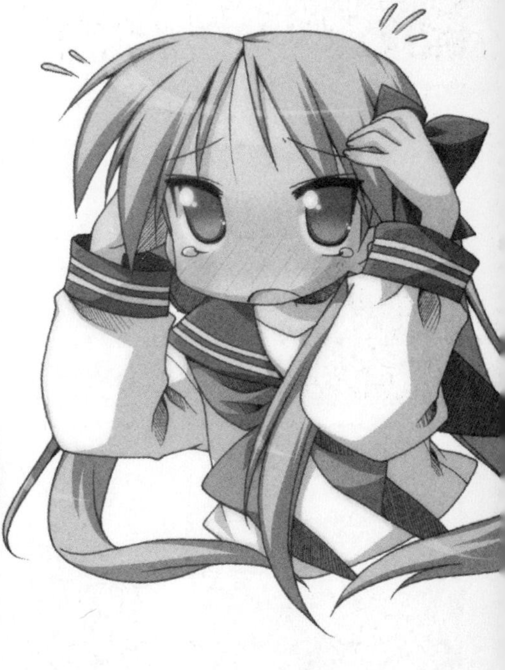

●Comptiq, March 2007 issue

a trick of fate 1

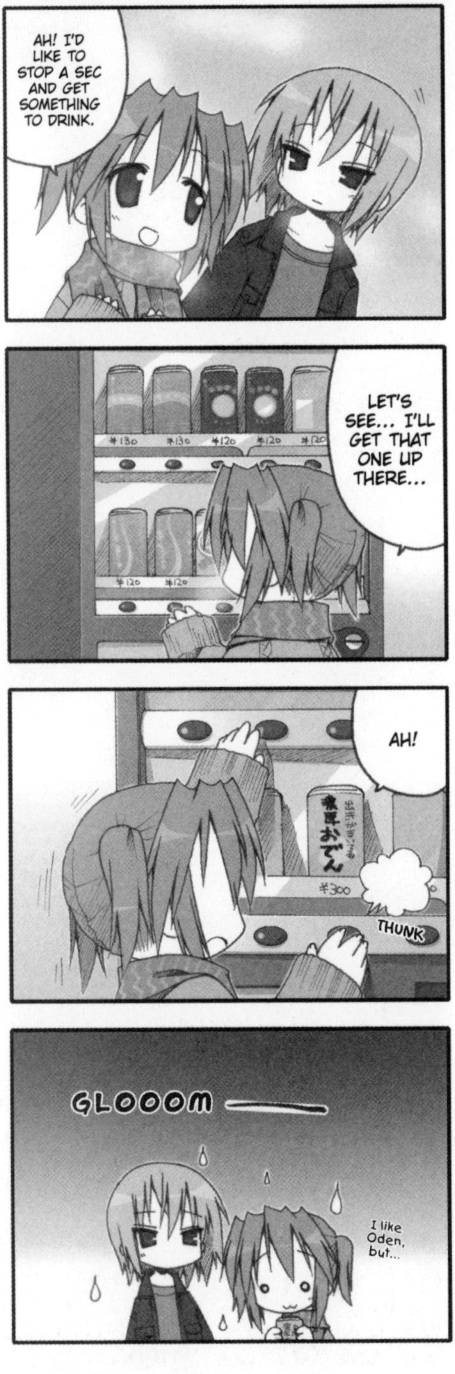
AH! I'D LIKE TO STOP A SEC AND GET SOMETHING TO DRINK.
LET'S SEE... I'LL GET THAT ONE UP THERE...
AH!
THUNK
GLOOOM ——
I like Oden, but...

a trick of fate 2

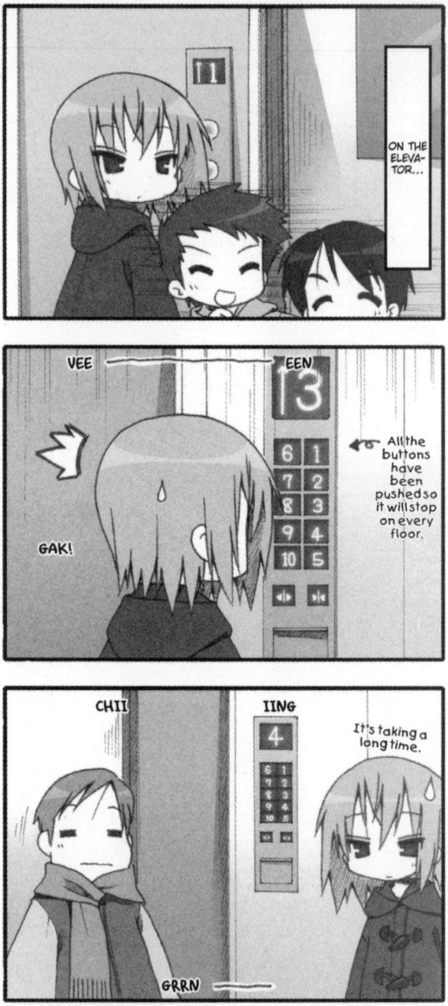
ON THE ELEVATOR...
VEE EEN
All the buttons have been pushed so it will stop on every floor.
GAK!
CHII IING
It's taking a long time.
GRRN
PANIC PANIC
......
IT WASN'T ME... IT WASN'T ME...

a trick of fate 3

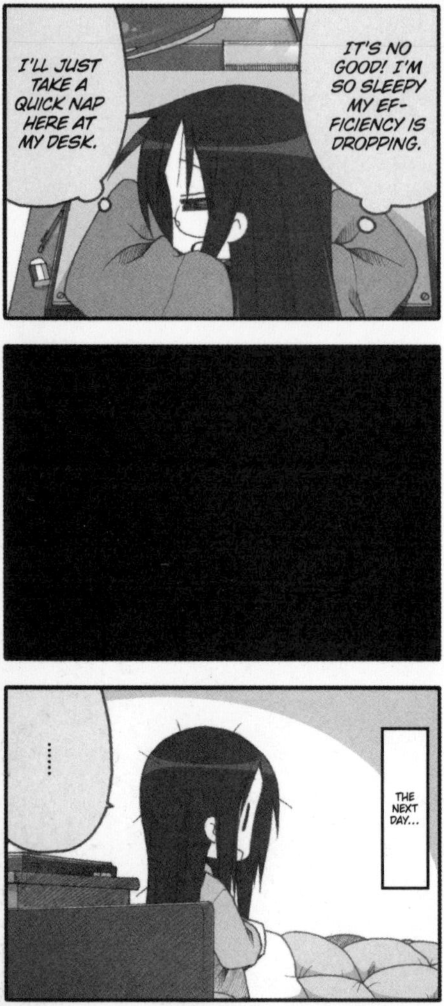
IT'S NO GOOD! I'M SO SLEEPY MY EFFICIENCY IS DROPPING.
I'LL JUST TAKE A QUICK NAP HERE AT MY DESK.
THE NEXT DAY...
......
HUHHH? THAT'S SO WEIRD... I DOZED OFF AT MY DESK, RIGHT? SO WHEN...?
What's going on here, Hiyorin? With the deadline almost here, your club project isn't getting any closer to being finished!
Are you listening to me?
Hey!
I'm sorry! I'm sorry!
SLAPP
KSH KSH

memory of 100 days earlier

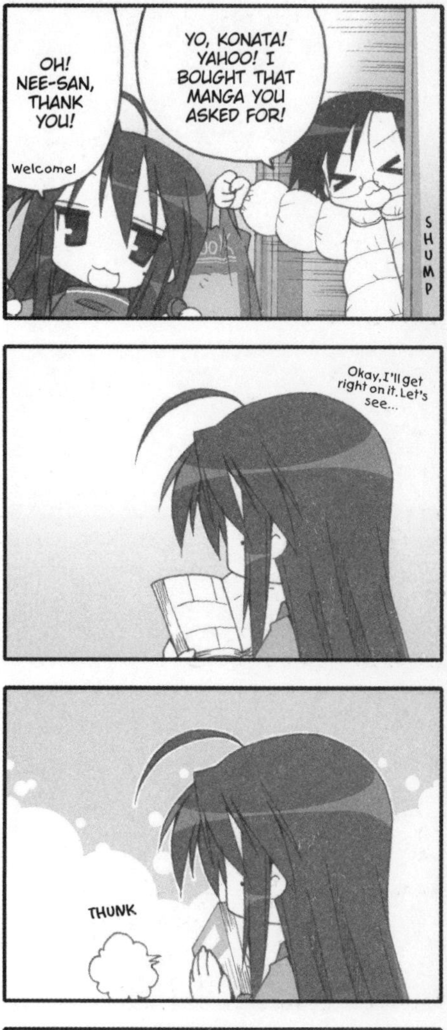
YO, KONATA! YAHOO! I BOUGHT THAT MANGA YOU ASKED FOR!
OH! NEE-SAN, THANK YOU!
Welcome!
SHUMP
Okay, I'll get right on it. Let's see...
THUNK
FIRST I'LL HAVE TO FIND...
...THE PREVIOUS VOLUME!!
I forgot what the plot was about!

treasure hunt

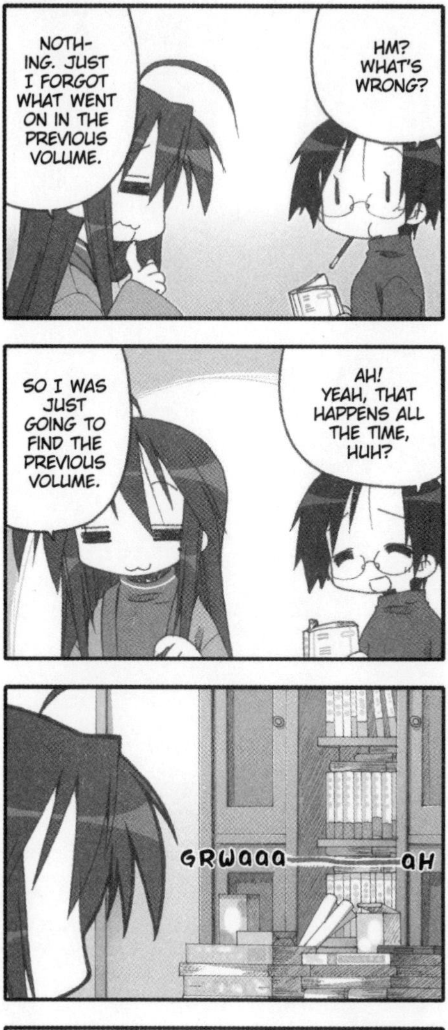
HM? WHAT'S WRONG?
NOTH-ING. JUST I FORGOT WHAT WENT ON IN THE PREVIOUS VOLUME.
AH! YEAH, THAT HAPPENS ALL THE TIME, HUH?
SO I WAS JUST GOING TO FIND THE PREVIOUS VOLUME.
GRWaaa——aH
...AND I COULDN'T STOP UNTIL I FOUND IT. SO I DIDN'T GET ENOUGH SLEEP LAST NIGHT.
DIDN'T I TELL YOU A LOAD OF TIMES TO CLEAN UP THAT MESS OF A ROOM YOU HAVE... (NAG NAG)
BLEAGH

the unheard voice

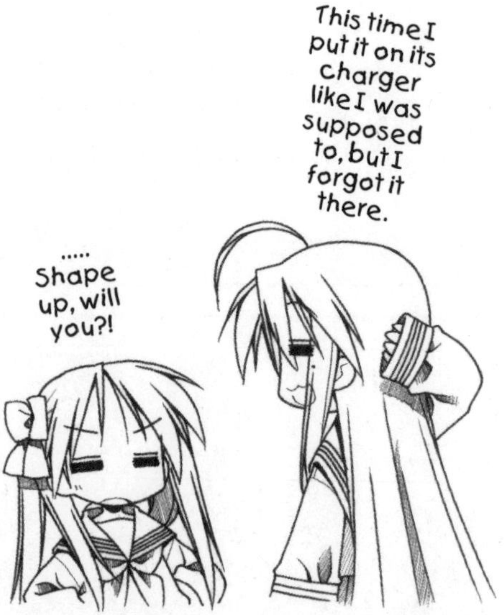
This time I put it on its charger like I was supposed to, but I forgot it there.
..... Shape up, will you?!

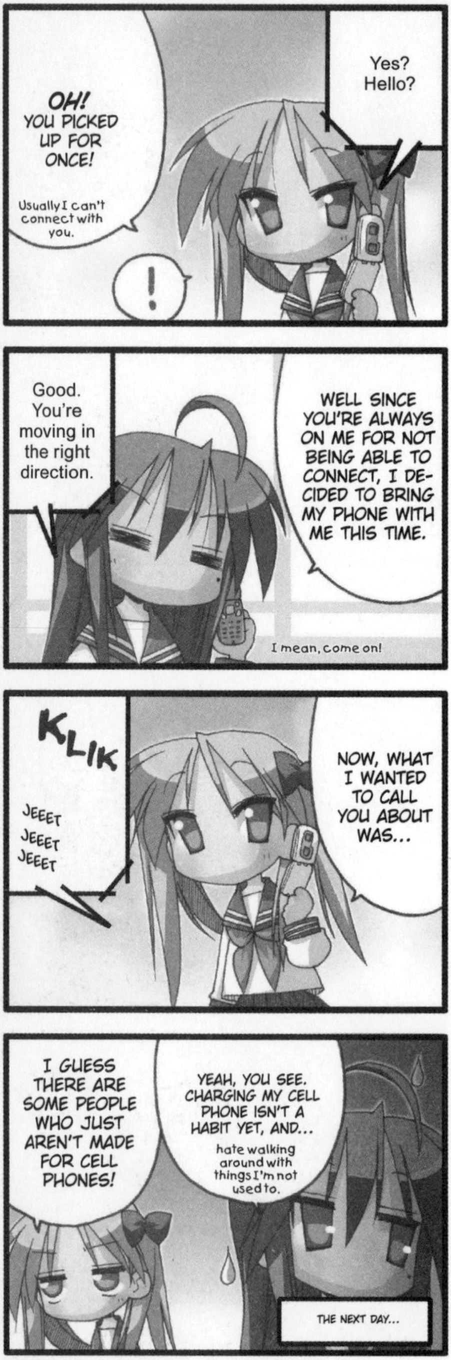
Yes? Hello?
OH! YOU PICKED UP FOR ONCE!
Usually I can't connect with you.
!
WELL SINCE YOU'RE ALWAYS ON ME FOR NOT BEING ABLE TO CONNECT, I DE-CIDED TO BRING MY PHONE WITH ME THIS TIME.
Good. You're moving in the right direction.
I mean, come on!
NOW, WHAT I WANTED TO CALL YOU ABOUT WAS...
KLIK
JEEET JEEET JEEET
YEAH, YOU SEE. CHARGING MY CELL PHONE ISN'T A HABIT YET, AND...
hate walking around with things I'm not used to.
I GUESS THERE ARE SOME PEOPLE WHO JUST AREN'T MADE FOR CELL PHONES!
THE NEXT DAY...

● **Mobile Newtype, June 2006 issue**

Lucky☆Star

episode 115
comparative brightness

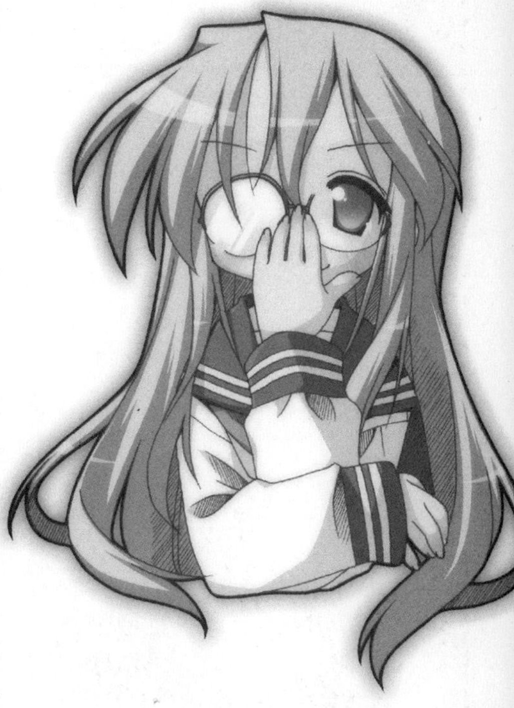

●Comptiq, April 2007 issue

big plan

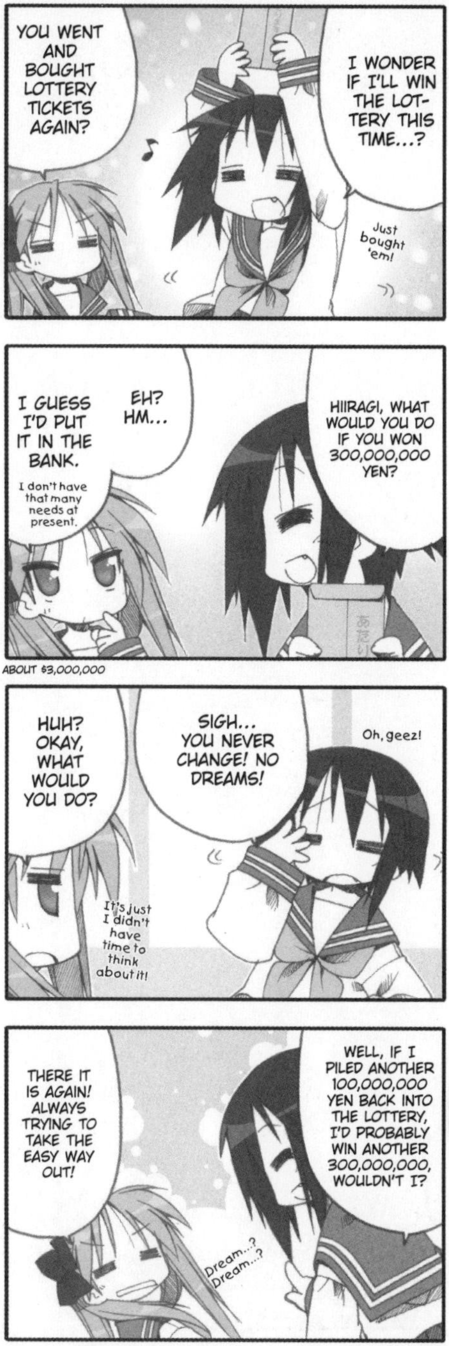
I WONDER IF I'LL WIN THE LOTTERY THIS TIME...?
Just bought 'em!
YOU WENT AND BOUGHT LOTTERY TICKETS AGAIN?
HIIRAGI, WHAT WOULD YOU DO IF YOU WON 300,000,000 YEN?
EH? HM...
I GUESS I'D PUT IT IN THE BANK.
I don't have that many needs at present.
ABOUT $3,000,000
Oh, geez!
SIGH... YOU NEVER CHANGE! NO DREAMS!
HUH? OKAY, WHAT WOULD YOU DO?
It's just I didn't have time to think about it!
WELL, IF I PILED ANOTHER 100,000,000 YEN BACK INTO THE LOTTERY, I'D PROBABLY WIN ANOTHER 300,000,000, WOULDN'T I?
Dream...? Dream...?
THERE IT IS AGAIN! ALWAYS TRYING TO TAKE THE EASY WAY OUT!

concern

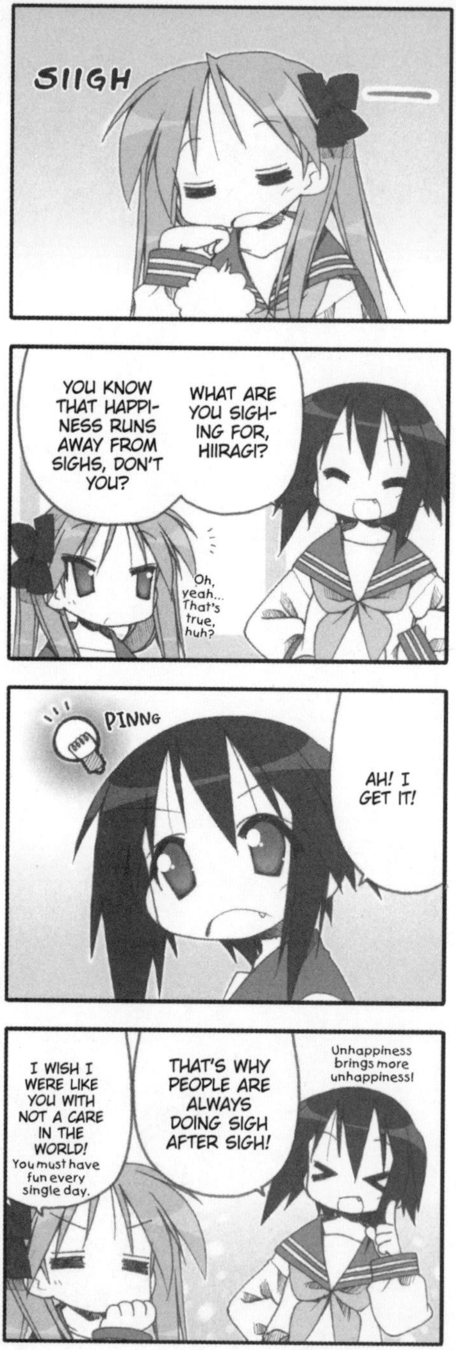
SIIGH
WHAT ARE YOU SIGHING FOR, HIIRAGI?
YOU KNOW THAT HAPPINESS RUNS AWAY FROM SIGHS, DON'T YOU?
Oh, yeah... That's true, huh?
AH! I GET IT!
PINNG
Unhappiness brings more unhappiness!
THAT'S WHY PEOPLE ARE ALWAYS DOING SIGH AFTER SIGH!
I WISH I WERE LIKE YOU WITH NOT A CARE IN THE WORLD!
You must have fun every single day.

fishing

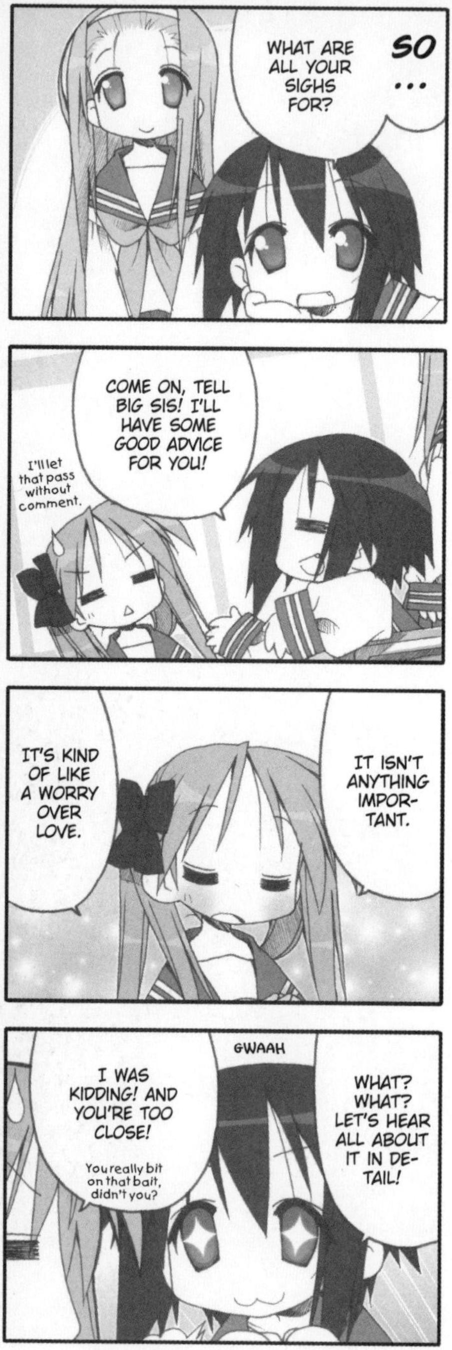
SO...
WHAT ARE ALL YOUR SIGHS FOR?
COME ON, TELL BIG SIS! I'LL HAVE SOME GOOD ADVICE FOR YOU!
I'll let that pass without comment.
IT ISN'T ANYTHING IMPORTANT.
IT'S KIND OF LIKE A WORRY OVER LOVE.
WHAT? WHAT? LET'S HEAR ALL ABOUT IT IN DETAIL!
GWAAH
I WAS KIDDING! AND YOU'RE TOO CLOSE!
You really bit on that bait, didn't you?

surprise attack

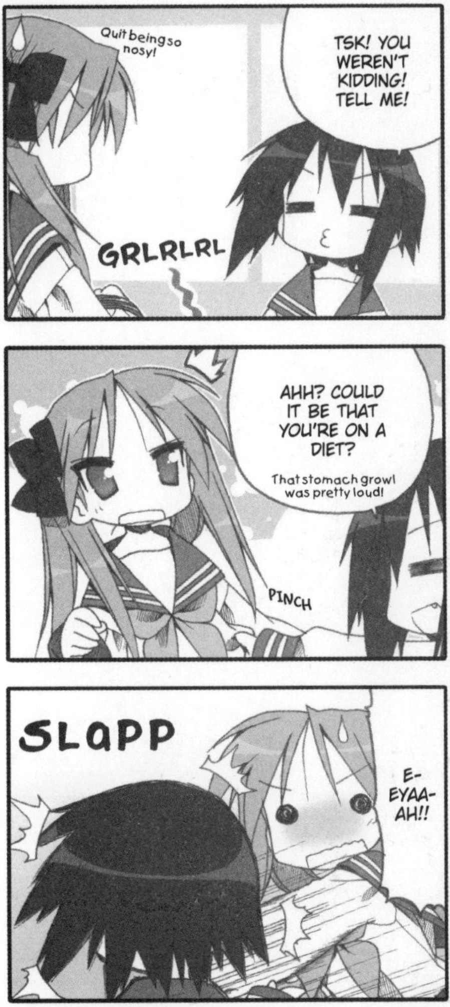
TSK! YOU WEREN'T KIDDING! TELL ME!
Quit being so nosy!
GRLRLRL
AHH? COULD IT BE THAT YOU'RE ON A DIET?
That stomach growl was pretty loud!
PINCH
E-EYAAA-AH!!
SLAPP
S-SORRY. IT WAS RE-FLEX...
It really shocked me!
HAHHH HAHH
FLAP FLAP

predictable action

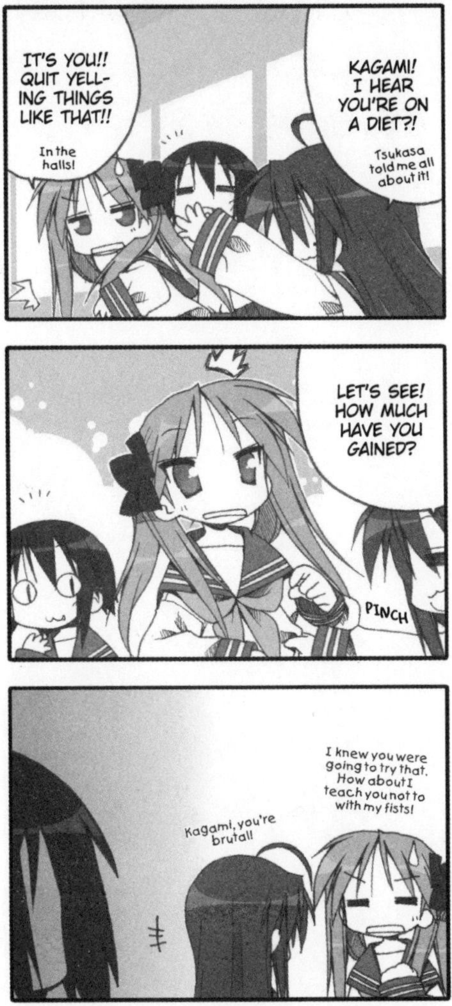
KAGAMI! I HEAR YOU'RE ON A DIET?!
Tsukasa told me all about it!
IT'S YOU!! QUIT YELL-ING THINGS LIKE THAT!!
In the halls!
LET'S SEE! HOW MUCH HAVE YOU GAINED?
PINCH
I knew you were going to try that. How about I teach you not to with my fists!
Kagami, you're brutal!
AYANO... I KNOW THOSE TWO HAVE BEEN FRIENDS LONGER THAN I HAVE, BUT...
Isn't this discrimi-nation?
There, there...
GLOO
——oom

Lucky☆Star

episode 116
everybody's classroom

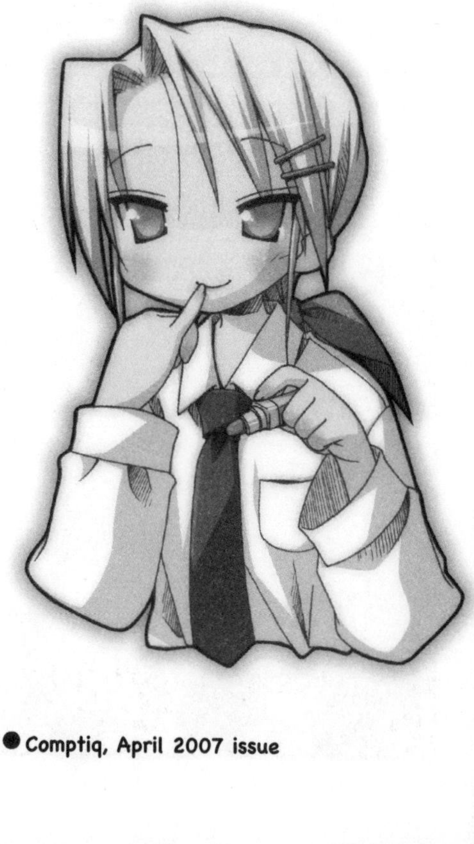

● Comptiq, April 2007 issue

mine and mine

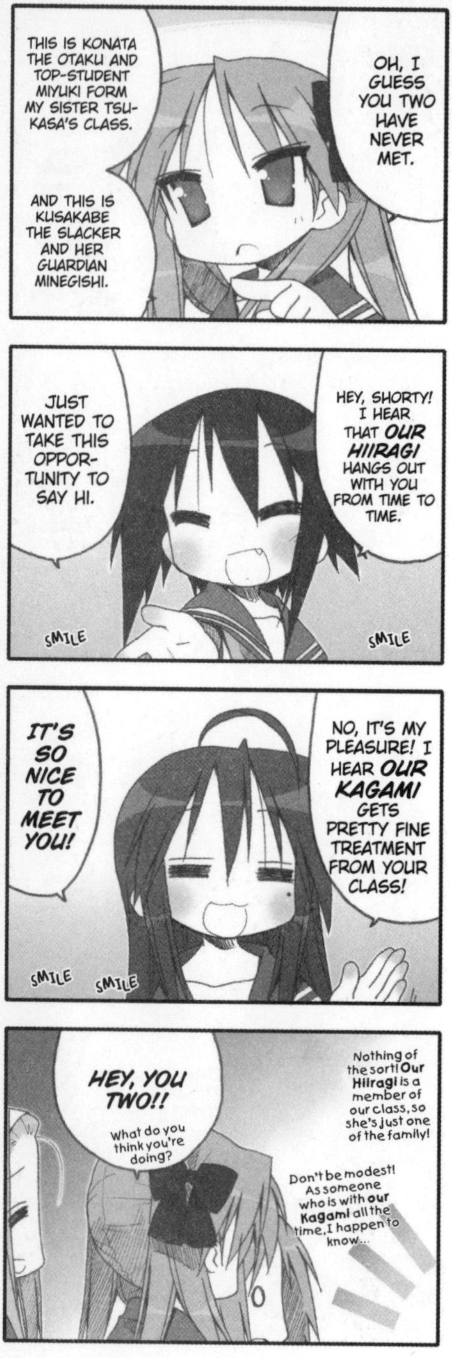
OH, I GUESS YOU TWO HAVE NEVER MET.
THIS IS KONATA THE OTAKU AND TOP-STUDENT MIYUKI FORM MY SISTER TSUKASA'S CLASS.
AND THIS IS KUSAKABE THE SLACKER AND HER GUARDIAN MINEGISHI.
HEY, SHORTY! I HEAR THAT OUR HIIRAGI HANGS OUT WITH YOU FROM TIME TO TIME.
JUST WANTED TO TAKE THIS OPPORTUNITY TO SAY HI.
SMILE
SMILE
NO, IT'S MY PLEASURE! I HEAR OUR KAGAMI GETS PRETTY FINE TREATMENT FROM YOUR CLASS!
IT'S SO NICE TO MEET YOU!
SMILE
SMILE
Nothing of the sort! Our Hiiragi is a member of our class, so she's just one of the family!
HEY, YOU TWO!!
What do you think you're doing?
Don't be modest! As someone who is with our Kagami all the time, I happen to know...

everybody's toy (3rd-year chapter)

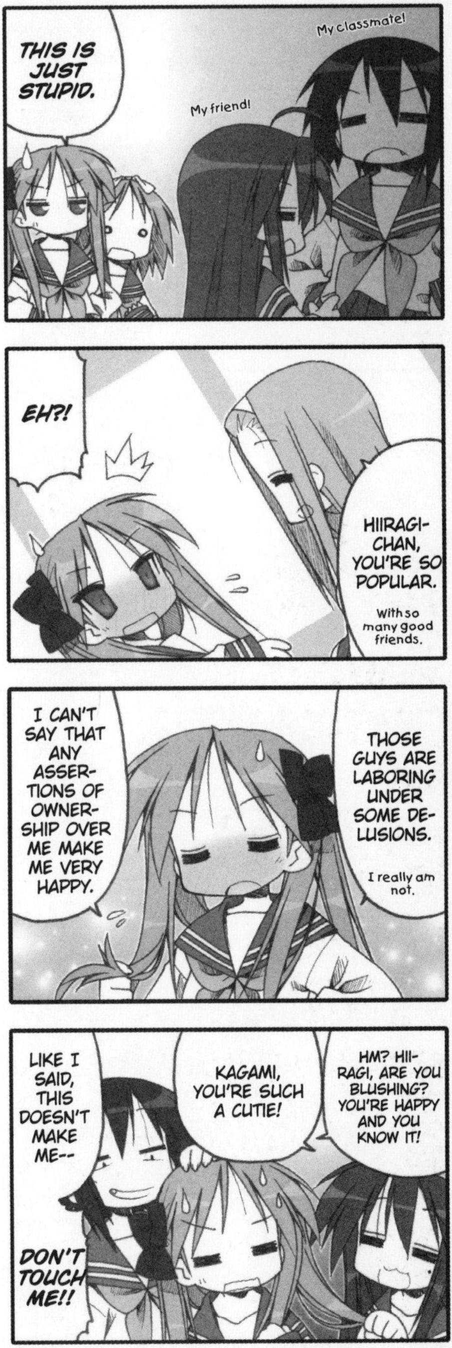
My classmate!
My friend!
THIS IS JUST STUPID.
HIIRAGI-CHAN, YOU'RE SO POPULAR.
With so many good friends.
EH?!
THOSE GUYS ARE LABORING UNDER SOME DELUSIONS.
I really am not.
I CAN'T SAY THAT ANY ASSERTIONS OF OWNERSHIP OVER ME MAKE ME VERY HAPPY.
HM? HIIRAGI, ARE YOU BLUSHING? YOU'RE HAPPY AND YOU KNOW IT!
KAGAMI, YOU'RE SUCH A CUTIE!
LIKE I SAID, THIS DOESN'T MAKE ME--
DON'T TOUCH ME!!

similar odd folks

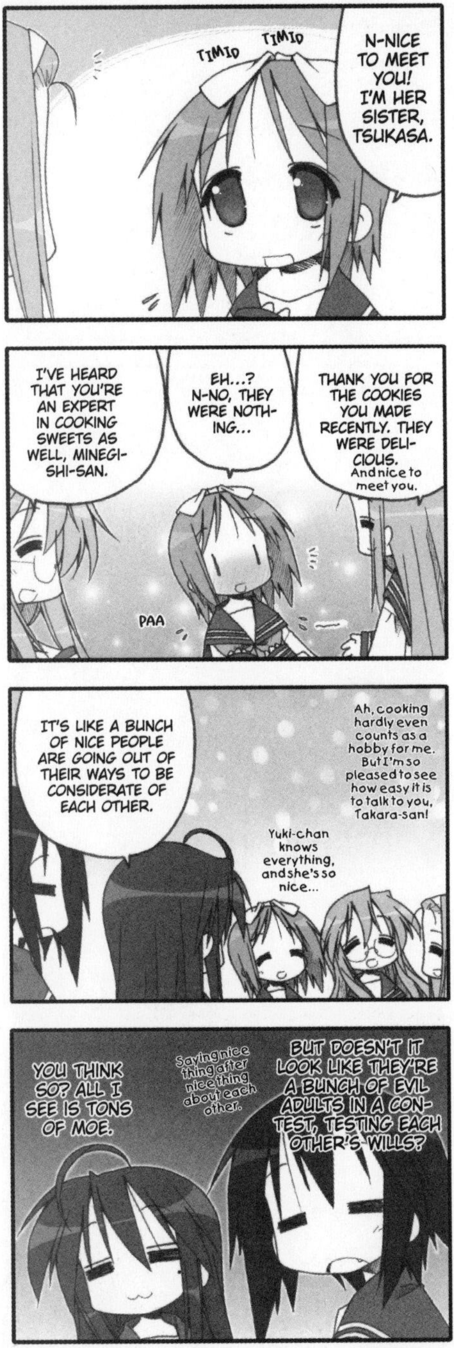
N-NICE TO MEET YOU! I'M HER SISTER, TSUKASA.
TIMID TIMID
THANK YOU FOR THE COOKIES YOU MADE RECENTLY. THEY WERE DELICIOUS.
And nice to meet you.
EH...? N-NO, THEY WERE NOTHING...
I'VE HEARD THAT YOU'RE AN EXPERT IN COOKING SWEETS AS WELL, MINEGISHI-SAN.
PAA
Ah, cooking hardly even counts as a hobby for me. But I'm so pleased to see how easy it is to talk to you, Takara-san!
Yuki-chan knows everything, and she's so nice...
IT'S LIKE A BUNCH OF NICE PEOPLE ARE GOING OUT OF THEIR WAYS TO BE CONSIDERATE OF EACH OTHER.
BUT DOESN'T IT LOOK LIKE THEY'RE A BUNCH OF EVIL ADULTS IN A CONTEST, TESTING EACH OTHER'S WILLS?
Saying nice thing after nice thing about each other.
YOU THINK SO? ALL I SEE IS TONS OF MOE.

a huge catch

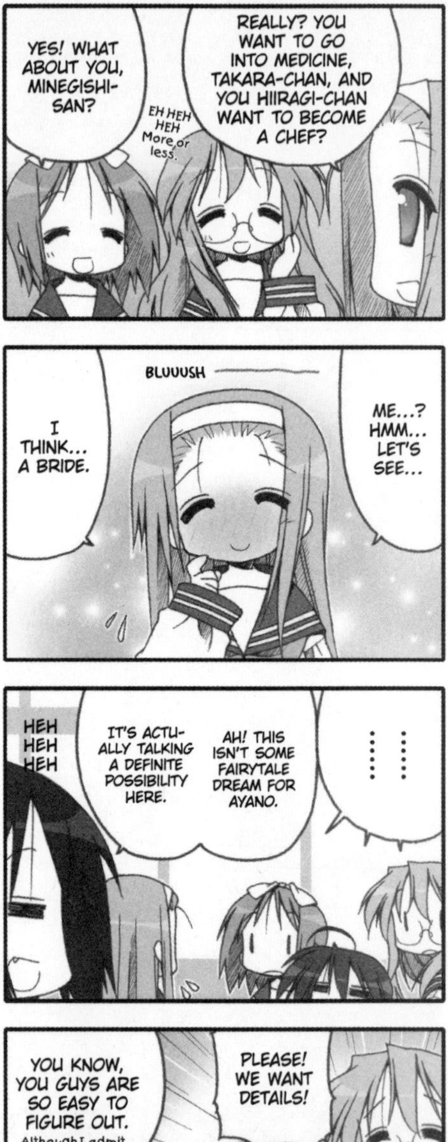
REALLY? YOU WANT TO GO INTO MEDICINE, TAKARA-CHAN, AND YOU HIIRAGI-CHAN WANT TO BECOME A CHEF?
EH HEH HEH More or less.
YES! WHAT ABOUT YOU, MINEGISHI-SAN?
ME...? HMM... LET'S SEE...
BLUUUSH
I THINK... A BRIDE.
......
AH! THIS ISN'T SOME FAIRYTALE DREAM FOR AYANO.
IT'S ACTU-ALLY TALKING A DEFINITE POSSIBILITY HERE.
HEH HEH HEH
PLEASE! WE WANT DETAILS!
YOU KNOW, YOU GUYS ARE SO EASY TO FIGURE OUT.
Although I admit that I'm inter-ested too.

a working man

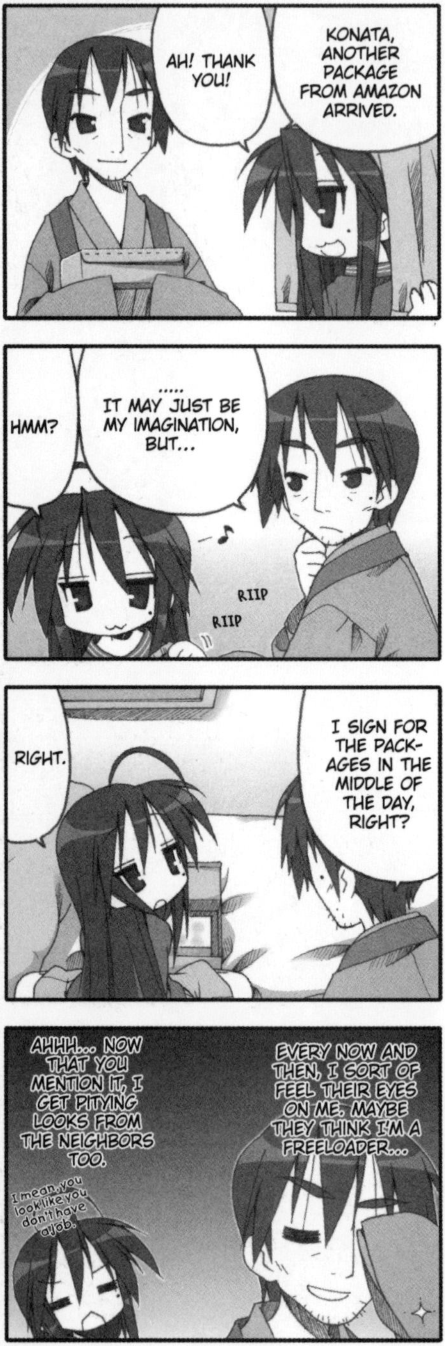
KONATA, ANOTHER PACKAGE FROM AMAZON ARRIVED.
AH! THANK YOU!
..... IT MAY JUST BE MY IMAGINATION, BUT...
HMM?
RIIP
RIIP
I SIGN FOR THE PACK-AGES IN THE MIDDLE OF THE DAY, RIGHT?
RIGHT.
EVERY NOW AND THEN, I SORT OF FEEL THEIR EYES ON ME. MAYBE THEY THINK I'M A FREELOADER...
AHHH... NOW THAT YOU MENTION IT, I GET PITYING LOOKS FROM THE NEIGHBORS TOO.
I mean, you look like you don't have a job.

Lucky☆Star

episode 117
so what happens now?

●Comptiq, April 2007 issue

one's dark history

HELLO!
OH. HIYORIN? YO.
? YOU LOOK A LITTLE BLUE. IS SOME-THING THE MATTER?
I DID SOME CLEANING YESTERDAY.
AND MY OLD PLOTS NOTEBOOK TURNED UP.
DOOM
OH, HO!
PLOTS
KOU YASAKA
IT'S JUST... HOW COME I WAS SO CHAOTIC WHEN I WAS YOUNGER?
I really want to see that!
AH... I THINK I KNOW WHAT YOU MEAN.
And why can't I throw this out now?
I flatly refuse.

everybody's toy (1st-year chapter)

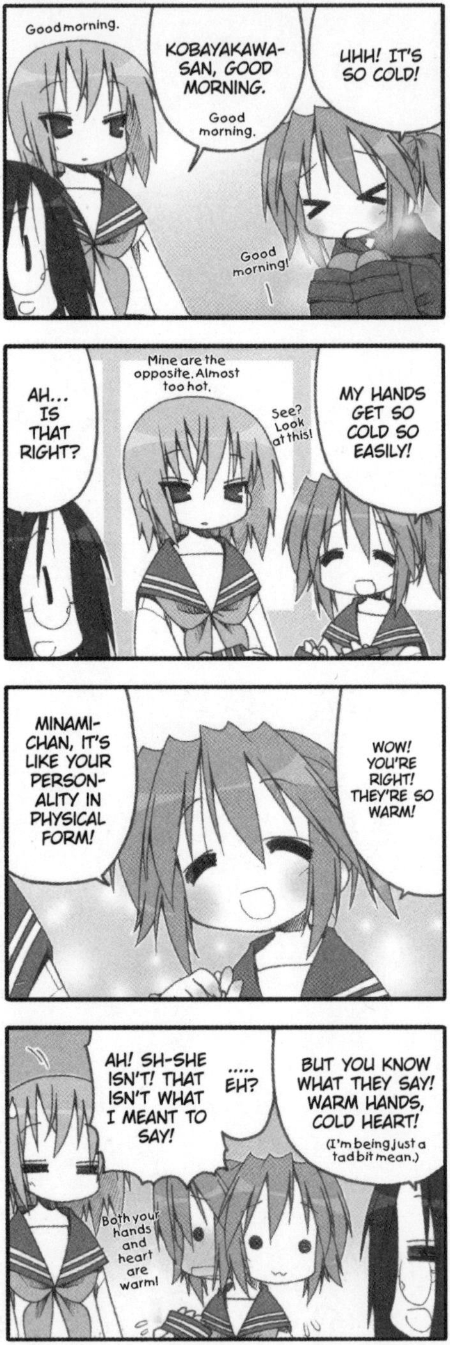
UHH! IT'S SO COLD!
KOBAYAKAWA-SAN, GOOD MORNING.
Good morning.
Good morning.
Good morning!
MY HANDS GET SO COLD SO EASILY!
See? Look at this!
Mine are the opposite. Almost too hot.
AH... IS THAT RIGHT?
WOW! YOU'RE RIGHT! THEY'RE SO WARM!
MINAMI-CHAN, IT'S LIKE YOUR PERSONALITY IN PHYSICAL FORM!
BUT YOU KNOW WHAT THEY SAY! WARM HANDS, COLD HEART!
(I'm being just a tad bit mean.)
..... EH?
AH! SH-SHE ISN'T! THAT ISN'T WHAT I MEANT TO SAY!
Both your hands and heart are warm!

otaku killer

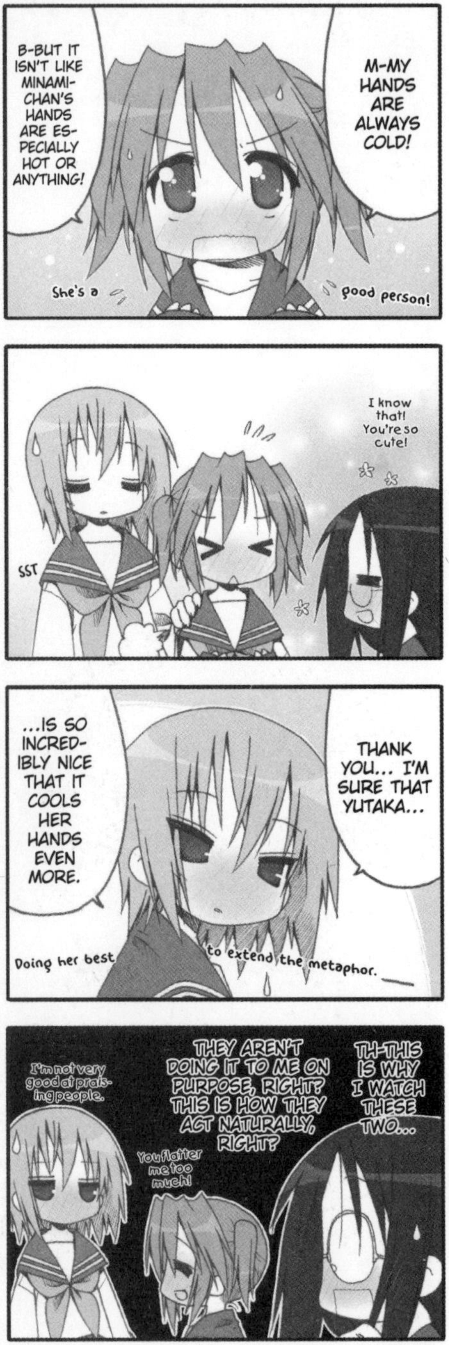
M-MY HANDS ARE ALWAYS COLD!
B-BUT IT ISN'T LIKE MINAMI-CHAN'S HANDS ARE ESPECIALLY HOT OR ANYTHING!
She's a good person!
I know that! You're so cute!
SST
THANK YOU... I'M SURE THAT YUTAKA...
...IS SO INCREDIBLY NICE THAT IT COOLS HER HANDS EVEN MORE.
Doing her best to extend the metaphor.
TH-THIS IS WHY I WATCH THESE TWO...
THEY AREN'T DOING IT TO ME ON PURPOSE, RIGHT? THIS IS HOW THEY ACT NATURALLY, RIGHT?
I'm not very good at praising people.
You flatter me too much!

the spirit of entertainment

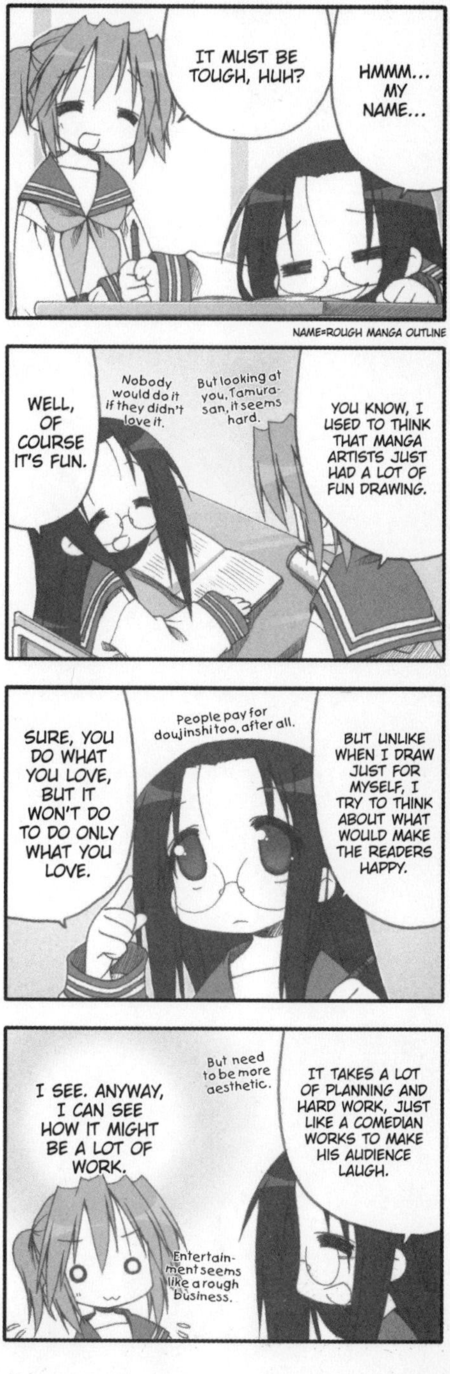
HMMM... MY NAME...
IT MUST BE TOUGH, HUH?
NAME=ROUGH MANGA OUTLINE
YOU KNOW, I USED TO THINK THAT MANGA ARTISTS JUST HAD A LOT OF FUN DRAWING.
But looking at you, Tamura-san, it seems hard.
Nobody would do it if they didn't love it.
WELL, OF COURSE IT'S FUN.
BUT UNLIKE WHEN I DRAW JUST FOR MYSELF, I TRY TO THINK ABOUT WHAT WOULD MAKE THE READERS HAPPY.
People pay for doujinshi too, after all.
SURE, YOU DO WHAT YOU LOVE, BUT IT WON'T DO TO DO ONLY WHAT YOU LOVE.
IT TAKES A LOT OF PLANNING AND HARD WORK, JUST LIKE A COMEDIAN WORKS TO MAKE HIS AUDIENCE LAUGH.
But need to be more aesthetic.
I SEE. ANYWAY, I CAN SEE HOW IT MIGHT BE A LOT OF WORK.
Entertain-ment seems like a rough business.

their turn

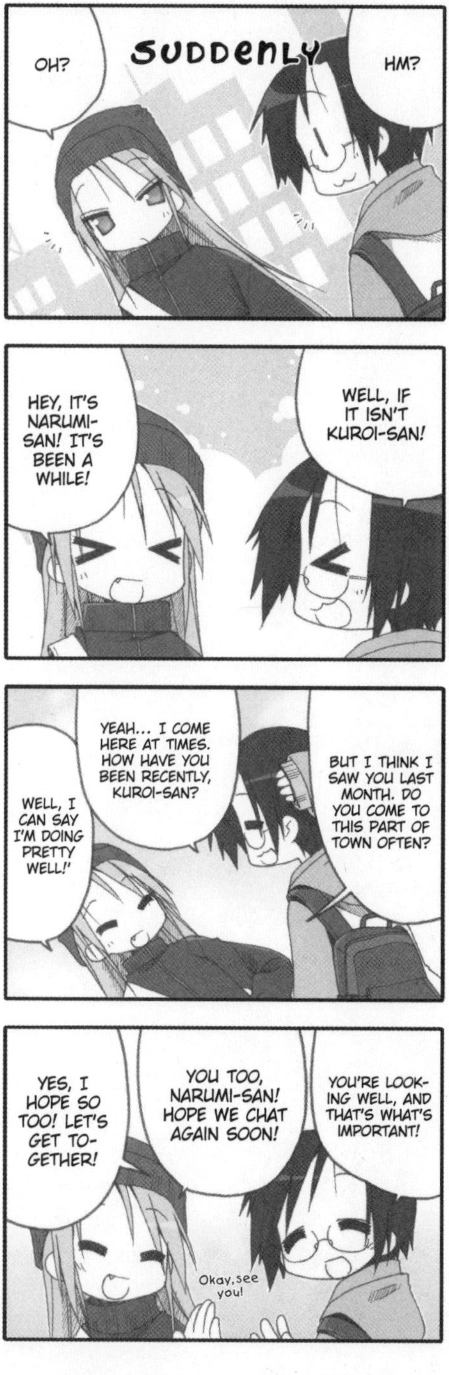
HM?
SUDDENLY
OH?
WELL, IF IT ISN'T KUROI-SAN!
HEY, IT'S NARUMI-SAN! IT'S BEEN A WHILE!
BUT I THINK I SAW YOU LAST MONTH. DO YOU COME TO THIS PART OF TOWN OFTEN?
YEAH... I COME HERE AT TIMES. HOW HAVE YOU BEEN RECENTLY, KUROI-SAN?
WELL, I CAN SAY I'M DOING PRETTY WELL!'
YOU'RE LOOK-ING WELL, AND THAT'S WHAT'S IMPORTANT!
YOU TOO, NARUMI-SAN! HOPE WE CHAT AGAIN SOON!
YES, I HOPE SO TOO! LET'S GET TO-GETHER!
Okay, see you!

The Tale of the Ice Princess

STORY BY: YUTAKA KOBAYAKAWA

LONG AGO IN A FAR-AWAY LAND, THERE LIVED A KIND AND GENTLE PRINCESS. BUT THE PRINCESS WAS SICKLY, AND SOON FELL ILL TO DISEASES.

MANY DAYS SHE WOULD FEEL POORLY AND CAST HER EYES DOWNWARD.

"OH, ISN'T THAT A SHAME!" SAID SOME PEOPLE IN THE KINGDOM. OTHERS WOULD SAY, "POOR PRINCESS-SAMA." AND EVERYONE WOULD PITY THE PRINCESS AND TREAT HER KINDLY.

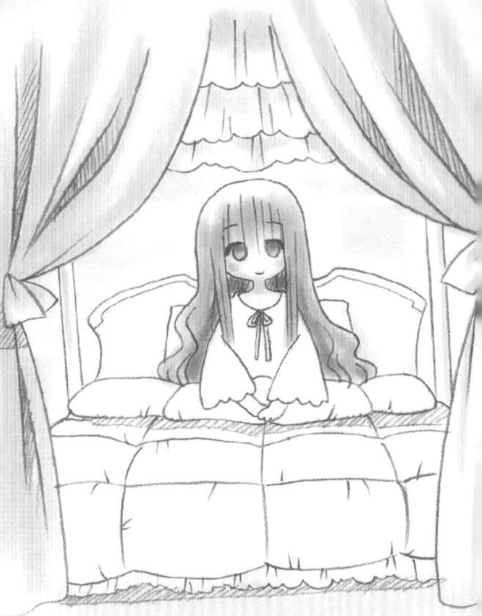

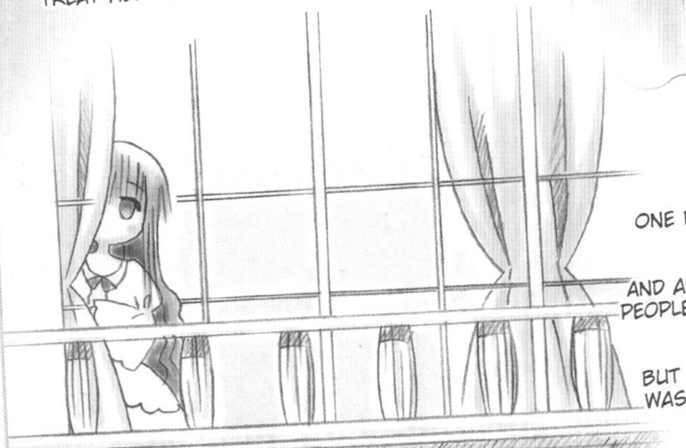

ONE DAY SHE CONTRACTED A DISEASE THAT BEGAN TO TURN HER BODY TO ICE.

AND AS HER CONDITION BECAME WORSE, THE PEOPLE TREATED HER WITH EVEN MORE KINDNESS.

BUT THAT ALSO MEANT THAT THE PRINCESS WAS ALWAYS FOUND OUTSIDE THE PEOPLE'S CIRCLES OF FRIENDS.

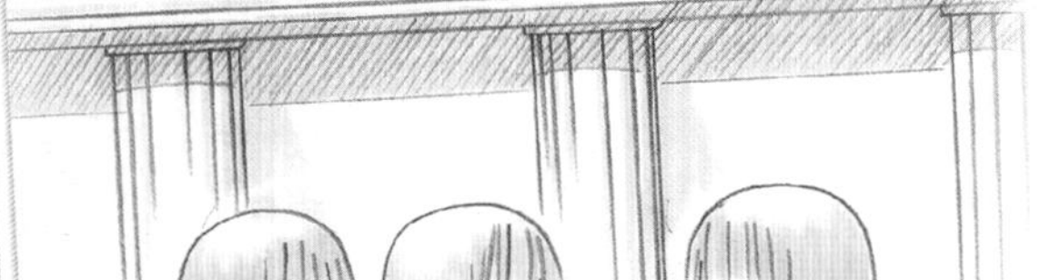

"I CAN'T GO OUT AND PLAY LIKE EVERYBODY ELSE DOES. I CAN'T STUDY MY LESSONS LIKE EVERYBODY ELSE DOES," THE PRINCESS CRIED.

AS THE PRINCESS LOST CONFIDENCE IN HERSELF, LITTLE-BY-LITTLE, THE ICE COVERED HER FACE, AND SHE COULDN'T EVEN SMILE ANYMORE.

POOR PRINCESS-SAMA! POOR PRINCESS-SAMA!" THE PEOPLE WOULD SAY EVEN MORE, AND THEY TREATED HER WITH EVEN MORE KINDNESS. BUT THAT VERY KINDNESS PILED UP ON TOP OF THE PRINCESS.

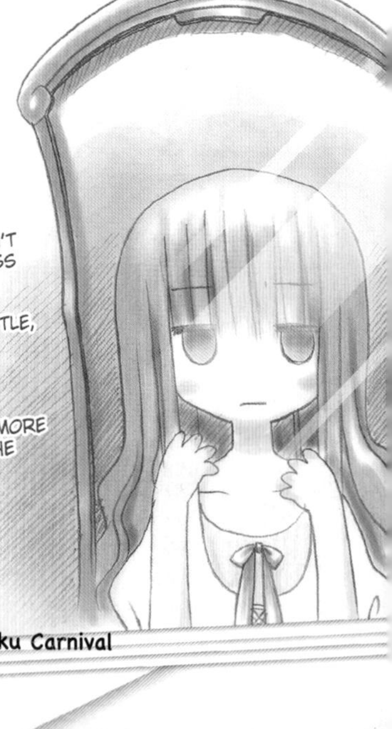

episode 118 the flower that melted the snow

● Lucky Star: Okiraku Carnival

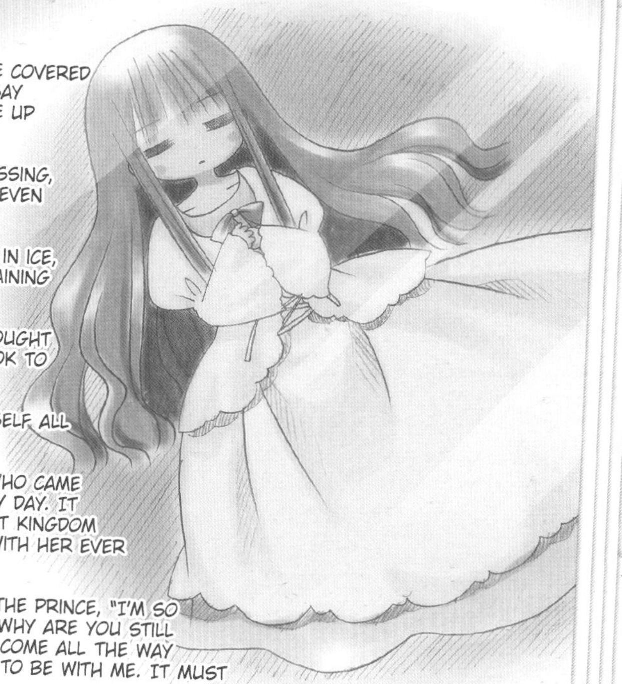

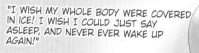

"I WISH MY WHOLE BODY WERE COVERED IN ICE! I WISH I COULD JUST SAY ASLEEP, AND NEVER EVER WAKE UP AGAIN!"

THE DISEASE KEPT ON PROGRESSING, AND SOON THE ICE HAD CREPT EVEN TO HER HEART.

AND WITH HER HEART COVERED IN ICE, THE PRINCESS STARTED COMPLAINING AND ACTING SELFISH.

THE PEOPLE, WHO AT FIRST THOUGHT SHE WAS SO PITIABLE, NOW TOOK TO AVOIDING HER.

AND THE PRINCESS FOUND HERSELF ALL ALONE.

BUT THERE WAS ONE PERSON WHO CAME TO THE PRINCESS'S ROOM EVERY DAY. IT WAS THE PRINCE FROM THE NEXT KINGDOM OVER WHO HAD BEEN FRIENDS WITH HER EVER SINCE THEY BOTH WERE BORN.

ONE DAY, THE PRINCESS ASKED THE PRINCE, "I'M SO SELFISH AND SUCH A BAD GIRL! WHY ARE YOU STILL FRIENDS WITH ME? WHY DO YOU COME ALL THE WAY FROM YOUR KINGDOM EVERYDAY TO BE WITH ME. IT MUST BE SO DIFFICULT ON YOU."

AND THE PRINCE ANSWERED, "I NEVER CAME TO SEE YOU OUT OF PITY. I CAME TO SEE YOU BECAUSE I LIKE BEING WITH YOU. I COME BECAUSE I LOVE YOU."

AFTER CASTING HER EYES DOWNWARD FOR SO LONG, THE PRINCESS, AS IF FOR THE FIRST TIME, LOOKED UP AND STRAIGHT AHEAD.

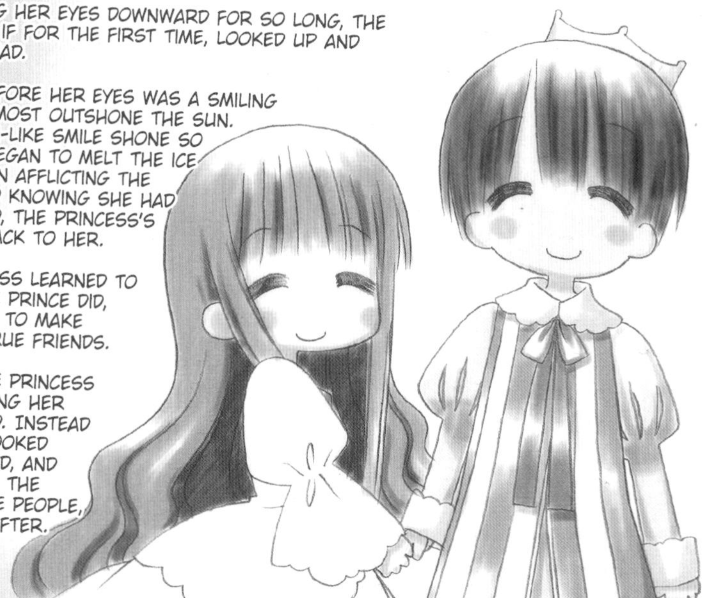

AND RIGHT BEFORE HER EYES WAS A SMILING FACE THAT ALMOST OUTSHONE THE SUN. AND THAT SUN-LIKE SMILE SHONE SO BRIGHTLY IT BEGAN TO MELT THE ICE THAT HAD BEEN AFFLICTING THE PRINCESS. AND KNOWING SHE HAD A TRUE FRIEND, THE PRINCESS'S SMILE CAME BACK TO HER.

AS THE PRINCESS LEARNED TO SMILE LIKE THE PRINCE DID, SHE WAS ABLE TO MAKE MANY MORE TRUE FRIENDS.

WITH THAT, THE PRINCESS STOPPED CASTING HER EYE DOWNWARD. INSTEAD SHE ALWAYS LOOKED STRAIGHT AHEAD, AND SHE LIVED WITH THE PRINCE AND THE PEOPLE, HAPPILY EVER AFTER.

THE END

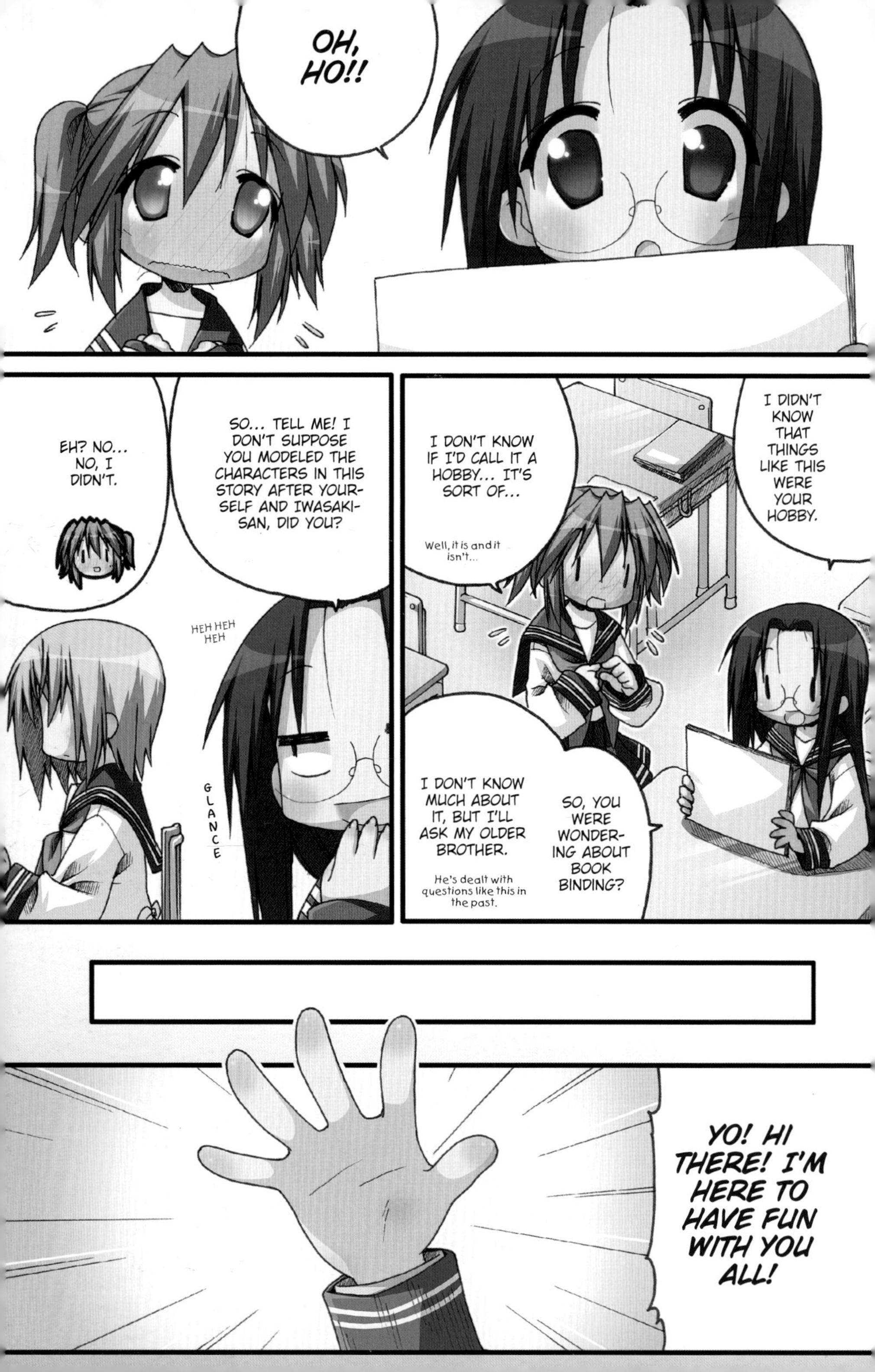
OH, HO!!
I DIDN'T KNOW THAT THINGS LIKE THIS WERE YOUR HOBBY.
I DON'T KNOW IF I'D CALL IT A HOBBY... IT'S SORT OF...
Well, it is and it isn't...
SO, YOU WERE WONDERING ABOUT BOOK BINDING?
I DON'T KNOW MUCH ABOUT IT, BUT I'LL ASK MY OLDER BROTHER.
He's dealt with questions like this in the past.
SO... TELL ME! I DON'T SUPPOSE YOU MODELED THE CHARACTERS IN THIS STORY AFTER YOURSELF AND IWASAKI-SAN, DID YOU?
EH? NO... NO, I DIDN'T.
HEH HEH HEH
GLANCE
YO! HI THERE! I'M HERE TO HAVE FUN WITH YOU ALL!

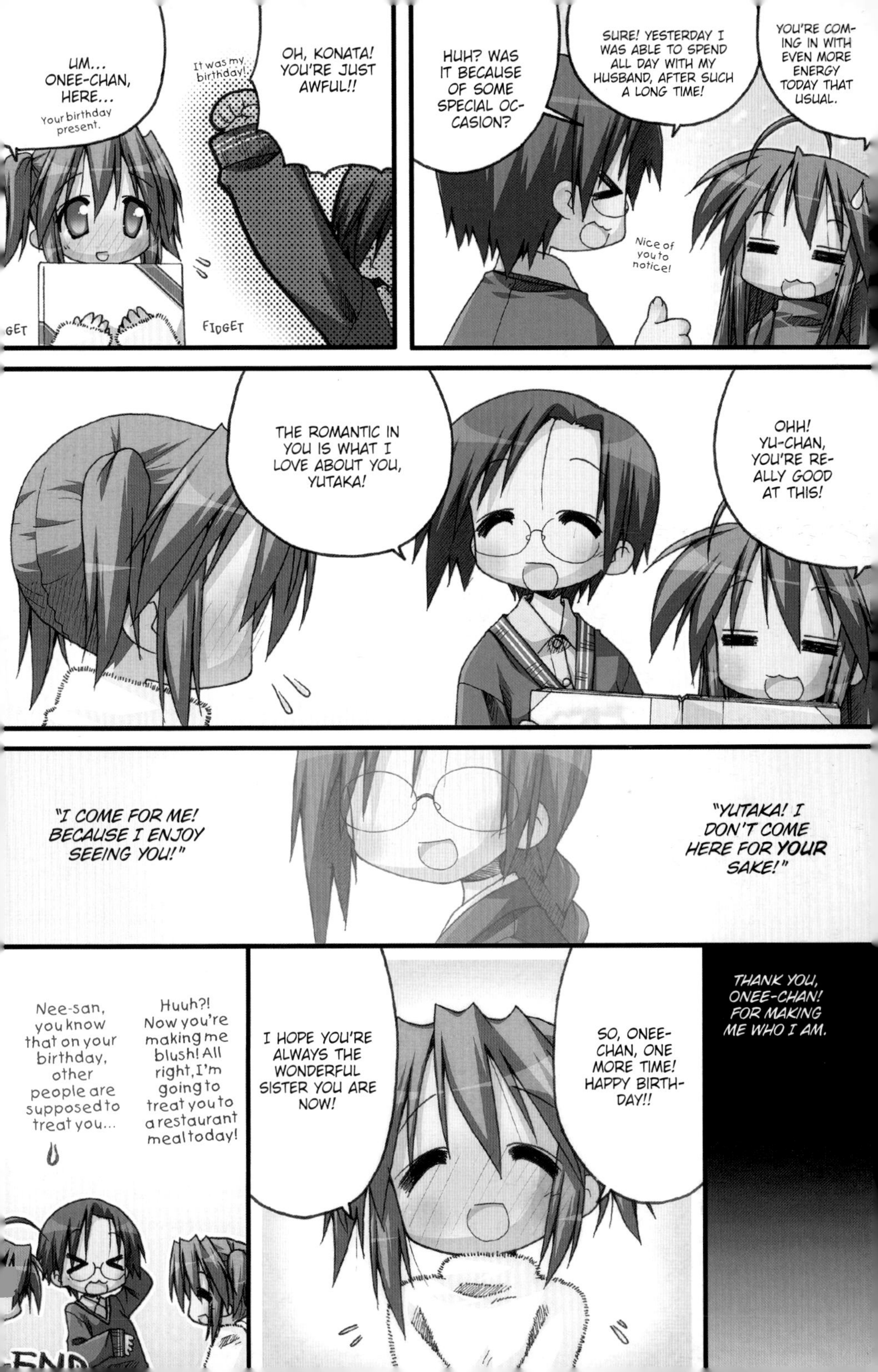
YOU'RE COMING IN WITH EVEN MORE ENERGY TODAY THAT USUAL.
SURE! YESTERDAY I WAS ABLE TO SPEND ALL DAY WITH MY HUSBAND, AFTER SUCH A LONG TIME!
HUH? WAS IT BECAUSE OF SOME SPECIAL OCCASION?
Nice of you to notice!
OH, KONATA! YOU'RE JUST AWFUL!!
It was my birthday!
UM... ONEE-CHAN, HERE...
Your birthday present.
FIDGET
GET
OHH! YU-CHAN, YOU'RE REALLY GOOD AT THIS!
THE ROMANTIC IN YOU IS WHAT I LOVE ABOUT YOU, YUTAKA!
"YUTAKA! I DON'T COME HERE FOR YOUR SAKE!"
"I COME FOR ME! BECAUSE I ENJOY SEEING YOU!"
THANK YOU, ONEE-CHAN! FOR MAKING ME WHO I AM.
SO, ONEE-CHAN, ONE MORE TIME! HAPPY BIRTHDAY!!
I HOPE YOU'RE ALWAYS THE WONDERFUL SISTER YOU ARE NOW!
Huuh?! Now you're making me blush! All right, I'm going to treat you to a restaurant meal today!
Nee-san, you know that on your birthday, other people are supposed to treat you...
END

Lucky☆Star

episode 119
purity

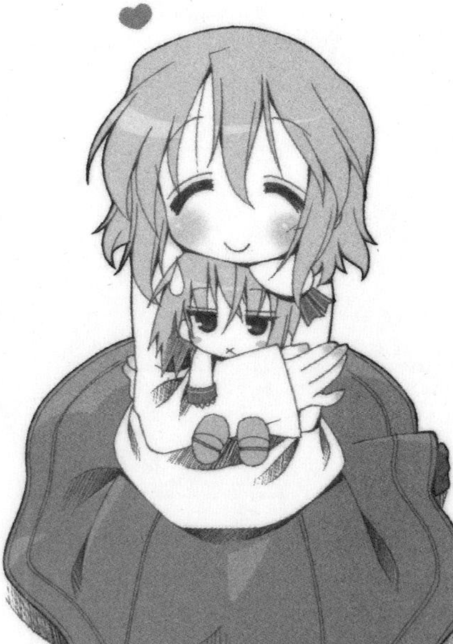

● Comp Ace, Vol. 006, Extra edition, May 2006

with the doggy

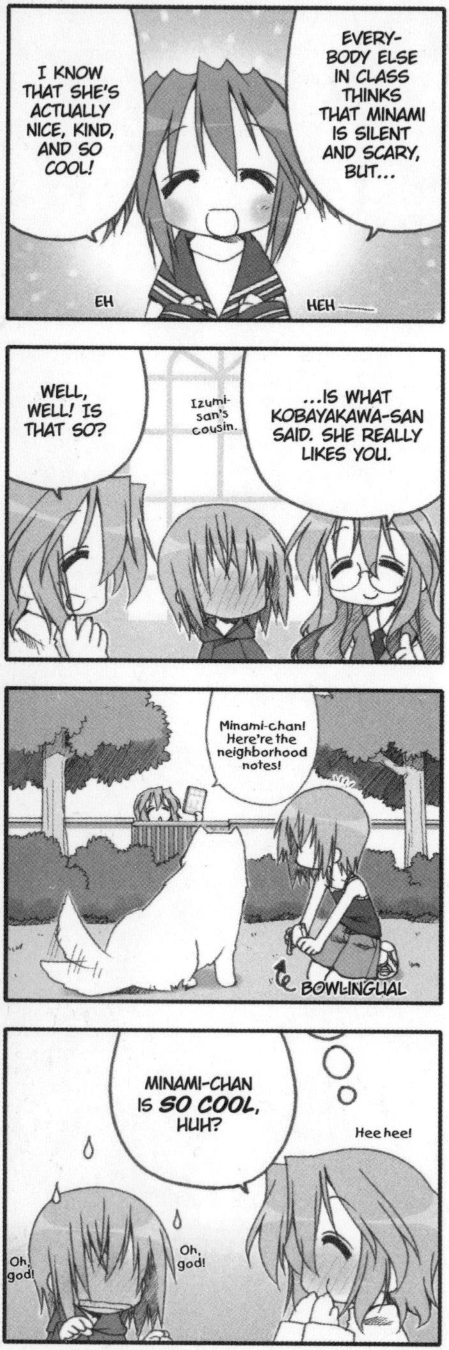
EVERY-BODY ELSE IN CLASS THINKS THAT MINAMI IS SILENT AND SCARY, BUT...
I KNOW THAT SHE'S ACTUALLY NICE, KIND, AND SO COOL!
HEH ——
EH
...IS WHAT KOBAYAKAWA-SAN SAID. SHE REALLY LIKES YOU.
Izumi-san's cousin.
WELL, WELL! IS THAT SO?
Minami-chan! Here're the neighborhood notes!
BOWLINGUAL
Hee hee!
MINAMI-CHAN IS SO COOL, HUH?
Oh, god!
Oh, god!

perseverance

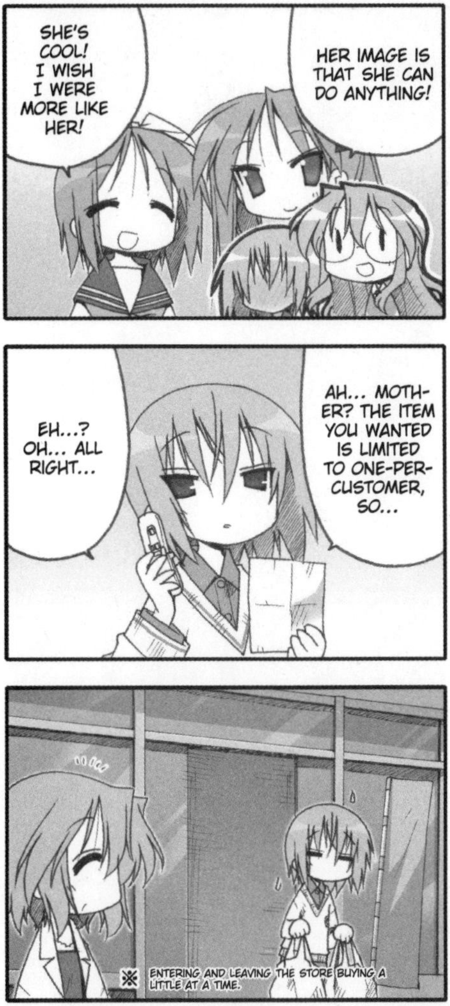
HER IMAGE IS THAT SHE CAN DO ANYTHING!
SHE'S COOL! I WISH I WERE MORE LIKE HER!
AH... MOTH-ER? THE ITEM YOU WANTED IS LIMITED TO ONE-PER-CUSTOMER, SO...
EH...? OH... ALL RIGHT...
※ ENTERING AND LEAVING THE STORE BUYING A LITTLE AT A TIME.
Hee hee hee!
MINAMI-CHAN IS SO COOL!
When she's actually just cute.

embarrassing

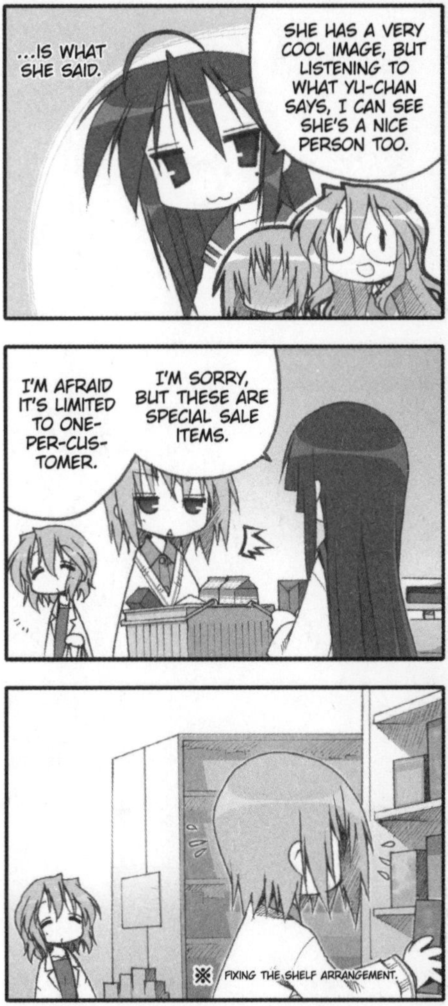
SHE HAS A VERY COOL IMAGE, BUT LISTENING TO WHAT YU-CHAN SAYS, I CAN SEE SHE'S A NICE PERSON TOO.
...IS WHAT SHE SAID.
I'M SORRY, BUT THESE ARE SPECIAL SALE ITEMS.
I'M AFRAID IT'S LIMITED TO ONE-PER-CUS-TOMER.
※ FIXING THE SHELF ARRANGEMENT.
Hee hee!
MINAMI-CHAN IS SO COOL!

in the same league

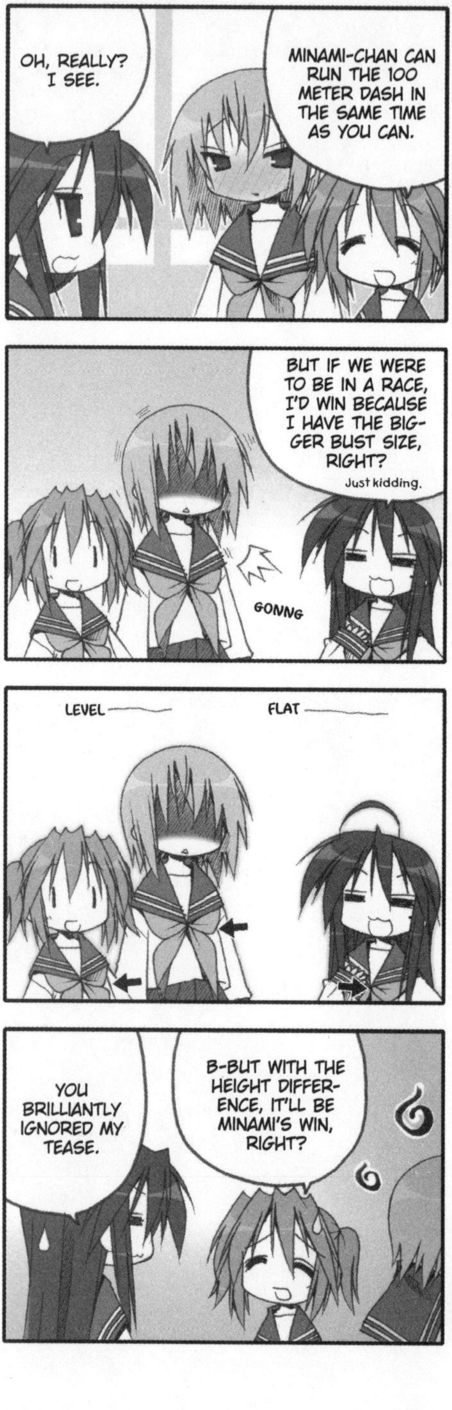
MINAMI-CHAN CAN RUN THE 100 METER DASH IN THE SAME TIME AS YOU CAN.
OH, REALLY? I SEE.
BUT IF WE WERE TO BE IN A RACE, I'D WIN BECAUSE I HAVE THE BIG-GER BUST SIZE, RIGHT?
Just kidding.
GONNG
FLAT
LEVEL
B-BUT WITH THE HEIGHT DIFFER-ENCE, IT'LL BE MINAMI'S WIN, RIGHT?
YOU BRILLIANTLY IGNORED MY TEASE.

the pure world

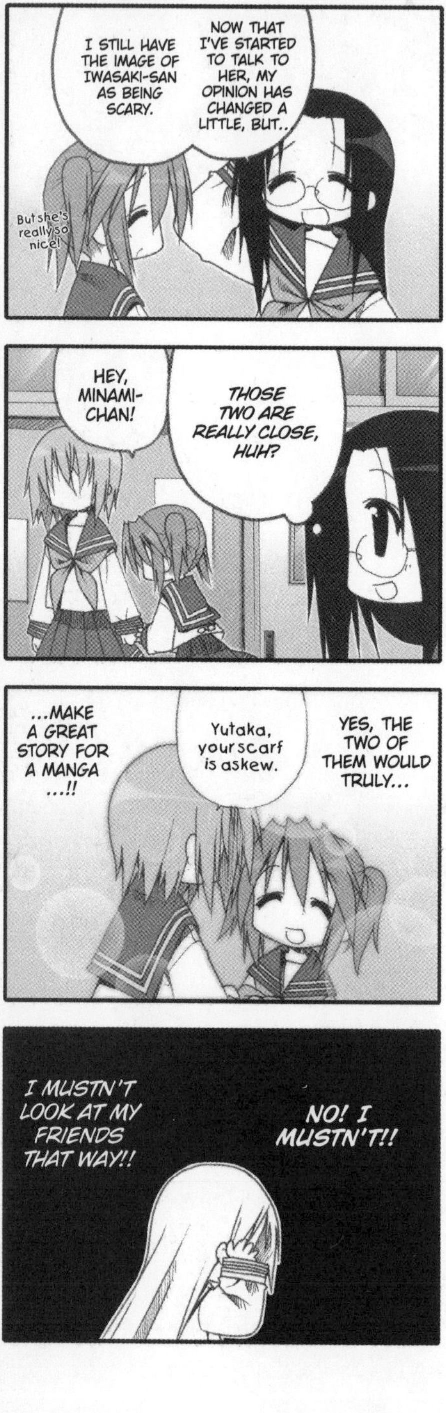
NOW THAT I'VE STARTED TO TALK TO HER, MY OPINION HAS CHANGED A LITTLE, BUT...
I STILL HAVE THE IMAGE OF IWASAKI-SAN AS BEING SCARY.
But she's really so nice!
THOSE TWO ARE REALLY CLOSE, HUH?
HEY, MINAMI-CHAN!
YES, THE TWO OF THEM WOULD TRULY...
Yutaka, your scarf is askew.
...MAKE A GREAT STORY FOR A MANGA ...!!
NO! I MUSTN'T!!
I MUSTN'T LOOK AT MY FRIENDS THAT WAY!!

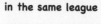

Lucky☆Star

episode 120
psychological warfare

sketch book
HIYORI TAMURA

● Comp Ace Vol. 007, Extra Edition, June 2006

sense of loss

SORRY! I CAN'T GIVE THIS TO YOU.
Oily food's not good for you.
STAAARE—
CHIN ON THE TABLE
YOU KNOW THAT MINAMI IS A SOFTIE, SO YOU KEEP BEGGING FROM HER, HUH?
I GUESS THERE'S NO CHOICE. COME HERE. I'LL GIVE YOU SOME!
WUFF WUFF
Calm down and eat.
SIGH
THERE'S SOMETHING ABOUT THIS...
...THAT MAKES ME LONELY.
It's like my dog's affections were stolen away by food.

in writing

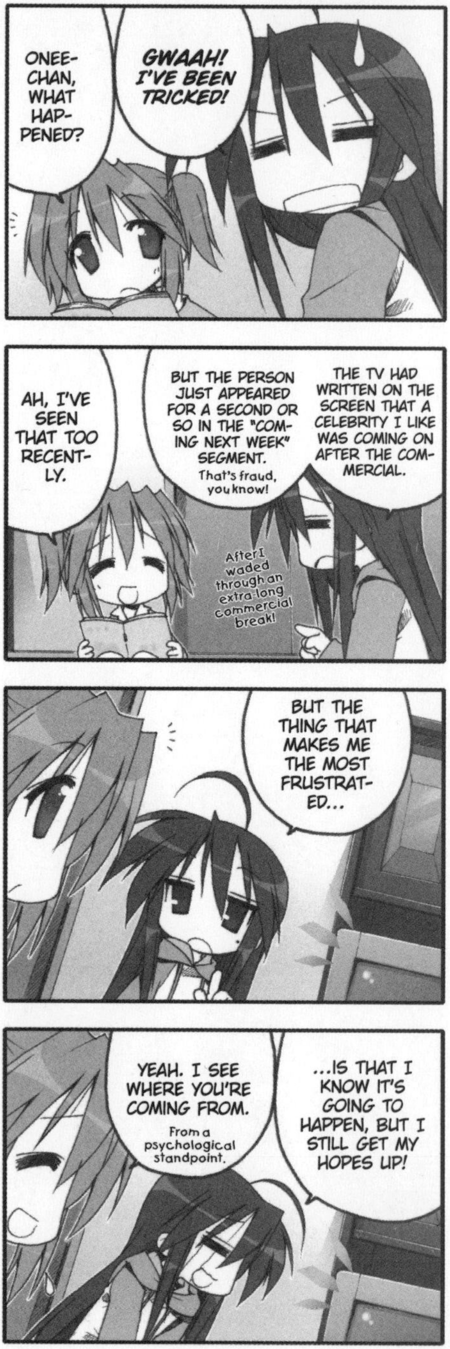
GWAAH! I'VE BEEN TRICKED!
ONEE-CHAN, WHAT HAPPENED?
THE TV HAD WRITTEN ON THE SCREEN THAT A CELEBRITY I LIKE WAS COMING ON AFTER THE COMMERCIAL.
BUT THE PERSON JUST APPEARED FOR A SECOND OR SO IN THE "COMING NEXT WEEK" SEGMENT.
That's fraud, you know!
After I waded through an extra-long commercial break!
AH, I'VE SEEN THAT TOO RECENTLY.
BUT THE THING THAT MAKES ME THE MOST FRUSTRATED...
...IS THAT I KNOW IT'S GOING TO HAPPEN, BUT I STILL GET MY HOPES UP!
YEAH. I SEE WHERE YOU'RE COMING FROM.
From a psychological standpoint.

attack on a fleeing enemy

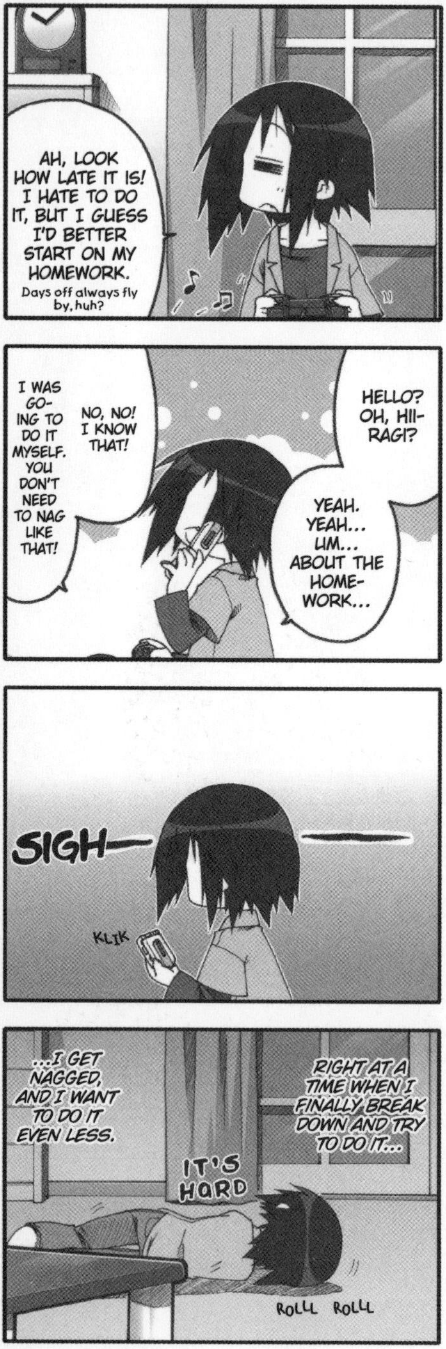
AH, LOOK HOW LATE IT IS! I HATE TO DO IT, BUT I GUESS I'D BETTER START ON MY HOMEWORK.
Days off always fly by, huh?
HELLO? OH, HIIRAGI?
YEAH. YEAH... UM... ABOUT THE HOMEWORK...
NO, NO! I KNOW THAT!
I WAS GOING TO DO IT MYSELF. YOU DON'T NEED TO NAG LIKE THAT!
SIGH—
KLIK
RIGHT AT A TIME WHEN I FINALLY BREAK DOWN AND TRY TO DO IT...
...I GET NAGGED, AND I WANT TO DO IT EVEN LESS.
IT'S HARD
ROLL ROLL

almost there

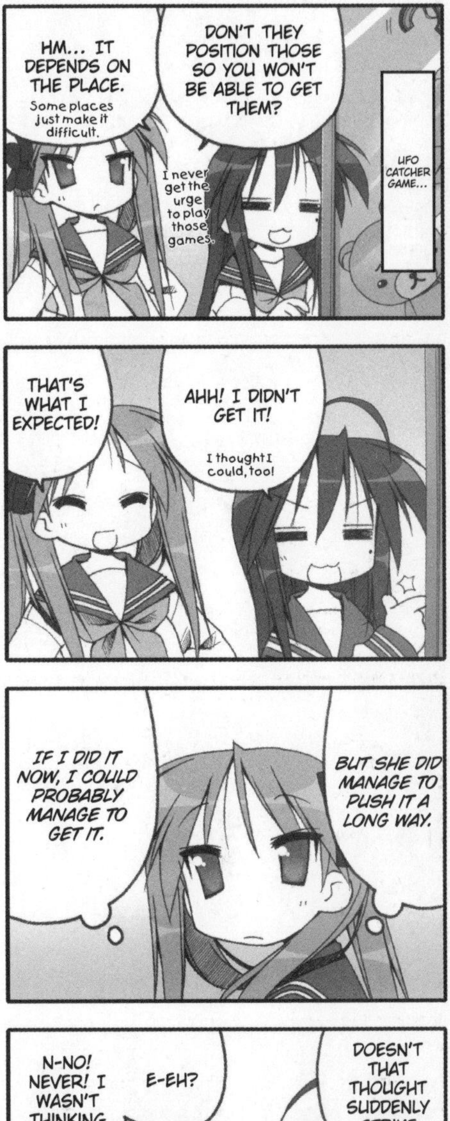
UFO CATCHER GAME...
DON'T THEY POSITION THOSE SO YOU WON'T BE ABLE TO GET THEM?
I never get the urge to play those games.
HM... IT DEPENDS ON THE PLACE.
Some places just make it difficult.
AHH! I DIDN'T GET IT!
I thought I could, too!
THAT'S WHAT I EXPECTED!
BUT SHE DID MANAGE TO PUSH IT A LONG WAY.
IF I DID IT NOW, I COULD PROBABLY MANAGE TO GET IT.
DOESN'T THAT THOUGHT SUDDENLY STRIKE YOU?
E-EH?
N-NO! NEVER! I WASN'T THINKING THAT AT ALL!
GAK

welcome, customer

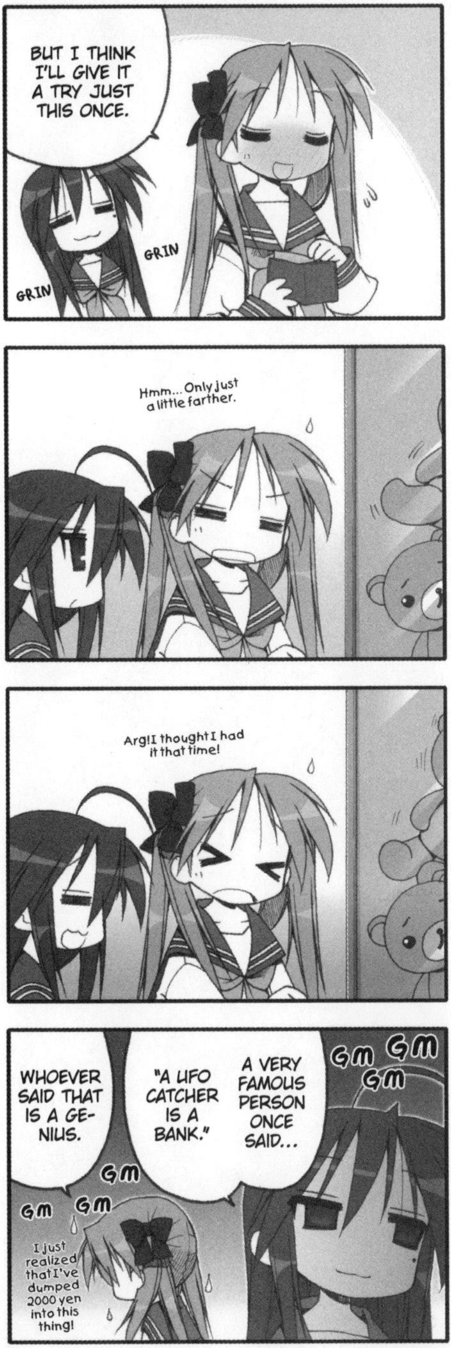
BUT I THINK I'LL GIVE IT A TRY JUST THIS ONCE.
GRIN
GRIN
Hmm... Only just a little farther.
Arg! I thought I had it that time!
GM GM GM
A VERY FAMOUS PERSON ONCE SAID...
"A UFO CATCHER IS A BANK."
WHOEVER SAID THAT IS A GE-NIUS.
GM
GM GM
I just realized that I've dumped 2000 yen into this thing!

ABOUT $20

Lucky☆Star

episode 121
don't give up until it's over

● Comp Ace Vol. 008, Extra edition, September 2006

effort

I THINK ONE OF THE REASONS I'VE GROWN IS BECAUSE I SLEEP QUITE A LOT.
And as the saying goes, a sleeping child grows up big and strong.
EVEN NOW, I GET TO BED BEFORE 11:00 PM.
And it was 10:00 PM until I was a 2nd-year student.
...IS WHAT MIYUKI TOLD ME A WHILE BACK.
BUT YOU SLEEP A LOT TOO, YU-CHAN, BUT YOU DON'T GROW AT ALL!
AH!
...IS WHAT ONEE-CHAN SAID TO ME!
And she knows I'm sensitive about that!
GRR
I'M SORRY TO CALL SO LATE! THIS IS KOBAYAKAWA. IS IWASAKI-SAN THERE?
EH? MINAMI-CHAN IS ALREADY IN BED?
THAT NIGHT AROUND 9:00 PM.

writing implements

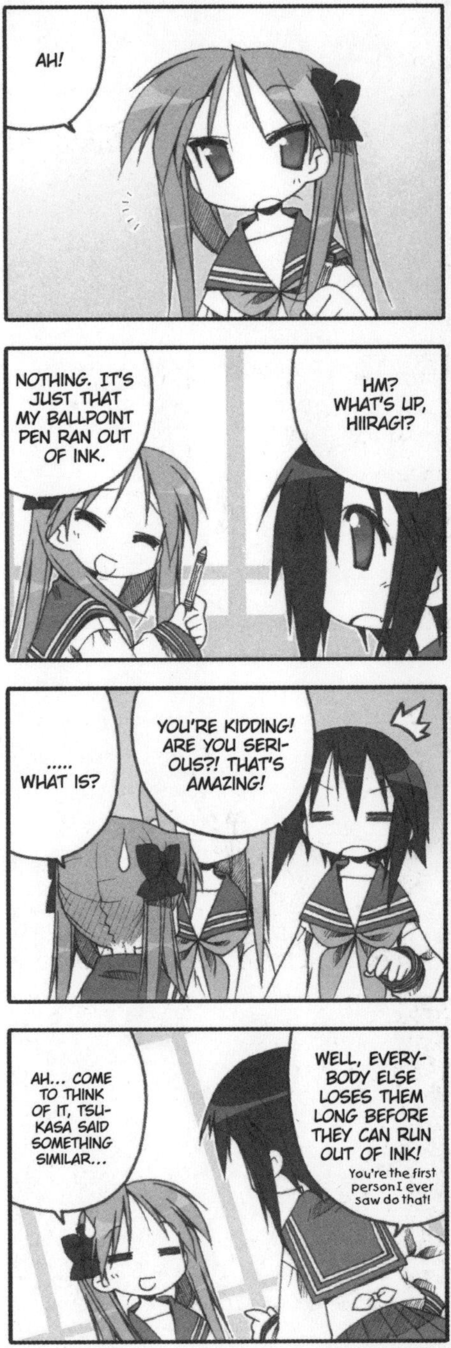
AH!
HM? WHAT'S UP, HIIRAGI?
NOTHING. IT'S JUST THAT MY BALLPOINT PEN RAN OUT OF INK.
YOU'RE KIDDING! ARE YOU SERIOUS?! THAT'S AMAZING!
..... WHAT IS?
WELL, EVERYBODY ELSE LOSES THEM LONG BEFORE THEY CAN RUN OUT OF INK!
You're the first person I ever saw do that!
AH... COME TO THINK OF IT, TSUKASA SAID SOMETHING SIMILAR...

suicide attack

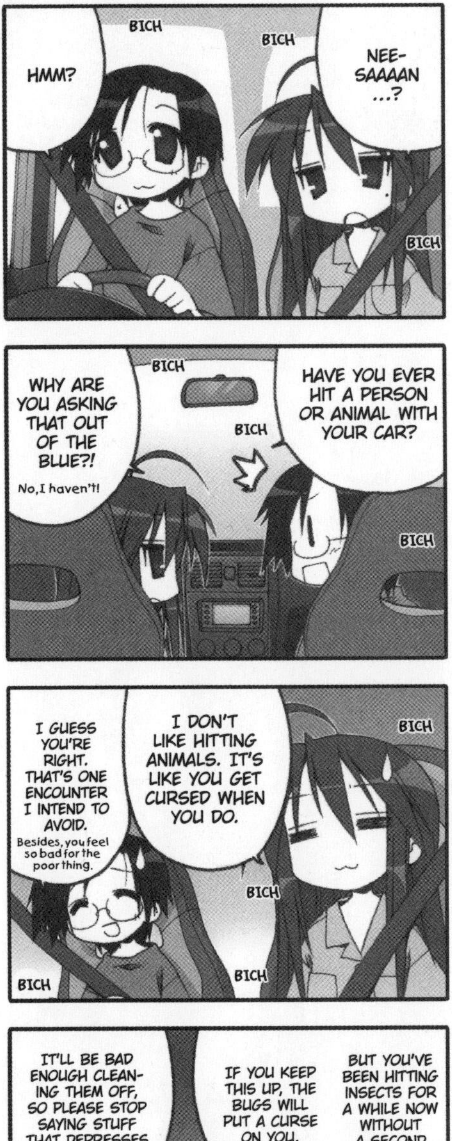
BICH
BICH
NEE-SAAAAN ...?
HMM?
BICH
HAVE YOU EVER HIT A PERSON OR ANIMAL WITH YOUR CAR?
BICH
BICH
WHY ARE YOU ASKING THAT OUT OF THE BLUE?!
No, I haven't!
BICH
BICH
I DON'T LIKE HITTING ANIMALS. IT'S LIKE YOU GET CURSED WHEN YOU DO.
I GUESS YOU'RE RIGHT. THAT'S ONE ENCOUNTER I INTEND TO AVOID.
Besides, you feel so bad for the poor thing.
BICH
BICH
BICH
BUT YOU'VE BEEN HITTING INSECTS FOR A WHILE NOW WITHOUT A SECOND THOUGHT.
IF YOU KEEP THIS UP, THE BUGS WILL PUT A CURSE ON YOU.
IT'LL BE BAD ENOUGH CLEANING THEM OFF, SO PLEASE STOP SAYING STUFF THAT DEPRESSES ME!
That's what I hate about Summer.
BICH
BICH

it's punishment

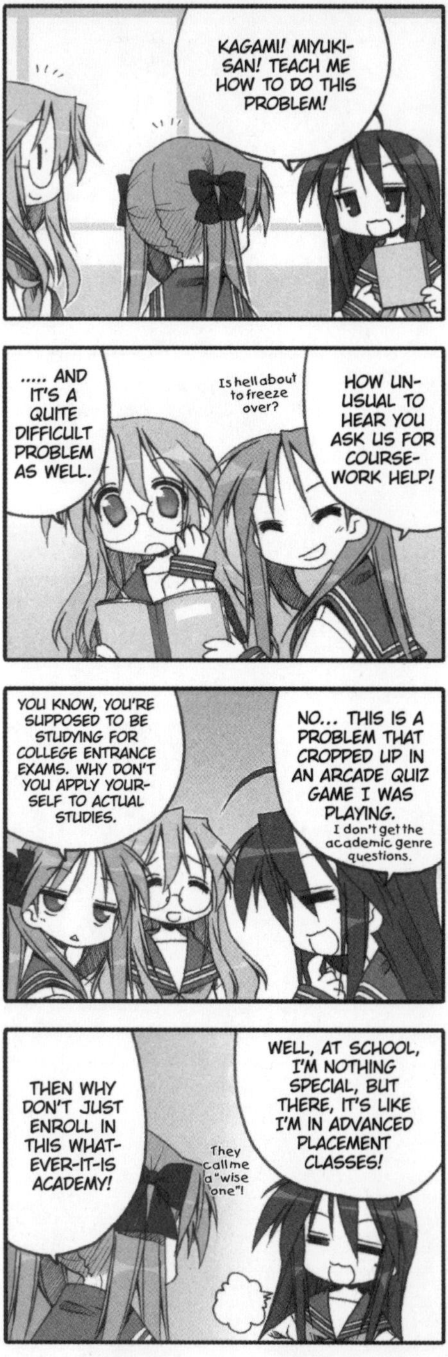
KAGAMI! MIYUKI-SAN! TEACH ME HOW TO DO THIS PROBLEM!
HOW UN-USUAL TO HEAR YOU ASK US FOR COURSE-WORK HELP!
Is hell about to freeze over?
..... AND IT'S A QUITE DIFFICULT PROBLEM AS WELL.
NO... THIS IS A PROBLEM THAT CROPPED UP IN AN ARCADE QUIZ GAME I WAS PLAYING.
I don't get the academic genre questions.
YOU KNOW, YOU'RE SUPPOSED TO BE STUDYING FOR COLLEGE ENTRANCE EXAMS. WHY DON'T YOU APPLY YOUR-SELF TO ACTUAL STUDIES.
WELL, AT SCHOOL, I'M NOTHING SPECIAL, BUT THERE, IT'S LIKE I'M IN ADVANCED PLACEMENT CLASSES!
They call me a "wise one"!
THEN WHY DON'T JUST ENROLL IN THIS WHAT-EVER-IT-IS ACADEMY!

Nice Sleeping Face

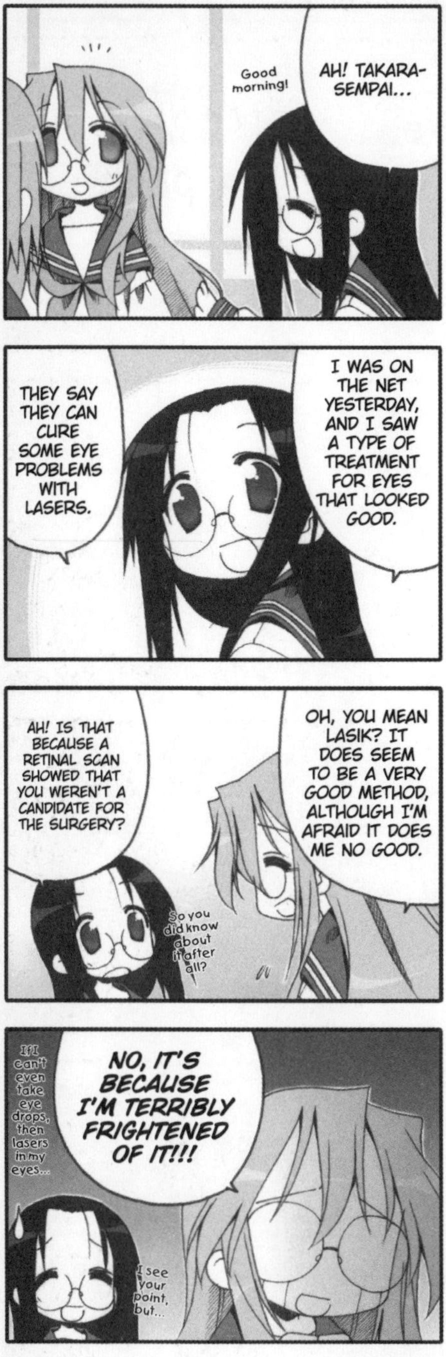
AH! TAKARA-SEMPAI...
Good morning!
I WAS ON THE NET YESTERDAY, AND I SAW A TYPE OF TREATMENT FOR EYES THAT LOOKED GOOD.
THEY SAY THEY CAN CURE SOME EYE PROBLEMS WITH LASERS.
OH, YOU MEAN LASIK? IT DOES SEEM TO BE A VERY GOOD METHOD, ALTHOUGH I'M AFRAID IT DOES ME NO GOOD.
So you did know about it after all?
AH! IS THAT BECAUSE A RETINAL SCAN SHOWED THAT YOU WEREN'T A CANDIDATE FOR THE SURGERY?
NO, IT'S BECAUSE I'M TERRIBLY FRIGHTENED OF IT!!!
If I can't even take eye drops, then lasers in my eyes...
I see your point, but...

Lucky☆Star

episode 122
i hate the phone

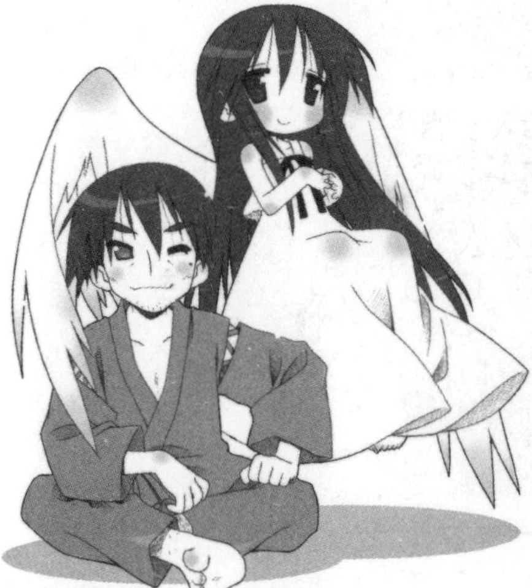

●Comp Ace Vol. 009, Extra Edition, October 2006

slow going

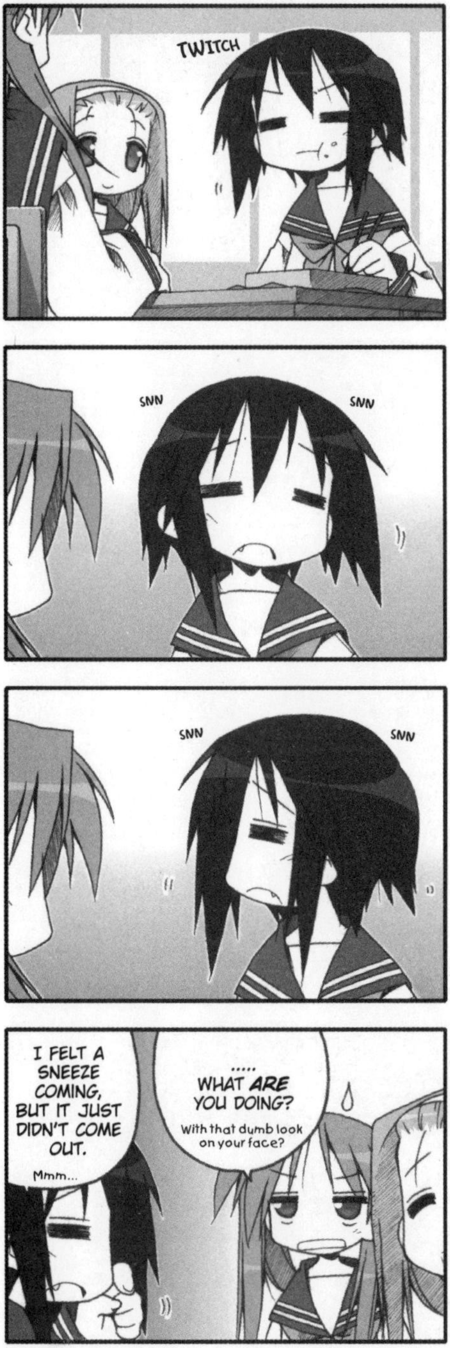
TWITCH
SNN
SNN
SNN
SNN
..... WHAT *ARE* YOU DOING?
With that dumb look on your face?
I FELT A SNEEZE COMING, BUT IT JUST DIDN'T COME OUT.
Mmm...

surgical strike

cause and effect

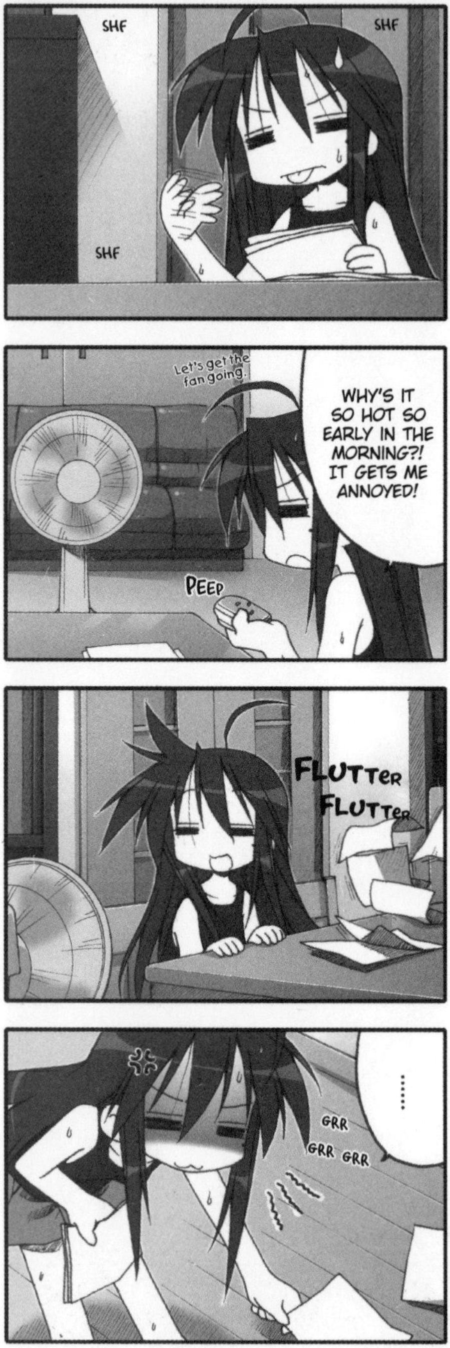
SHF
SHF
SHF
WHY'S IT SO HOT SO EARLY IN THE MORNING?! IT GETS ME ANNOYED!
Let's get the fan going.
PEEP
FLUTTer
FLUTTer
......
GRR
GRR GRR

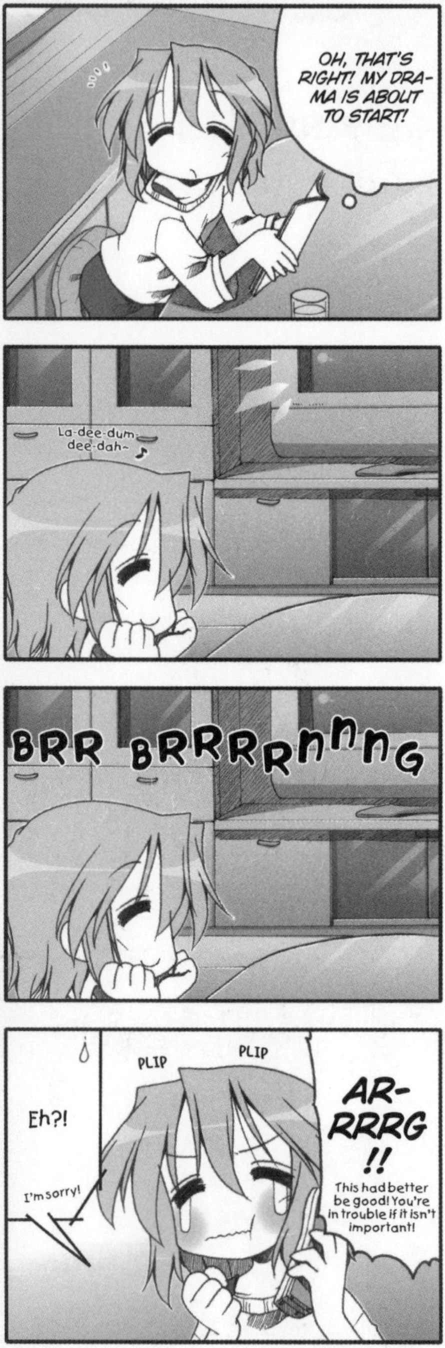
OH, THAT'S RIGHT! MY DRA-MA IS ABOUT TO START!
La-dee-dum-dee-dah~ ♪
BRR BRRRRRnnnG
AR-RRRG!!
This had better be good! You're in trouble if it isn't important!
PLIP
PLIP
Eh?!
I'm sorry!

back attack

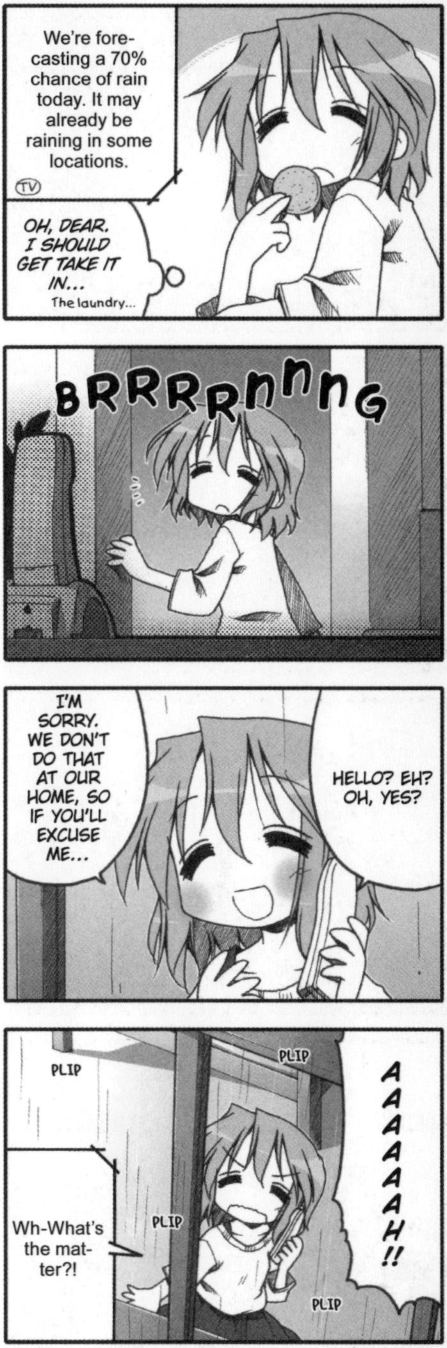

We're fore-casting a 70% chance of rain today. It may already be raining in some locations.
TV
OH, DEAR. I SHOULD GET TAKE IT IN...
The laundry...
BRRRRnnnG
HELLO? EH? OH, YES?
I'M SORRY. WE DON'T DO THAT AT OUR HOME, SO IF YOU'LL EXCUSE ME...
AAAAAAAH!!
PLIP
PLIP
PLIP
Wh-What's the mat-ter?!
PLIP

practical joke

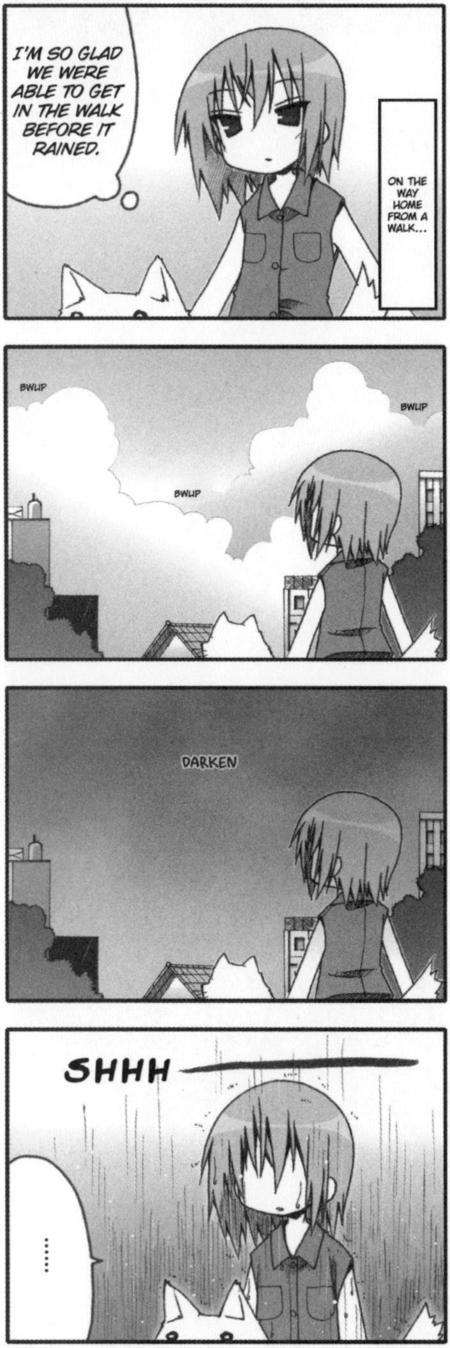

ON THE WAY HOME FROM A WALK...
I'M SO GLAD WE WERE ABLE TO GET IN THE WALK BEFORE IT RAINED.
BWUP
BWUP
BWUP
DARKEN
SHHH
......

Lucky☆Star

LIMITED TIME ONLY SET PRICE! NORI-MAKI! 3 ROLL SET!
1140円
NORI-MAKI 1 ROLL, 380 YEN
HMM
ONEE-CHAN, WHAT IS IT?
NOTHING. IT'S JUST THAT WHEN THEY'RE SELLING SEVERAL IN A SET, I JUST THINK THAT NATURALLY THE PRICE SHOULD BE LOWER. I GUESS MY THINKING'S WRONG.
AHHH ...

episode 123
at my pace

●Comp Ace Vol. 011, Extra Edition, February 2007

trap

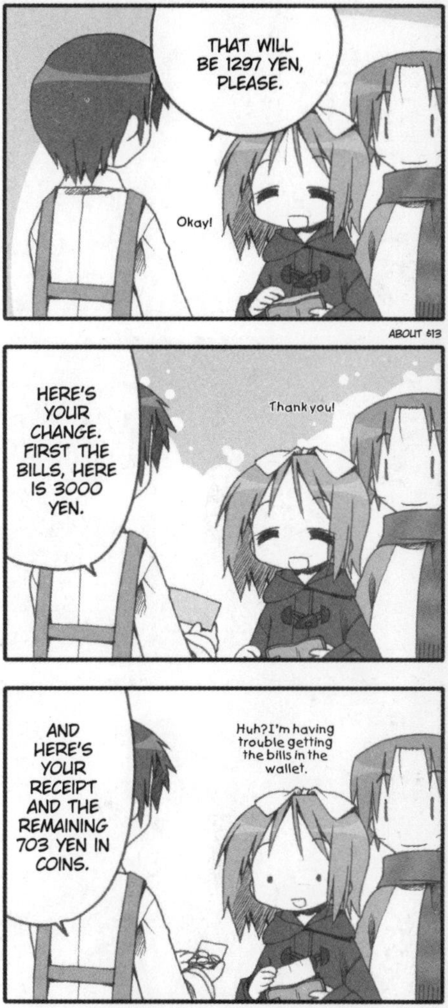
THAT WILL BE 1297 YEN, PLEASE.
Okay!
ABOUT $13
HERE'S YOUR CHANGE. FIRST THE BILLS, HERE IS 3000 YEN.
Thank you!
AND HERE'S YOUR RECEIPT AND THE REMAINING 703 YEN IN COINS.
Huh? I'm having trouble getting the bills in the wallet.
WHY DOES THIS ONLY HAPPEN AT TIMES LIKE THIS?
UMPH UMPH
They won't go in!

a tiny happiness

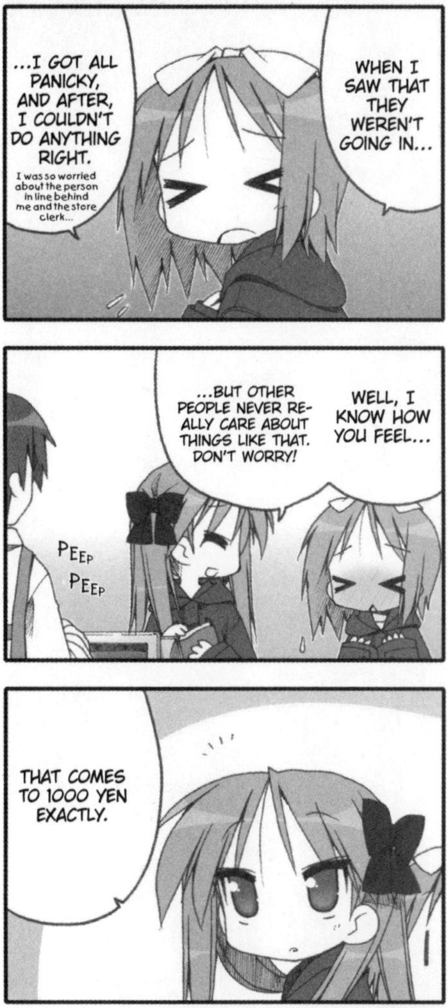
WHEN I SAW THAT THEY WEREN'T GOING IN...
...I GOT ALL PANICKY, AND AFTER, I COULDN'T DO ANYTHING RIGHT.
I was so worried about the person in line behind me and the store clerk...
WELL, I KNOW HOW YOU FEEL...
...BUT OTHER PEOPLE NEVER RE-ALLY CARE ABOUT THINGS LIKE THAT. DON'T WORRY!
PEEP PEEP
THAT COMES TO 1000 YEN EXACTLY.
ABOUT $10
YOU KNOW, WHEN IT COMES OUT TO A ROUND NUMBER LIKE THAT, YOU FEEL KIND OF HAPPY.
OR WHEN IT COMES OUT TO SOME-THING LIKE 777 TOO!
You get through the line quickly too.

a feeling of defeat

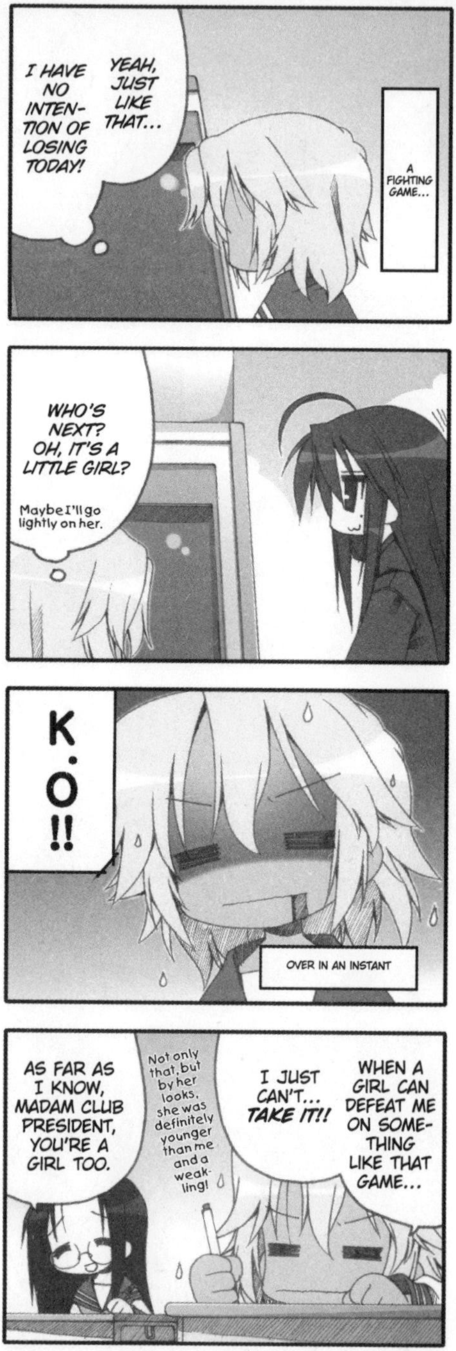
A FIGHTING GAME...
YEAH, JUST LIKE THAT...
I HAVE NO INTENTION OF LOSING TODAY!
WHO'S NEXT? OH, IT'S A LITTLE GIRL?
Maybe I'll go lightly on her.
K.O!!
OVER IN AN INSTANT
WHEN A GIRL CAN DEFEAT ME ON SOMETHING LIKE THAT GAME...
I JUST CAN'T... TAKE IT!!
Not only that, but by her looks, she was definitely younger than me and a weakling!
AS FAR AS I KNOW, MADAM CLUB PRESIDENT, YOU'RE A GIRL TOO.

clown

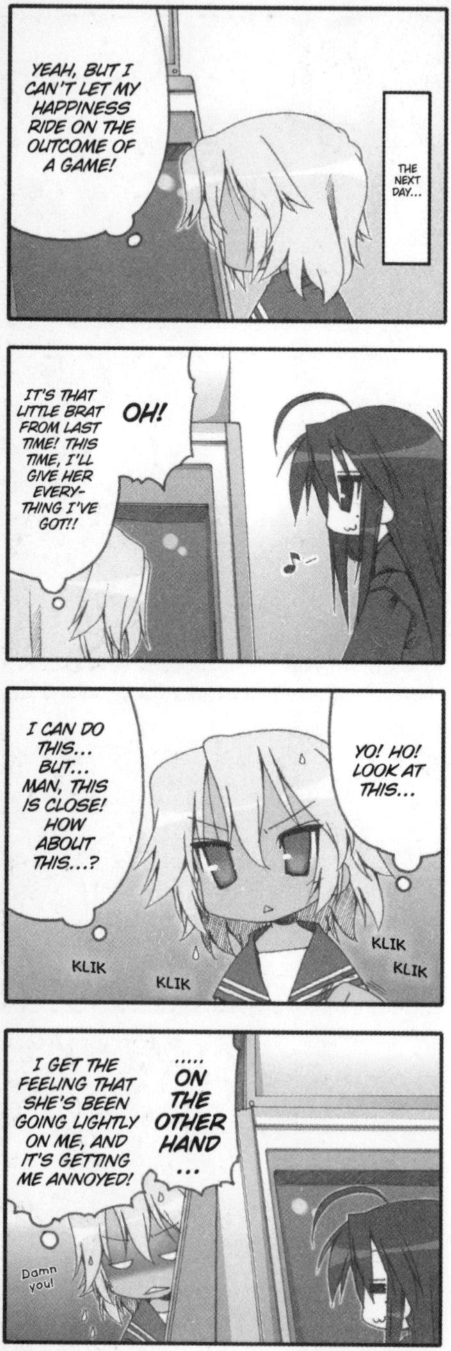
THE NEXT DAY...
YEAH, BUT I CAN'T LET MY HAPPINESS RIDE ON THE OUTCOME OF A GAME!
OH!
IT'S THAT LITTLE BRAT FROM LAST TIME! THIS TIME, I'LL GIVE HER EVERYTHING I'VE GOT!!
YO! HO! LOOK AT THIS...
I CAN DO THIS... BUT... MAN, THIS IS CLOSE! HOW ABOUT THIS...?
KLIK
KLIK
KLIK
KLIK
..... ON THE OTHER HAND ...
I GET THE FEELING THAT SHE'S BEEN GOING LIGHTLY ON ME, AND IT'S GETTING ME ANNOYED!
Damn you!

Lucky☆Star

episode 124
this is my pace

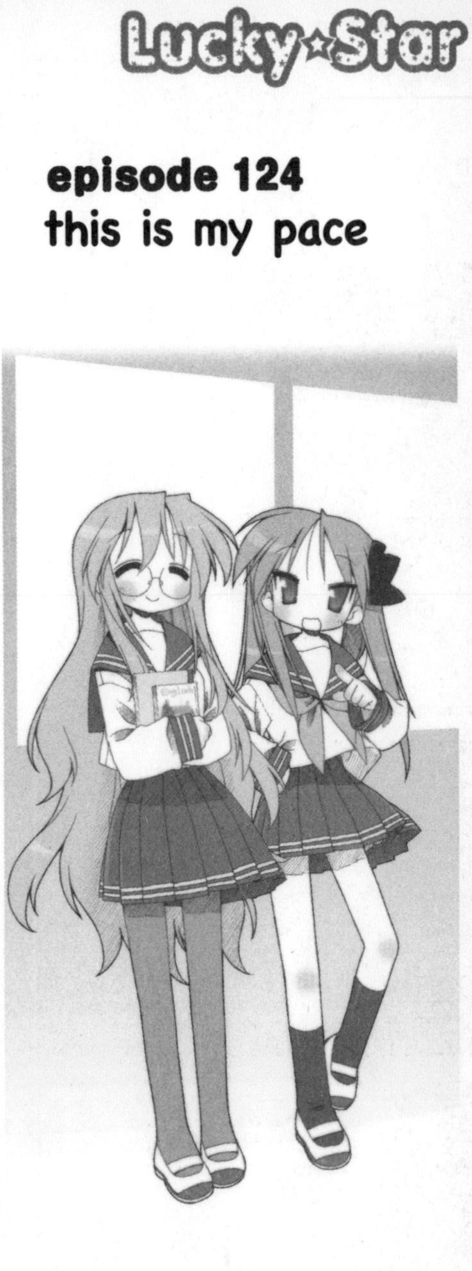
English

●Comp Ace Vol. 012, Extra Edition, April 2007

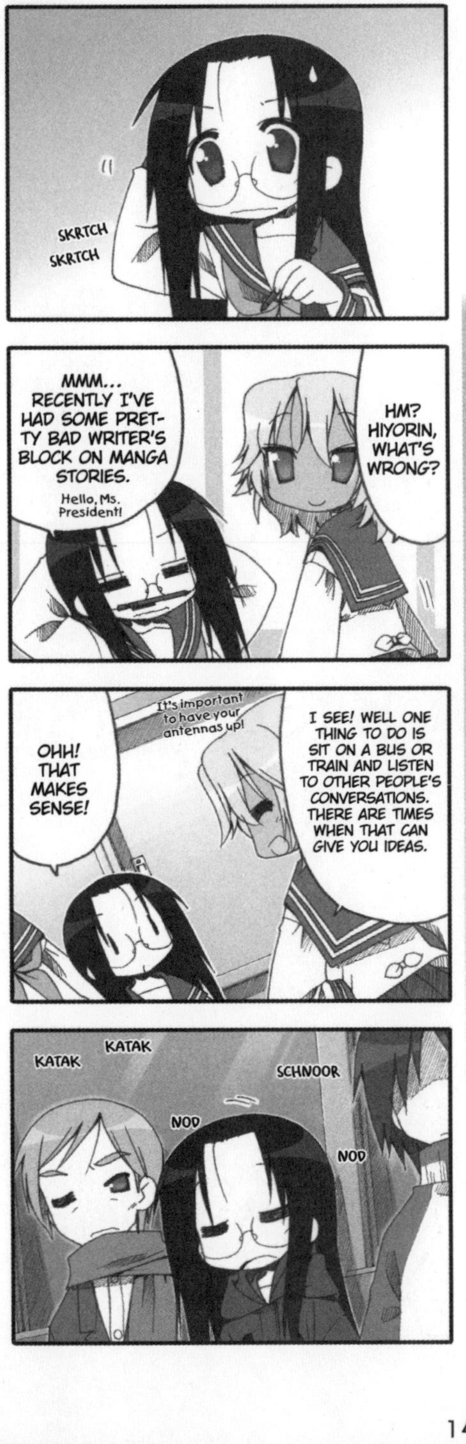
SKRTCH
SKRTCH
HM? HIYORIN, WHAT'S WRONG?
MMM... RECENTLY I'VE HAD SOME PRETTY BAD WRITER'S BLOCK ON MANGA STORIES.
Hello, Ms. President!
I SEE! WELL ONE THING TO DO IS SIT ON A BUS OR TRAIN AND LISTEN TO OTHER PEOPLE'S CONVERSATIONS. THERE ARE TIMES WHEN THAT CAN GIVE YOU IDEAS.
It's important to have your antennas up!
OHH! THAT MAKES SENSE!
SCHNOOR
NOD
NOD
KATAK
KATAK

nightmare

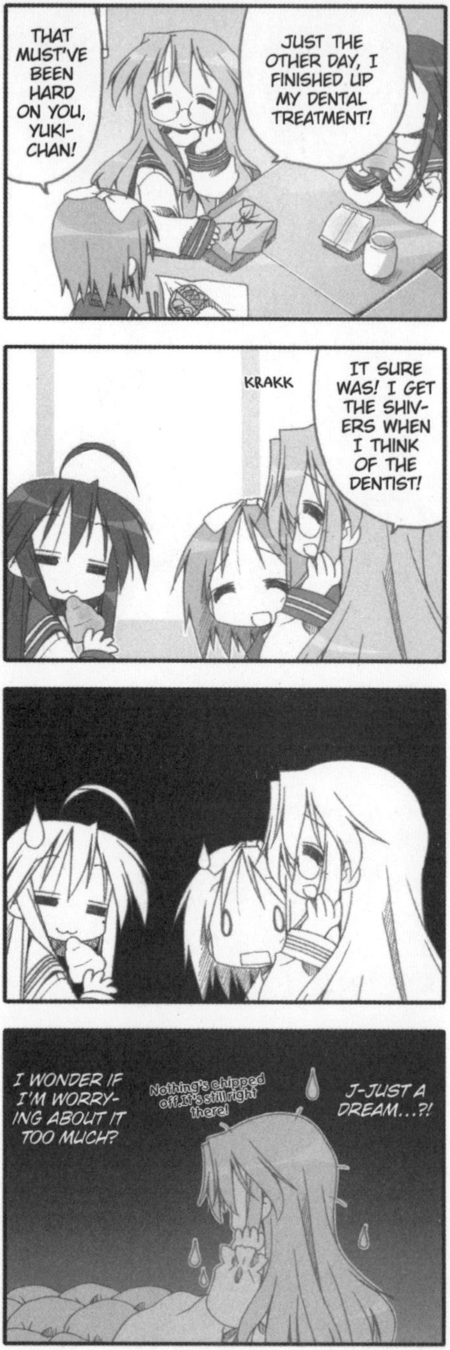
JUST THE OTHER DAY, I FINISHED UP MY DENTAL TREATMENT!
THAT MUST'VE BEEN HARD ON YOU, YUKI-CHAN!
IT SURE WAS! I GET THE SHIVERS WHEN I THINK OF THE DENTIST!
KRAKK
J-JUST A DREAM...?!
Nothing's chipped off. It's still right there!
I WONDER IF I'M WORRYING ABOUT IT TOO MUCH?

A kanagawa user of a fake kansai dialect

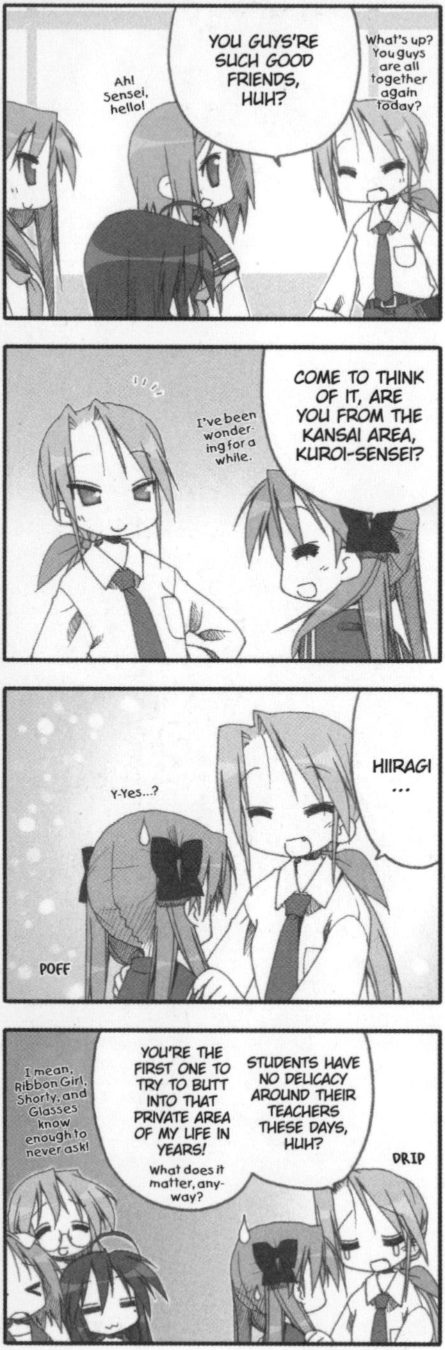
What's up? You guys are all together again today?
YOU GUYS'RE SUCH GOOD FRIENDS, HUH?
Ah! Sensei, hello!
COME TO THINK OF IT, ARE YOU FROM THE KANSAI AREA, KUROI-SENSEI?
I've been wondering for a while.
HIIRAGI ...
Y-Yes...?
POFF
DRIP
STUDENTS HAVE NO DELICACY AROUND THEIR TEACHERS THESE DAYS, HUH?
YOU'RE THE FIRST ONE TO TRY TO BUTT INTO THAT PRIVATE AREA OF MY LIFE IN YEARS!
What does it matter, anyway?
I mean, Ribbon Girl, Shorty, and Glasses know enough to never ask!

prime minister hiiragi

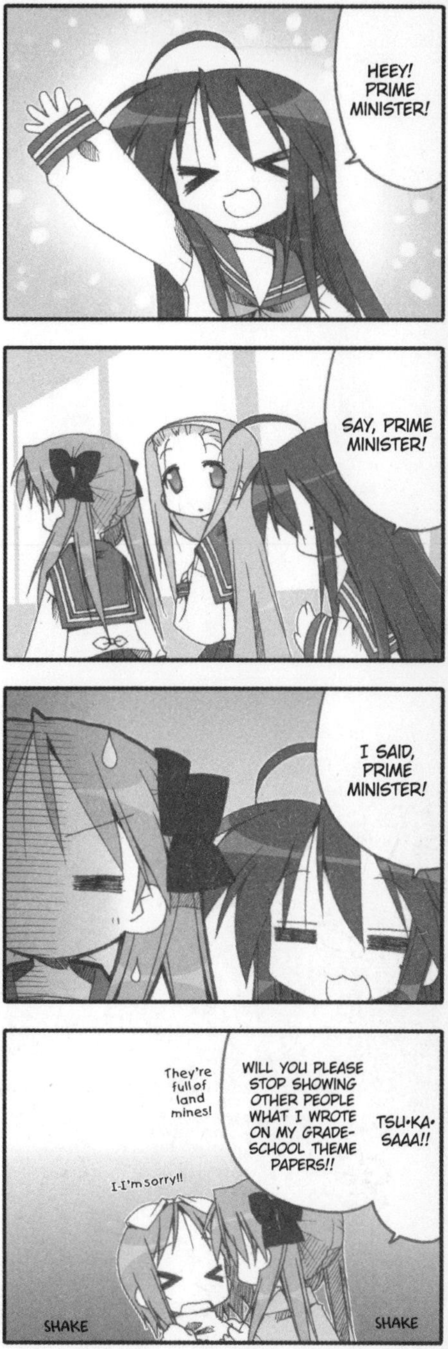
HEEY! PRIME MINISTER!
SAY, PRIME MINISTER!
I SAID, PRIME MINISTER!
TSU•KA•SAAA!!
WILL YOU PLEASE STOP SHOWING OTHER PEOPLE WHAT I WROTE ON MY GRADE-SCHOOL THEME PAPERS!!
They're full of land mines!
I-I'm sorry!!
SHAKE
SHAKE

evil eyes

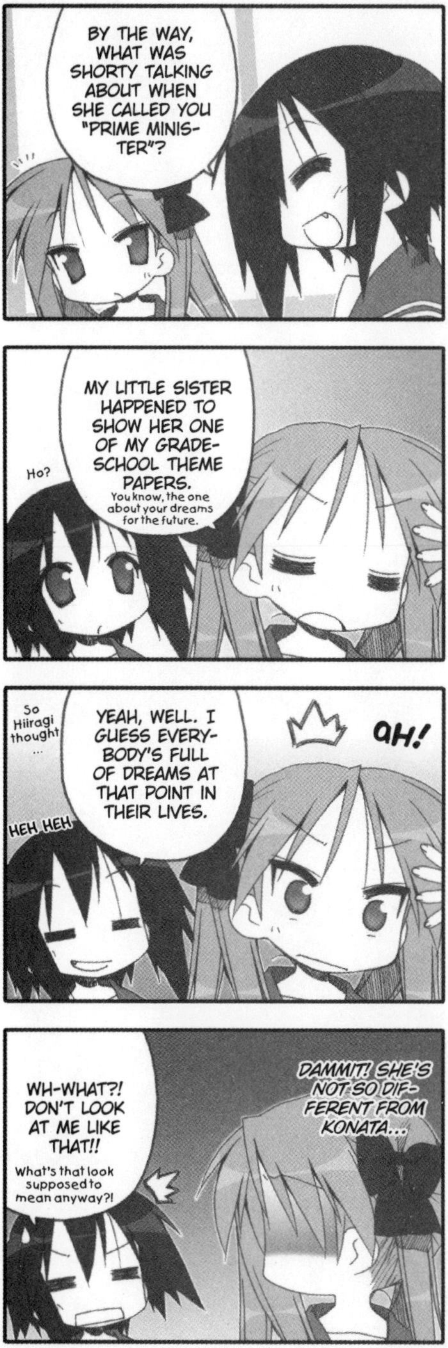
BY THE WAY, WHAT WAS SHORTY TALKING ABOUT WHEN SHE CALLED YOU "PRIME MINISTER"?
MY LITTLE SISTER HAPPENED TO SHOW HER ONE OF MY GRADE-SCHOOL THEME PAPERS.
You know, the one about your dreams for the future.
Ho?
AH!
YEAH, WELL. I GUESS EVERYBODY'S FULL OF DREAMS AT THAT POINT IN THEIR LIVES.
So Hiiragi thought...
HEH HEH
DAMMIT! SHE'S NOT SO DIFFERENT FROM KONATA...
WH-WHAT?! DON'T LOOK AT ME LIKE THAT!!
What's that look supposed to mean anyway?!

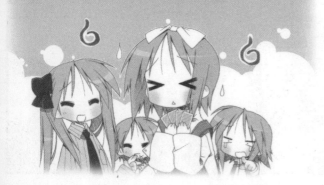

~~sale~~ special extras

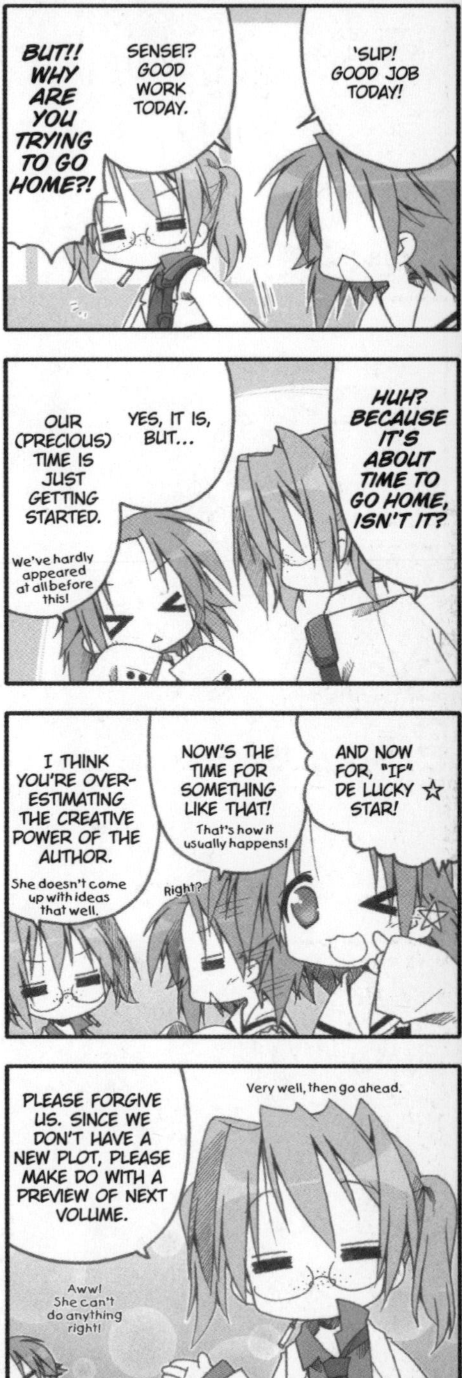
'SUP! GOOD JOB TODAY!
SENSEI? GOOD WORK TODAY.
BUT!! WHY ARE YOU TRYING TO GO HOME?!
HUH? BECAUSE IT'S ABOUT TIME TO GO HOME, ISN'T IT?
YES, IT IS, BUT...
OUR (PRECIOUS) TIME IS JUST GETTING STARTED.
We've hardly appeared at all before this!
AND NOW FOR, "IF" DE LUCKY ☆ STAR!
NOW'S THE TIME FOR SOMETHING LIKE THAT!
That's how it usually happens!
Right?
I THINK YOU'RE OVER-ESTIMATING THE CREATIVE POWER OF THE AUTHOR.
She doesn't come up with ideas that well.
Very well, then go ahead.
PLEASE FORGIVE US. SINCE WE DON'T HAVE A NEW PLOT, PLEASE MAKE DO WITH A PREVIEW OF NEXT VOLUME.
Aww! She can't do anything right!

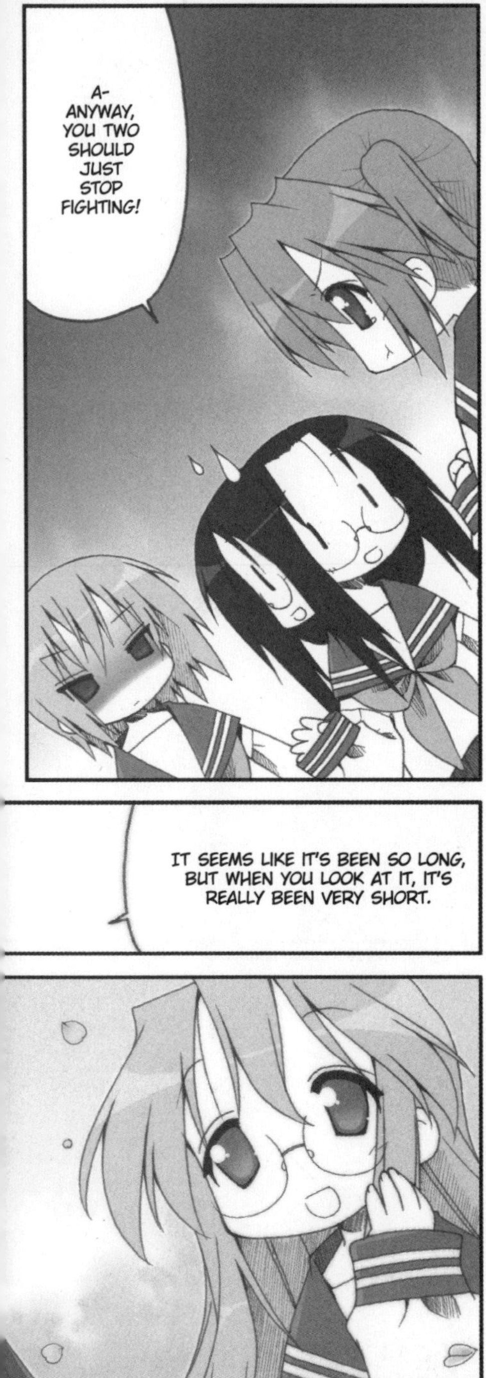
A- ANYWAY, YOU TWO SHOULD JUST STOP FIGHTING!
IT SEEMS LIKE IT'S BEEN SO LONG, BUT WHEN YOU LOOK AT IT, IT'S REALLY BEEN VERY SHORT.

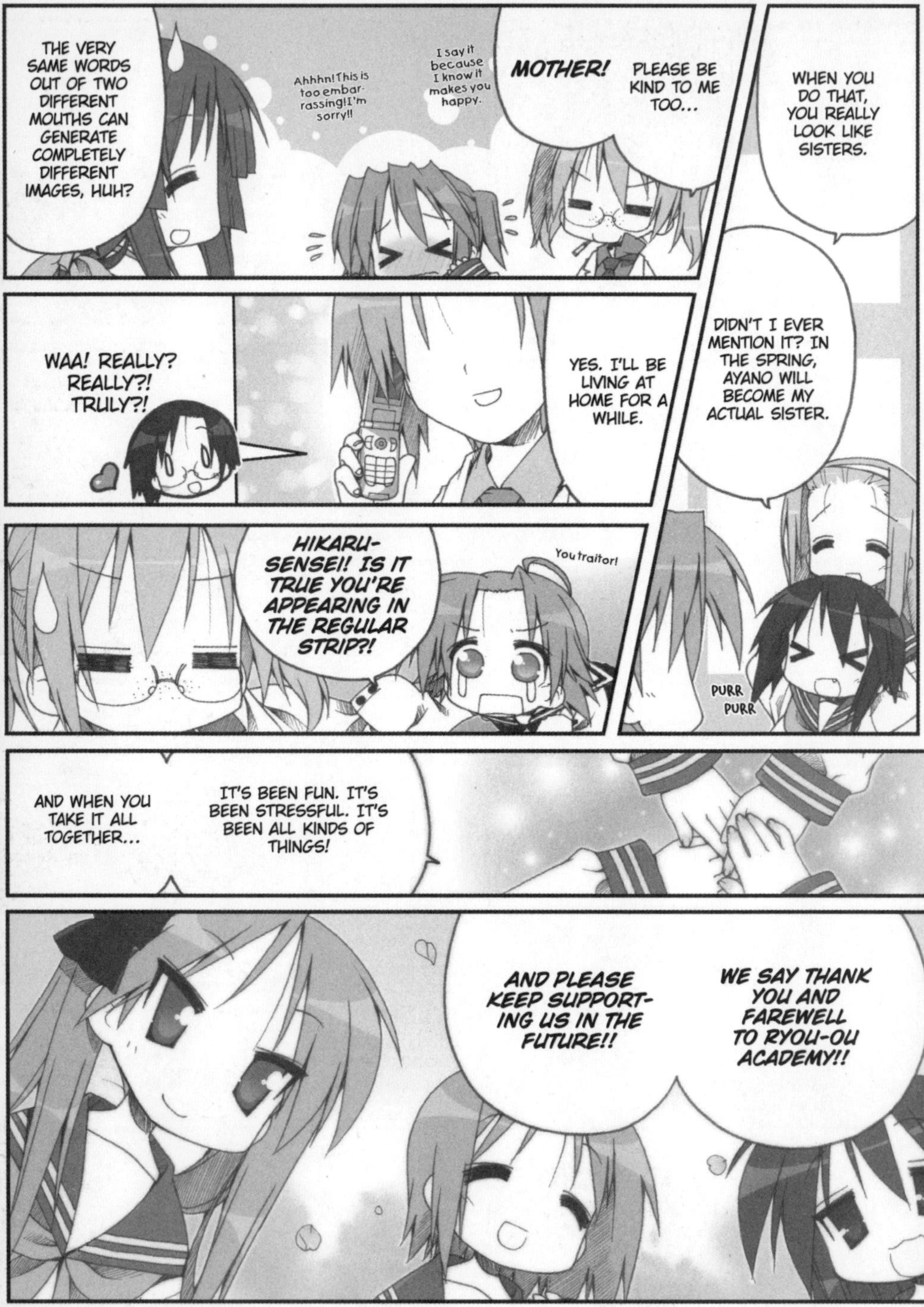
WHEN YOU DO THAT, YOU REALLY LOOK LIKE SISTERS.
DIDN'T I EVER MENTION IT? IN THE SPRING, AYANO WILL BECOME MY ACTUAL SISTER.
PURR PURR
MOTHER!
PLEASE BE KIND TO ME TOO...
I say it because I know it makes you happy.
Ahhhn! This is too embarrassing! I'm sorry!!
THE VERY SAME WORDS OUT OF TWO DIFFERENT MOUTHS CAN GENERATE COMPLETELY DIFFERENT IMAGES, HUH?
YES. I'LL BE LIVING AT HOME FOR A WHILE.
WAA! REALLY? REALLY?! TRULY?!
You traitor!
HIKARU-SENSEI!! IS IT TRUE YOU'RE APPEARING IN THE REGULAR STRIP?!
IT'S BEEN FUN. IT'S BEEN STRESSFUL. IT'S BEEN ALL KINDS OF THINGS!
AND WHEN YOU TAKE IT ALL TOGETHER...
WE SAY THANK YOU AND FAREWELL TO RYOU-OU ACADEMY!!
AND PLEASE KEEP SUPPORTING US IN THE FUTURE!!

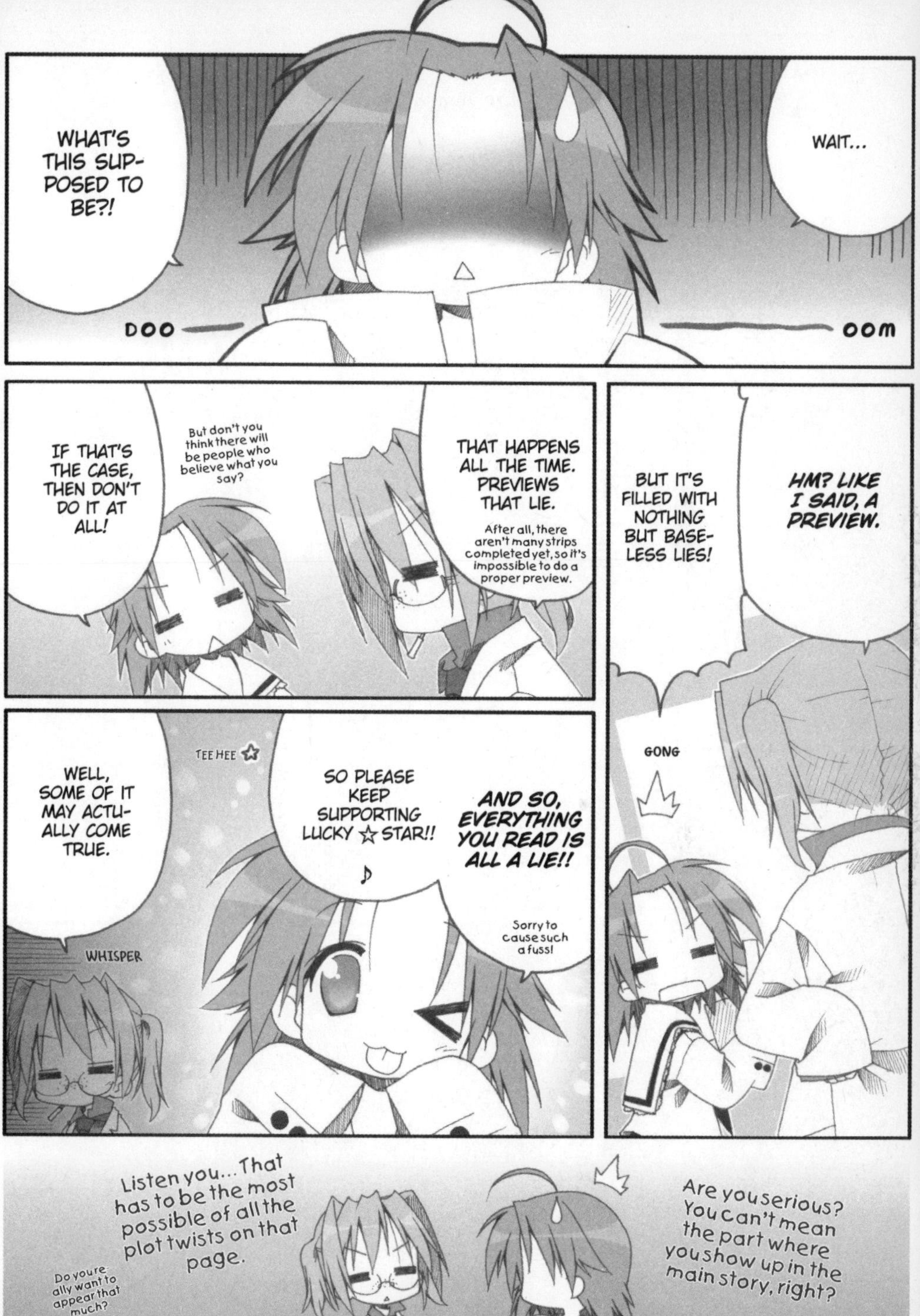
WAIT...
WHAT'S THIS SUP-POSED TO BE?!
DOO——OOM
HM? LIKE I SAID, A PREVIEW.
BUT IT'S FILLED WITH NOTHING BUT BASE-LESS LIES!
GONG
THAT HAPPENS ALL THE TIME. PREVIEWS THAT LIE.
After all, there aren't many strips completed yet, so it's impossible to do a proper preview.
But don't you think there will be people who believe what you say?
IF THAT'S THE CASE, THEN DON'T DO IT AT ALL!
AND SO, EVERYTHING YOU READ IS ALL A LIE!!
SO PLEASE KEEP SUPPORTING LUCKY ☆ STAR!!
♪
Sorry to cause such a fuss!
TEE HEE ☆
WELL, SOME OF IT MAY ACTU-ALLY COME TRUE.
WHISPER
Are you serious? You can't mean the part where you show up in the main story, right?
Listen you... That has to be the most possible of all the plot twists on that page.
Do you really want to appear that much?

•My very thankful feelings 4(th volume)•

- NICE TO MEET YOU. OR, LONG TIME NO SEE. THIS IS YOSHIMIZU. THANK YOU SO MUCH FOR PICKING UP THIS BOOK!

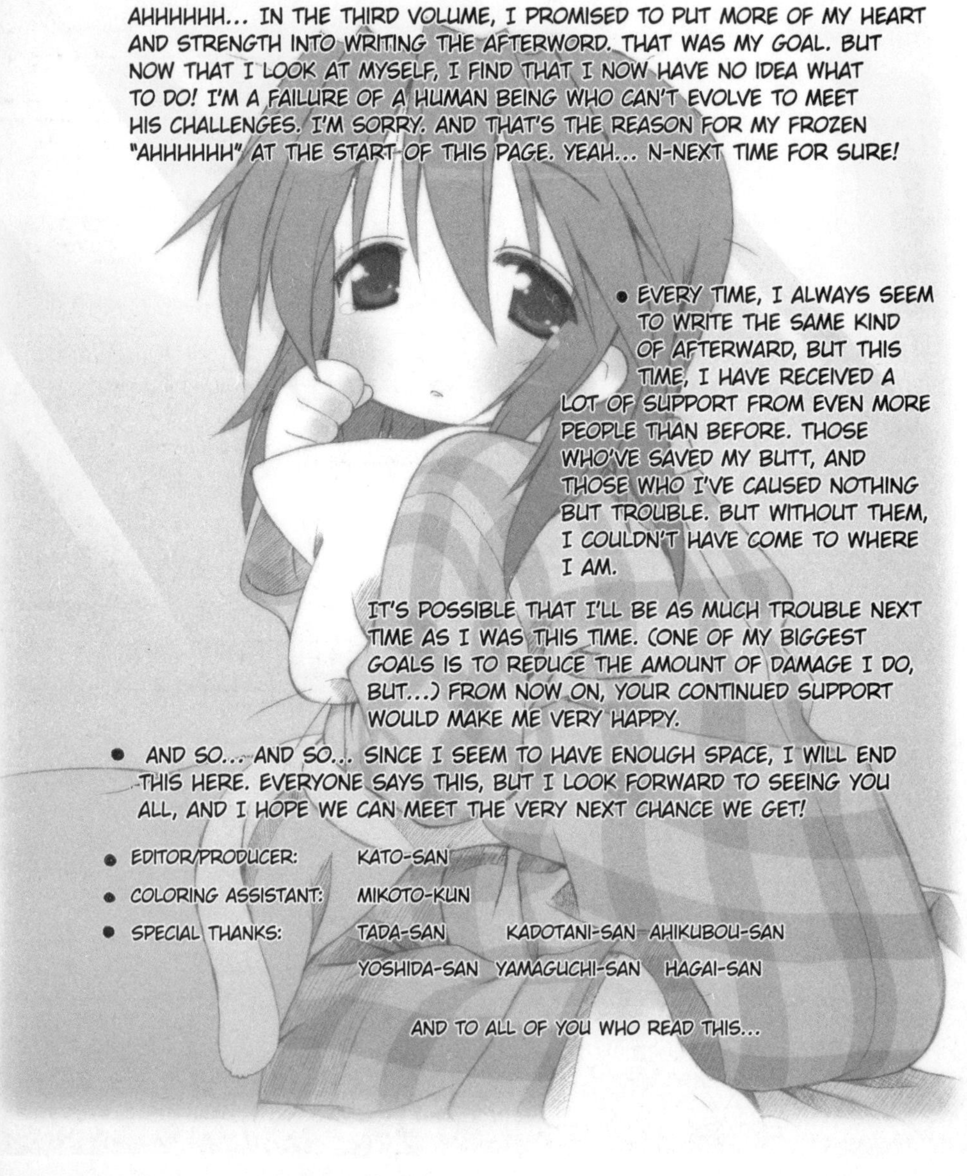

AHHHHHH… IN THE THIRD VOLUME, I PROMISED TO PUT MORE OF MY HEART AND STRENGTH INTO WRITING THE AFTERWORD. THAT WAS MY GOAL. BUT NOW THAT I LOOK AT MYSELF, I FIND THAT I NOW HAVE NO IDEA WHAT TO DO! I'M A FAILURE OF A HUMAN BEING WHO CAN'T EVOLVE TO MEET HIS CHALLENGES. I'M SORRY. AND THAT'S THE REASON FOR MY FROZEN "AHHHHHH" AT THE START OF THIS PAGE. YEAH… N-NEXT TIME FOR SURE!

- EVERY TIME, I ALWAYS SEEM TO WRITE THE SAME KIND OF AFTERWARD, BUT THIS TIME, I HAVE RECEIVED A LOT OF SUPPORT FROM EVEN MORE PEOPLE THAN BEFORE. THOSE WHO'VE SAVED MY BUTT, AND THOSE WHO I'VE CAUSED NOTHING BUT TROUBLE. BUT WITHOUT THEM, I COULDN'T HAVE COME TO WHERE I AM.

IT'S POSSIBLE THAT I'LL BE AS MUCH TROUBLE NEXT TIME AS I WAS THIS TIME. (ONE OF MY BIGGEST GOALS IS TO REDUCE THE AMOUNT OF DAMAGE I DO, BUT…) FROM NOW ON, YOUR CONTINUED SUPPORT WOULD MAKE ME VERY HAPPY.

- AND SO… AND SO… SINCE I SEEM TO HAVE ENOUGH SPACE, I WILL END THIS HERE. EVERYONE SAYS THIS, BUT I LOOK FORWARD TO SEEING YOU ALL, AND I HOPE WE CAN MEET THE VERY NEXT CHANCE WE GET!

- EDITOR/PRODUCER: KATO-SAN
- COLORING ASSISTANT: MIKOTO-KUN
- SPECIAL THANKS: TADA-SAN KADOTANI-SAN AHIKUBOU-SAN YOSHIDA-SAN YAMAGUCHI-SAN HAGAI-SAN

AND TO ALL OF YOU WHO READ THIS…

TRANSLATOR NOTES

P.5 *AUTUMN SKY*   IN JAPAN, THE AUTUMN SKY IS CONSIDERED TO BE VERY "HIGH" AND ENDLESS.

P.7 *JAPANESE AMAZON*   AMAZON.CO.JP IS ALMOST AS FAMOUS AS AMERICAN AMAZON.COM. BUT WHEN YOU USE A CREDIT CARD ON THE SERVICE, YOU MUST PAY OFF THE ENTIRE AMOUNT CHARGED TO A JAPANESE CREDIT CARD AT THE END OF THE MONTH. MOST SHOPS GIVE YOU THE OPTION OF REVOLVING CREDIT.

P.10 *AUTUMN JUMBO*   A HIGH-JACKPOT LOTTERY MUCH LIKE THE SUMMER JUMBO FROM THE NOTES IN THE LAST VOLUME.

P.17 *GARI-GARI-KUN*   A LIGHT-BLUE COLORED POPSICLE-LIKE SNACK TREAT.

P.24 *HIYORIN*   ADDING AN "N" ON THE END OF CERTAIN NAMES IS SOMETHING OF A REPLACEMENT FOR THE -CHAN HONORIFIC.

P.26 *LOLI-CON*   AS DESCRIBED IN THE LAST VOLUME, LOLI-CON IS AN ATTRACTION TO CHILDREN OR CHILD-LIKE PEOPLE AND IMAGES.

P.27 *CHAWAN-MUSHI*   A NON-SWEET CUSTARD LIKE DINNER DISH FILLED WITH MEAT, VEGGIES, FISH, AND OTHER INGREDIENTS.

P.31 *KONNYAKU*   A NON-SWEET GELATIN-LIKE DISH MADE FROM A CERTAIN JAPANESE POTATO.

P.72 *TAMAGO-YAKI*   FRIED EGG DISHES IN SUSHI NORMALLY DON'T HAVE WASABI ON THEM.

P.73 *TORO-HAMACHI*   A SUSHI DELICACY AND USUALLY VERY EXPENSIVE.

     LIMIT CUT   THIS IS SORT OF A POWERING UP FROM THE GAME KINGDOM HEARTS.

P.77 *HOT-WATER BOTTLES*   NORMALLY HOT WATER BOTTLES WITHOUT ANY BRANDING WOULD COST NO MORE THAN ABOUT 2000 YEN ($20).

P.78 *KOTATSU*   A SPECIAL LOW TABLE WITH A FUTON COMFORTER ATTACHED AND A HEATER BELOW, SO PEOPLE CAN BE WARM IN THE WINTER.

P.87 *OBI*   TAKEN FROM THE WORD FOR "BELT," THIS IS A PAPER WRAPPER THAT WRAPS AROUND THE BOTTOM SECTIONS OF JAPANESE GRAPHIC NOVELS' OUTSIDE COVERS. THEY ARE USUALLY COVERED IN SOME SORT OF ADVERTISEMENT.

P. 93 *CELEBRITIES*   ONE COMMON JOB FOR TV CELEBRITIES IS TO DO SHOWS THAT INVOLVE GOING TO OUT-OF-THE WAY LOCATIONS, EATING IN THE RESTAURANTS THERE, AND GUSHING OVER HOW DELICIOUS THE RESTAURANT'S FARE IS.

     ONSEN   HOT-SPRINGS RESORTS FOUND IN THE MOUNTAINOUS REGIONS. THESE PLACES ARE WINTER REFUGES AND POPULAR VACATION SPOTS.

P.97 MIXI A JAPANESE FACEBOOK/MY SPACE-STYLE SOCIAL NETWORKING SITE.

P.98 TOASTED MOCHI RICE PASTE THAT, WHEN PUT IN THE TOASTER, BROWN TO A CRISP OUTSIDE AND CHEWY INTERIOR.

P.101 SKINSHIP THE WORD HAS ENGLISH ORIGINS, BUT IT IS NOW A JAPANESE WORD. IT MEANS THE SHOWING OF AFFECTION THROUGH THE TOUCH OF BODY ON BODY (SUCH AS HUGGING).

A CHILD NEVER KNOWS THIS IS A FAMOUS JAPANESE SAYING, THAT MEANS THAT CHILDREN NEVER KNOW WHAT THEIR PARENTS GO THROUGH FOR THEM.

P.108 CANNED ODEN ODEN IS A SOUPY DISH WITH VARIOUS DIFFERENT MEAT, EGG, VEGGIE, AND FISH-BASED INGREDIENTS IN IT. IT'S USUALLY CONSIDERED A WINTER DISH. BUT IT ISN'T REALLY A DRINK. CANNED ODEN ARE SAID TO BE VERY POPULAR IN AKIHABARA.

P.120 NAME BEFORE A MANGA-KA DRAWS A MANGA, THE FIRST STEP IS TO DO A ROUGH SKETCH OF ALL THE PANELS AND DIALOG SO THE EDITOR KNOWS WHAT THE STORY WILL BE AND CAN COMMENT ON IT. THAT ROUGH SKETCH IS CALLED A NAAMU, TAKEN FROM THE ENGLISH WORD, "NAME."

P.125 NEIGHBORHOOD NOTES THE KAIRANBAN IS A SET OF NOTES AND NOTICES THAT IS PASSED FROM HOUSE TO HOUSE IN A NEIGHBORHOOD ABOUT ONCE A WEEK.

BOWLINGUAL THIS WAS A NOVELTY DEVICE THAT CLAIMED TO BE ABLE TO DECODE DOG'S BARKS.

P.138 FIRST THE BILLS WHEN JAPANESE STORE CLERKS GIVE CHANGE, THEY ALMOST INVARIABLY HAND YOU THE BILLS FIRST TO ALLOW YOU TO PUT THEM IN YOUR WALLET. THEN THEY HAND YOU THE COINS AND RECEIPT NEXT.

Yeah, Yoshiko...
She's got it so good! Her name was Rinko or something like that? I hear she's doing something with Kimutaku and nominated for the Academy Awards? And here I am, never having ever sat on the Mariner's bench, and I don't even meet many guys! No teacher awards anywhere to be found. I guess they have like awards and medals for police, huh?

Yoshimizu★Kagami

Lucky☆Star

4

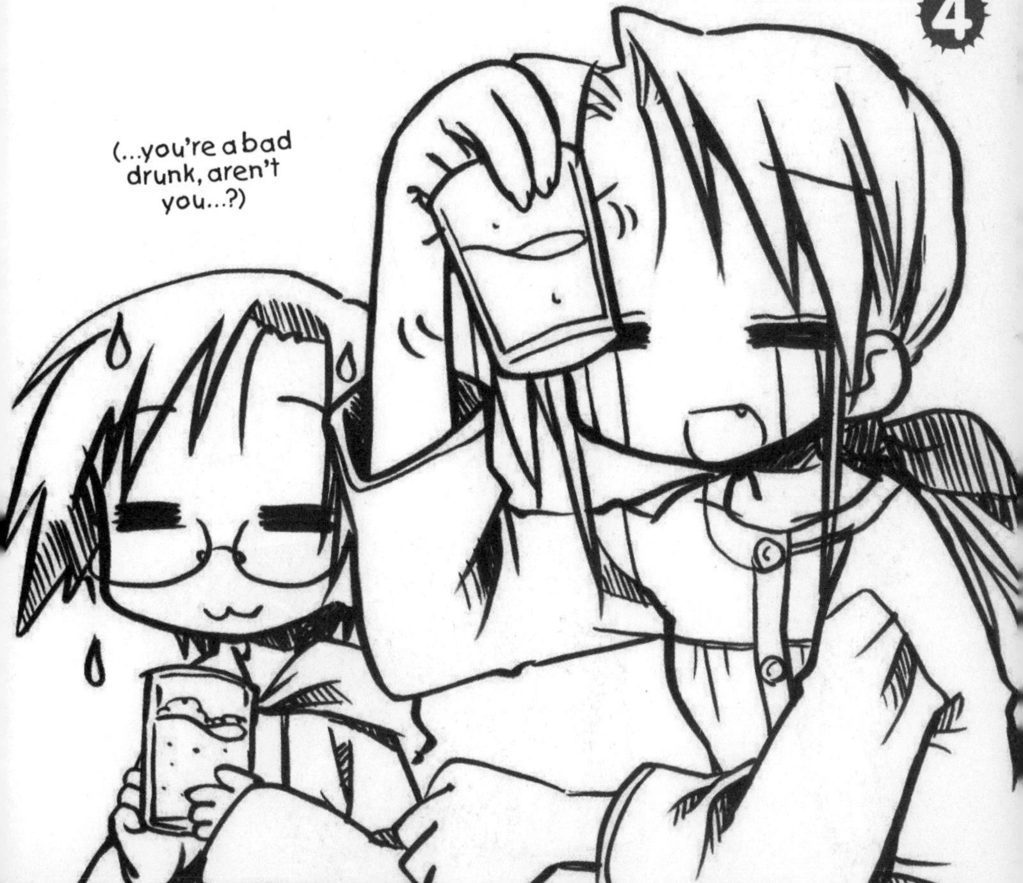
(...you're a bad drunk, aren't you...?)

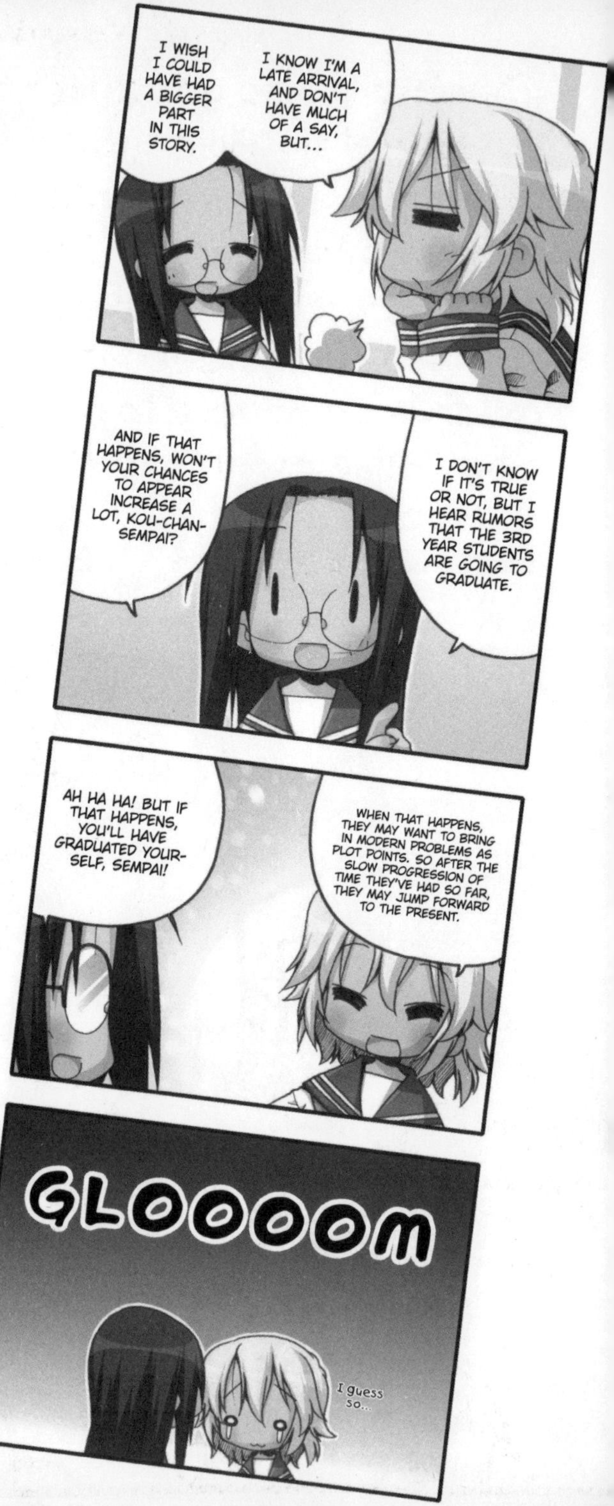
I KNOW I'M A LATE ARRIVAL, AND DON'T HAVE MUCH OF A SAY, BUT...
I WISH I COULD HAVE HAD A BIGGER PART IN THIS STORY.
I DON'T KNOW IF IT'S TRUE OR NOT, BUT I HEAR RUMORS THAT THE 3RD YEAR STUDENTS ARE GOING TO GRADUATE.
AND IF THAT HAPPENS, WON'T YOUR CHANCES TO APPEAR INCREASE A LOT, KOU-CHAN-SEMPAI?
WHEN THAT HAPPENS, THEY MAY WANT TO BRING IN MODERN PROBLEMS AS PLOT POINTS. SO AFTER THE SLOW PROGRESSION OF TIME THEY'VE HAD SO FAR, THEY MAY JUMP FORWARD TO THE PRESENT.
AH HA HA! BUT IF THAT HAPPENS, YOU'LL HAVE GRADUATED YOURSELF, SEMPAI!
GLOOOOM
I guess so...

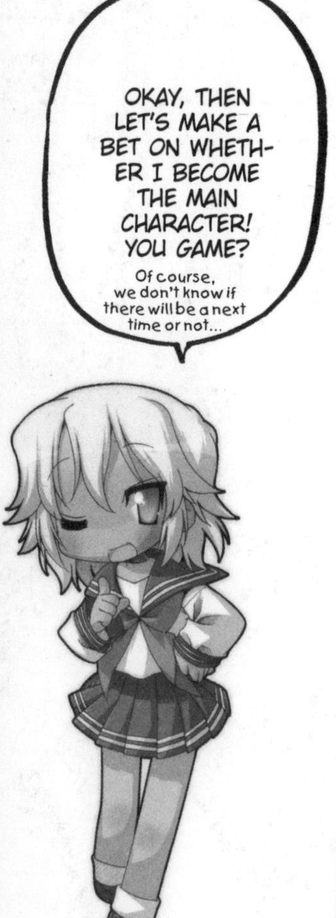
OKAY, THEN LET'S MAKE A BET ON WHETHER I BECOME THE MAIN CHARACTER! YOU GAME?
Of course, we don't know if there will be a next time or not...

If you liked this, then it would make me very happy if you could pick up the next one too!

Lucky★Star

MANGA BY KAGAMI YOSHIMIZU

4

© KAGAMI YOSHIMIZU 2006

FIRST PUBLISHED IN JAPAN IN 2007 BY KADOKAWA SHOTEN PUBLISHING CO., LTD., TOKYO.

ENGLISH TRANSLATION RIGHTS ARRANGED WITH KADOKAWA SHOTEN PUBLISHING CO., LTD., TOKYO.

ENGLISH CREDITS

TRANSLATION BY	WILLIAM FLANAGAN
LETTERING BY	ERIKA TERRIQUEZ
COVER PRODUCTION BY	KIT LOOSE
COPY EDITED BY	TAKU OTSUKA
EDITED BY	ROBERT PLACE NAPTON
PUBLISHED BY	KEN IYADOMI

FIRST BANDAI ENTERTAINMENT INC EDITION PUBLISHED IN FEBRUARY 2010

PRINTED IN CANADA

ISBN 1-978-1-60496-116-4

10, 9, 8, 7, 6, 5, 4, 3, 2, 1

**THE FINAL VOLUME OF THE SEASON
ONE ADAPTATION OF GUNDAM 00!
ON SALE IN FEBRUARY!**

THE SIDE STORY OF CODE GEASS THAT TELLS
AN ALTERNATIVE VERSION OF THE STORY!
NOW ON SALE!

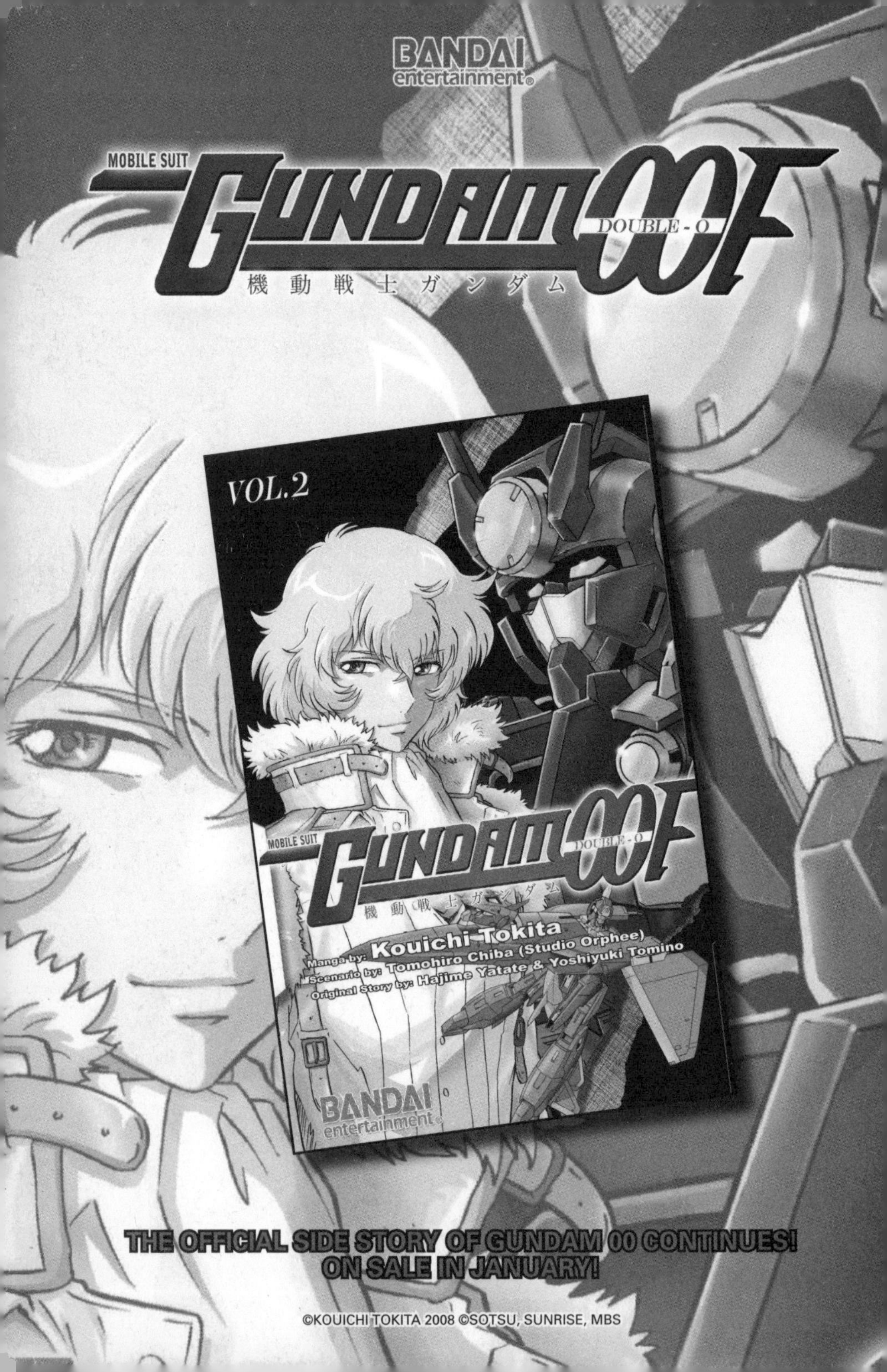
BANDAI entertainment
MOBILE SUIT GUNDAM 00F DOUBLE-O
機動戦士ガンダム
VOL.2
MOBILE SUIT GUNDAM 00F DOUBLE-O
機動戦士ガンダム
Manga by: Kouichi Tokita
Scenario by: Tomohiro Chiba (Studio Orphee)
Original Story by: Hajime Yatate & Yoshiyuki Tomino
BANDAI entertainment
THE OFFICIAL SIDE STORY OF GUNDAM 00 CONTINUES!
ON SALE IN JANUARY!
©KOUICHI TOKITA 2008 ©SOTSU, SUNRISE, MBS

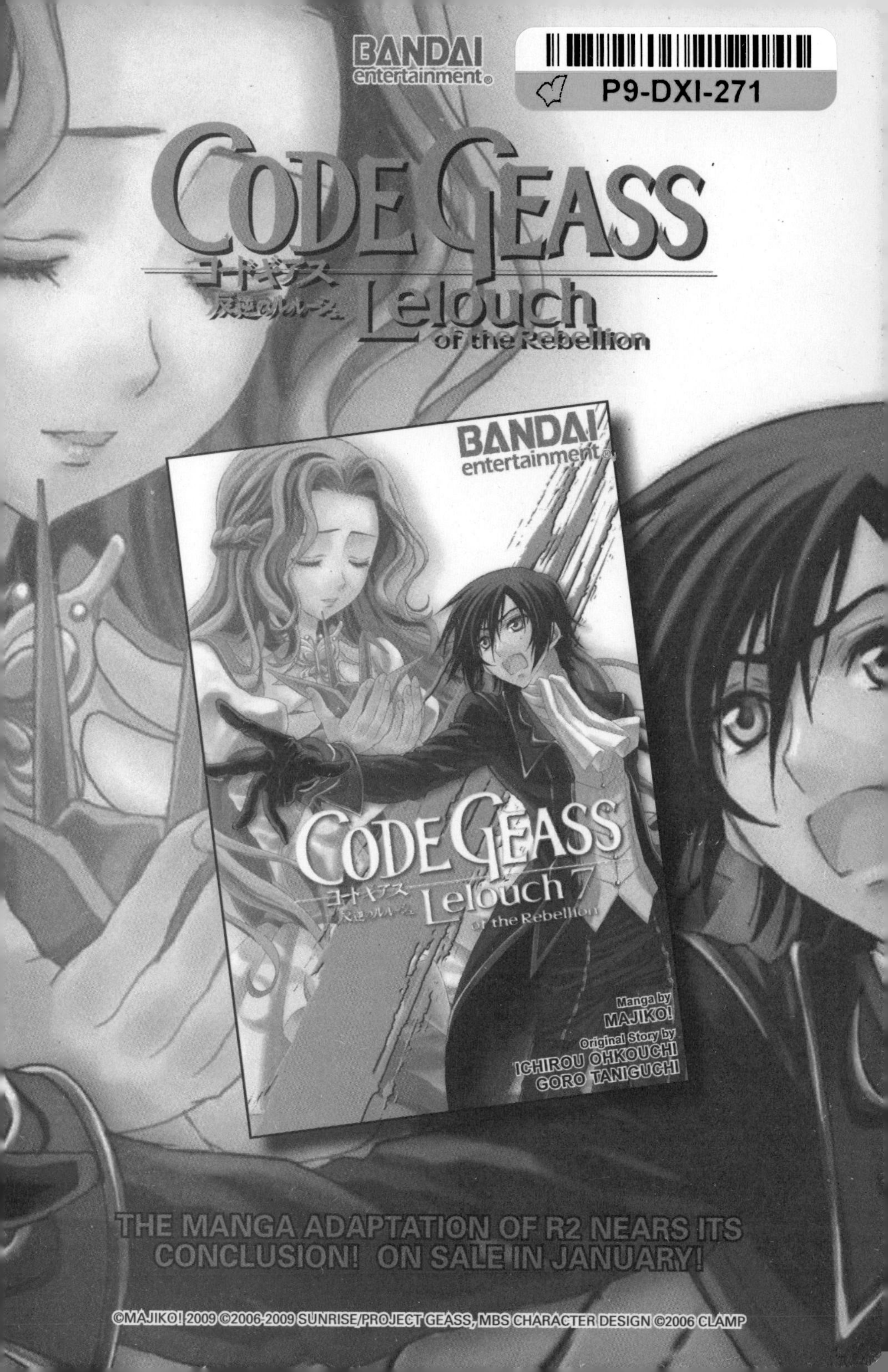
BANDAI entertainment
P9-DXI-271
CODE GEASS
コードギアス
反逆のルルーシュ
Lelouch of the Rebellion
BANDAI entertainment
CODE GEASS
コードギアス
反逆のルルーシュ
Lelouch 7 of the Rebellion
Manga by
MAJIKO!
Original Story by
ICHIROU OHKOUCHI
GORO TANIGUCHI
THE MANGA ADAPTATION OF R2 NEARS ITS CONCLUSION! ON SALE IN JANUARY!
©MAJIKO! 2009 ©2006-2009 SUNRISE/PROJECT GEASS, MBS CHARACTER DESIGN ©2006 CLAMP